With love and
Blessings
Sri Sathy Sai
15-12-87.

(Above) Bliss is not an uncommon occurrence in the presence of Sai. The author is wearing the japamala mentioned in Chapter Thirty-nine.

(Below) The ring manifested by Baba for the author. Description and story in Chapter Eighteen.

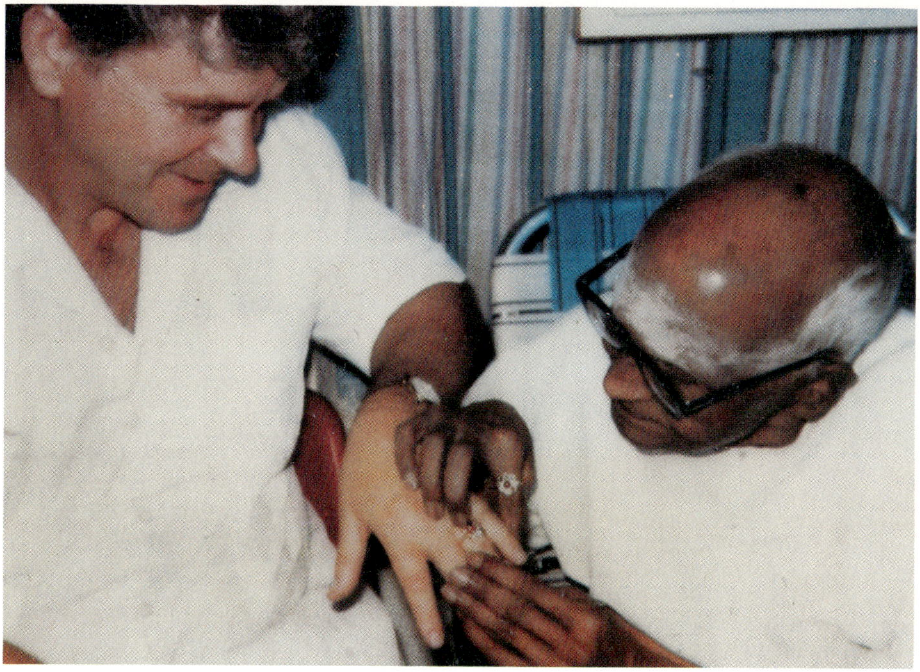

RAYE THOMAS AND SRI N. KASTURI compare the nine-gem rings materialized for them by Sathya Sai Baba. Story in Chapter Twenty-two.

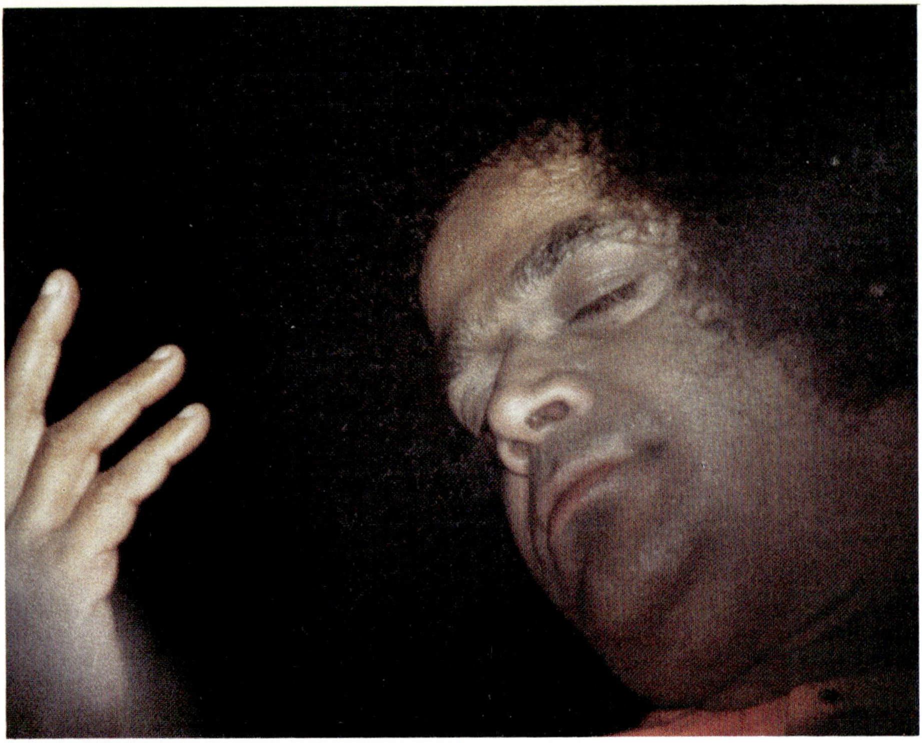

(Above) Bhagavan Sri Sathya Sai Baba

(Below) The story of this picture of Sathya Sai and Raye Thomas is related in Chapter Thirty-one.

LIFE IS A GAME, PLAY IT!

by
Joy Thomas

DISTRIBUTED BY
SATHYA SAI BOOK CENTER
OF AMERICA
305 W. FIRST ST
TUSTIN, CA 92680, USA

Copyright© 1989 by Joy Thomas

All rights reserved. No part of this publication may be reproduced or transmitted in any form or by any means without written permission from the author.

Cover design by William John Proud

ONTIC BOOK PUBLISHERS
P.O. Box 3291
Beaumont, California 92223
U.S.A.

Printed in the United States of America

With devotion to

Sri Sathya Sai Baba

"The wise man is he who keeps his reason sharp and clear and sees things as they really are. He listens to this advice:

Life is a challenge, meet it.
Life is Love, share it.
Life is a dream, realize it.
Life is a game, play it!

This is the real pilgrim's progress. This is the lion's march across the forest—fearless, masterful, and victorious."

—Bhagavan Sri Sathya Sai Baba
Sai Avatar, Vol. II

INTRODUCTION

Bhagavan Sri Sathya Sai Baba said in a discourse given at the Sri Sathya Sai Institute of Higher Learning on July 3, 1986, "The world is teaching man innumerable lessons all the time. Each one should try to discover for himself the secret of his life and the Universal Consciousness that is inherent in him. The first requisite for each one is to make himself his own guru." This book is the story of the efforts made by the author to be obedient to that instruction and of some of the ways she has been assisted in her inner search by Baba's simple but very effective teaching methods.

This book does not attempt to tell anyone else how to live his life. It does not include any experiences except those of which the author has first-hand knowledge. No attempt is made to describe or explain Sathya Sai Baba, but the author illustrates by incidents in her personal story what knowing Him has meant to her. Dr. John Hislop said in his book *My Baba and I*: "At one and the same time, in various regions of the world, great numbers of people experience direct contact and direct help from Baba by means of inner hearing and intuition, by dreams, by visions, by manifest appearance, [and] by leading events..." The author's experiences of help through these means are perhaps among the very least of those occurring throughout the world. It is for this reason that she relates them—not because they are unusual, but because they are **not**.

No effort has been made to arrange the book in chronological order. It is related in units of lessons, and a particular lesson may have spanned weeks, months, five years, or a lifetime. The author frequently refers back to learnings which took place during the time that she studied Christian Science. Baba has often stressed that, after coming to Him, one may find that his or her former religious training will become much more meaningful. This has been found to be true in the experience of the author.

Due to the personal nature of this story, no effort has been made to eliminate or reduce the use of the personal pronoun. The names of others involved have been included also. They have each been invaluable instruments in the unfolding of this narrative as well as in the author's own budding spiritual development. Very special gratitude is due to each one mentioned and to many who have not been mentioned.

It is hoped that the reader will never feel called upon to either agree or disagree with the author. The experiences which have been related are not put forward as anything other than learning incidents in the life of one ordinary person. However, if they stimulate the reader to contemplate any of the spiritual teachings which have been quoted in this text and, thereby, tap into his own Inner Wisdom, the purpose of the book will have been achieved.

******

"Old age is the fourth stage of life. By the time one reaches this stage of his journey, he must have discovered that the joys available in this world are trivial and fleeting. He must be equipped with the higher knowledge of spiritual joy available through delving into the inner spring of bliss through his experiences; his heart must have softened and filled with compassion. He has to be engrossed in promoting the progress of all beings without distinction. He must be eager to share with others the knowledge he has accumulated and to give them the benefit of his experiences.

—Sathya Sai Baba
Sathya Sai Vahini

TABLE OF CONTENTS

Chapter		
1	Beginnings	1
2	"Where Did You Come From?"	15
3	"I Am Prepared To Give You Whatever You Want"	21
4	"Life Is A Teacher"	29
5	"Bring Me Your Garbage"	37
6	"Where Is Your Husband?"	45
7	"I Have To Mother My Western Devotees"	55
8	"You Have Seven Children"	67
9	"Your Guidance Is As Good As Mine"	75
10	"Don't Try, Do"	87
11	"Don't Exhibit; Exemplify"	93
12	"Make The Mind Forget Itself"	101
13	"I Am The Doer"	109
14	"Not Sisters?"	119
15	"Living Is Not Necessary, But Navigation Is"	125
16	"Love My Uncertainty"	133
17	"I Will Come, And I Will Stay At Your House."	141
18	"Happy, Happy, Happy!"	145

19	"My Life Is My Message"	151
20	"You Are Only Witnessing My Play"	155
21	"Forget It...Just Repeat The Name!"	163
22	"Ask For What I Came To Give: Liberation"	171
23	"For You, Or For Me?"	181
24	"I Will Carry The Burden Of Your Welfare"	189
25	"You Are Mine"	201
26	He Called Me Beautiful	207
27	"Being Is Lost In Becoming"	213
28	"After Ecstasy, Laundry"	219
29	Through The Sai-Lens	227
30	"Be Careful For Nothing"	235
31	"The Process *Is* The Healing."	239
32	"I Will Take Care"	245
33	"Both Good Men"	255
34	"When The Tongue Is Conquered, Victory Is Yours"	259
35	"Life Is Awareness"	263
36	"What Is Religion?"	265
37	"You Will Experience Me In Different Manifestations Of My Form"	277
38	"Why Fear...Sin?"	281
39	The Miracle Of Miracles	285
40	"You Always Want To Do Everything Just Right"	291

41	"Blessed Are They That Mourn..."	301
42	"What Is Your Name?"	309
43	Dante Called You Beatrice	319

With special appreciation to Kathi de Mille for her help in establishing the point of view to be used in this book, to Cynthia Barlow for typing, to Sonia Nordenson for editing, to Yogesh Alekal for technical assistance, to Elizabeth and David Davidson, without whose friendship and support the book might never have become a reality, to Mahri Kintz and to Raye Thomas for unswerving faith in the book and continuing encouragement during the writing and publishing of it.

"The world we see around us cannot give us happiness. From moment to moment it is changing. The experiences the world gives us in the waking state get obliterated in the dream state, and those of the dream stage cease when we wake up from the dream. The dream experiences are our creation. And so are the waking state experiences. What we see is nothing but our own creations. The vision experience of the world is but a projection of our mind and the reflection of our inner thoughts. As the thought, so the vision. The color of the glasses you wear determines the color in which things appear to you. If you wear red glasses, everything will appear red. If you wear green glasses, everything will appear green. Pure thoughts make the whole world appear as pure. If you view everything with a loving heart, the whole world, the whole creation will appear to you as a reflection of Love."

—Sathya Sai Baba
Sathya Sai Speaks, Vol. XI

1
BEGINNINGS

Playing games has been a lifelong fascination. The first thirteen years of this incarnation were spent in Chattanooga, Tennessee, in the area referred to as the Bible Belt of the United States. One of my earliest memories is of playing cards with my stepsister. From time to time we were allowed to have real cards. When my father would get an attack of "old-time religion," he would throw our cards away, not willing for us to endanger our immortal souls with such dubious pastimes. Then we would patiently cut up our notebook paper, draw clubs, diamonds, hearts, and spades on the rectangles, and continue our game of Old Maid, Go Fishing, or whatever, as furtively as if we had been smoking cornsilks behind the barn.

After my father's passing, I went to live with my mother and stepfather in Coral Gables, Florida. My stepfather was an avid bridge player. He and my mother had friends in to make up two or three tables of bridge almost every week. Since a last-minute defection on the part of a player created a serious threat to the evening's entertainment, my stepfather viewed my arrival on their domestic scene as a potential asset. He set about with not-always-too-patient determination to teach me the game. Before I was fourteen years old, I became a fairly acceptable stand-in for an absent bridge player. My own interests at this stage of life probably leaned more toward swimming, diving, waterskiing, jitterbugging, and hanging out with friends. Still, I found pleasure in Monopoly, crossword puzzles, and card games.

While bringing up two children and pursuing a career as an educator, I rarely had time to play games, but solving puzzles of any kind always gave me pleasure. Finding a solution to a child's learning problems or a teacher's classroom-control problems became my favorite challenges for a while. After I passed the half-century mark and my children had established their own homes, I found myself faced with an unexpected puzzle. I wasn't even aware when the question began to insinuate itself into my consciousness. On a rare day when the time pressure was not too great, we had finished our lunch and were lingering over a cup of coffee, and I posed the question to my assistant: "When a person dies, what happens to all of the knowledge that he has accumulated in his lifetime?" She looked at me as if I might be suffering from some sort of mental problem and replied with a question of her own: "Do you realize that you have asked me that two or three dozen times in the last few months?" Now it was my turn to be surprised. I was not aware that I had been asking the question repetitively.

The surfacing of this question not only signified a major turning point in my life, but it also revealed one of the basic rules of the game. I had been quite disturbed thirty-five years earlier when the son of the principal of the high school I attended had been killed in a traffic accident. He was a young man working his way through college by driving an ambulance. I had never met him, nor was I at all closely acquainted with his father. However, when the news came that he had been in a fatal collision while driving an ambulance with its siren on and its lights flashing, my reaction had been out of proportion to my relation to the family. I had mourned his death for weeks, asking such questions as: "Was his whole life wasted, lost, in this high-speed crash? Was all of the knowledge, which he was working so hard to gain, wiped out? If it was, then what's the use of studying and striving to improve one's abilities? And if it wasn't, where is it now?" Gradually the discomfort and the question disappeared below the surface of consciousness. I was too busy going to college, caring for my family, teaching, counseling, and striving to get ahead in the world to spend much time mulling over such relatively impractical things. The seed which had been planted at that time, however, had been lying dormant, waiting for just the right moment to sprout. Now, here it was, whether I liked it or not.

According to the California State Retirement System and the general consensus of opinion, I had to work another fourteen years before retiring. I had a standard of living to which I had become accustomed—addicted might be a better word—and obviously the school district in which I worked would crumble and fall apart without me. So I resisted the urge to resign my position and take the next steps. I didn't know what those steps were, how to go about taking them, or where they would lead me, and I hadn't found a guide in whom I could completely place my trust, either.

I should say here that my spiritual development had not been totally neglected. Early in my high school years, I had voluntarily left a Protestant church, which offered many attractive social activities, and begun attending the Christian Science Sunday School. I applied myself diligently to the study of the King James version of the Bible, also to *Science and Health with Key to the Scriptures* by Mary Baker Eddy, and to other "authorized" Christian Science literature. I read a prepared lesson daily, attended lectures, took class instruction from an "authorized" teacher, and made an effort to put into practice everything I was exposed to in these activities.

But now something was happening for which I was totally unprepared. The demand had come to go up higher, and I resisted it with every bit of ego-strength I could muster. At first the only change in my outer circumstances was the "empty nest syndrome." I filled that void with buying a new house, decorating it, and spending longer hours on the job. I clung to the status quo with determination. But the game plan would not be denied.

In rapid succession, my best friend died, my husband died, and the superintendent of the school district, who had been very supportive of the way I was handling all of the programs under my direction, was replaced by one who had an entirely different agenda. I had come to a fork in the road, and life was not going to put up with my procrastination any longer. I had to make a choice no matter how repugnant it might seem. I could stay in the school district and stagnate, or leave and take a chance that there might be something else out there that I could discover. By taking a year's leave of absence, I postponed the decision as long as I could.

Other circumstances seemed to occur without my willing them. I remarried, sold my dream house, and moved fifty miles farther away from the school district. I had severed my connection with the church at the time of my friend's death, recognizing that when I put a large demand on my spiritual account it had quickly become depleted. Finding myself in a strange neighborhood, friendless, married to a man I barely knew, it seemed to me that I had not come to a fork in the road at all. I felt sure that I had come to the end of it.

I made an appointment with a psychiatrist, persuaded him to prescribe tranquilizers and sleeping pills, and prepared to swallow the contents of both bottles at once. I poured all of the pills out into my hand, but the thought came very insistently that there must be something that I hadn't discovered, something I hadn't tried. I finally put the pills down the drain and picked up the telephone book. I started thumbing through the Yellow Pages, not knowing where else to turn. As I ran my eye down the list of churches, the word "Unity" stood out to me. The church

Chapter One

was not located in the town where we lived, but that didn't seem to matter. When Raye came home, I asked him if he would go to church with me. He agreed right away, seeming to be as ready as I was, although we had never before been to church together. We had been married by a Lutheran minister someone had recommended to us, but the ceremony had taken place in a marriage chapel—not in a church.

So that Sunday we attended the Unity church service in a nearby town, found it to be as helpful as we had hoped it might be, and became regular attendants. The minister introduced me to Joel Goldsmith's writings, which I found inspiring as well as instructive, and Raye was elected president of the Board of Directors, which was very dharmic (pure, heartfelt) activity for him. It seemed we had selected the path along which we were to travel for a while, and our hearts were more at peace. The church was a stabilizing influence in our lives, but the search went on.

Another seed, which had been planted earlier, sprouted at this time. While I was still employed as Director of Compensatory Education, I had served as a member of a monitor and review team to evaluate the early childhood education program in Hemet, California. At that time, Hemet was foreign to us. So, while I performed my duties, Raye explored the area. He came across a strange-looking place with "no trespassing—do not enter" signs posted all around it, and his curiosity was piqued. He drove in, parked in front of what appeared to be an administration building, went in, and asked a very pleasant lady behind the desk, "What sort of place is this?" He was received very graciously, all of his questions answered, and he came away with some printed material on Transcendental Meditation (TM).

At the time, we had thought it a mildly interesting adventure into some strange hippie-type activity and had promptly forgotten all about it. Now, however, with my study of Joel

Goldsmith's writings and our new church affiliation, meditation was not sounding so weird to us anymore. I was trying to meditate according to Goldsmith's directions and having some experiences of deep peace, occasionally achieving glimpses into states of consciousness that seemed infinitely more desirable than the one in which I spent the majority of my waking hours. So, when Raye suggested that we go back to "that place in Hemet" together and see about learning to meditate, I agreed right away. We were soon initiated into TM and found ourselves establishing a regular habit of meditating together twice a day. It is a routine which we follow faithfully and which has blessed us immensely.

Studying and teaching had both been indispensable to my way of life for so long that the habits carried right over into my new activities. I studied biofeedback and practiced and taught in that field for a time. I became interested in Kirlian photography, bought equipment capable of photographing the electrical energy surrounding the fingertips, and enjoyed showing slides of some of the more interesting pictures. For a short time I was a mildly successful "New Age" lecturer, entertaining audiences with demonstrations of biofeedback equipment, teaching relaxation techniques, and showing slides. I even completed the doctorate on which I had been working at the time of my departure from the field of education. I may be the only person in history who ever did doctoral research sitting in a semi-lotus position with eyes closed for hours each day and then attempted to describe the indescribable in her dissertation.

Both Raye and I had become convinced that the only way we were going to find that which we now felt it was possible to find was by looking within ourselves. The next step seemed to be to try to improve our technique for doing that. It was possible to lower blood pressure, to warm or cool the fingertips, to reduce the galvanic skin response, to decrease muscle tension, and to slow down the brain's frantic pace, but what about peace, love, and joy? Where did these come in? Where, in fact, was God and how did we go about finding Him? We took advanced training in meditation, the TM Siddhis program, hoping that this technique might take us to our goal.

It was at the First World Peace Assembly, held at the University of Massachusetts in Amherst under the auspices of Maharishi Mahesh Yogi, that an unusual incident occurred which signalled the beginning of the end of our search. At about 3:00 A.M., during a rainstorm, I smelled an unfamiliar fragrance. The dorms in which we were housed were quite solidly built, and the windows were all tightly shut, but my room was filled with a smell which was strange to me. It seemed to be something like incense. I opened the door to see if it could be coming from the hallway, but it was only discernible inside the room. That was mysterious enough, but the next morning, while meditating with hundreds of others in a huge cafeteria containing nothing but foam rubber mats, I again became aware of the fragrance. It was nothing anyone could explain. It seemed to be just one of those odd, meaningless things which happen in everyone's life.

We had returned to California and almost forgotten the whole thing when, one night on the way home from Riverside, I suddenly smelled it again. This time we were on the freeway, traveling at about sixty-five miles per hour, with fresh air circulating through the car. As I pondered whether to mention it to Raye or not, he asked me, "Do you smell something?" I said, "Yes, what do you think it could be?" We agreed that we couldn't even imagine what it was. We rolled the windows all the way down to see if it would dissipate, but it seemed to get even more pronounced. When we arrived home in Cherry Valley, the fragrance was still in the car. We were not to learn its source for many months yet.

Meanwhile, I continued conducting seminars. Groups came together in our home to share experiences and attempt to find answers to basic questions. One day—August 18, 1981, to be precise—I mentioned to those who had come to study with me that I had seen an article about a man in Italy who could manifest objects. I repeated what the article had said about a blue light appearing first in his hand, then gradually the object about which he was thinking would seem to filter out of the light. The light would gradually fade and disappear and the object would remain. It might be a ring, a pendant, or some other small gift for a friend or relative. The article went on to say that this man was very reclusive, that this was the first interview that he had ever given, and that he rarely saw anyone except members of his immediate family.

Margaret Tucker, a member of the group, responded by saying that there was a holy man in India who manifested objects also. She said that he did it so rapidly that either there was no blue light or else it appeared and disappeared too quickly to be recognized by the thousands of people who went to see him. I asked where one might learn more about this holy man. She said that she volunteered in a metaphysical bookstore in Hemet where books about him could be purchased and where a class was held weekly to read such books and discuss them.

When the bookstore opened the following morning, I was waiting at the door. Margaret was on duty. I asked her to show me the book which they were studying in the class about this man who manifested things from the ether. She handed me a book. I paid for it and quickly started home. I wanted to get to a quiet place where I could read and read without being interupted. I felt a certain sense of excitement that something was about to happen—that a real breakthrough was coming.

On arriving home, I settled in my favorite chair and opened the book at random to get a feeling for what it might be like. The page I opened to was page 55 and the first words my eyes fell upon were: "I do go to my devotees first as light, then as fragrance, and, only then, much later, in person." What was happening? Was this the occurrence we had been praying for?

Chapter One

Our prayers had been something like: "Please, oh, please, if there's anybody out there, make Yourself known to us. We know that there is Love, Truth, Wisdom, Soul, Spirit, Principle, and Life, but sometimes we long for a God with skin on—One who will show us what Love is—One who will smooth away our roughness until we can be like Him—One who is here now so that we can see Him with our eyes, hear Him with our ears, and feel His touch upon our hands." We had prayed this way without believing for a minute that it could really happen.

When Raye came home, I met him at the door with the question: "How would you like to go to India?" Evidently sensing something more than small talk in the question, he agreed before even asking: "Why?" After hearing about the experience and seeing the words for himself in *The Golden Age 1980,* Raye was as eager as I, and we began making inquiries. After many calls, we finally were referred to the Sai Foundation in Los Angeles, and Janet Bock told us about a tour that would be leaving from San Francisco in early December. We promptly made arrangements to be members of that tour group. We didn't know much about the teachings of this holy man called Sri Sathya Sai Baba, but we knew that our experiences were undeniable.

When I had attended the class in Hemet, after buying *The Golden Age 1980*, Margaret apologized profusely for having sold me the wrong book. It was *The Golden Age 1979* which the group was reading. This incident only served to convince me that this Being who went to His devotees as fragrance and sold them the right wrong books, if not God incarnate, was at least more Godlike than anyone I had ever before experienced. I had to know Him, whatever the price.

Reading both of the Golden Age volumes gave me a wonderful overview of experiences and reactions to knowing Him, written by people from all walks of life. There were scientists, ministers, priests, educators, government officials, medical doctors, journalists, physicists, healers, parapsychologists, astrologers, lawyers, judges, military officers, a psychiatrist, Hollywood film producers, and even a Kirlian photographer. I quickly became aware that Raye's and my introduction to Him through the fragrance was quite tame compared to the many miraculous rescues and healings experienced by others.

An aerospace engineer, Al Drucker, reported hearing His voice coming from an inoperable radio during a snowstorm. The voice guided him to a safe landing when total destruction of his small plane and the loss of his life and that of his passenger seemed inevitable. Later, Al Drucker learned about Sri Sathya Sai Baba's existence on the planet and went to India to see Him in person as we now planned to do.

Due to my interest in Kirlian photography and the human aura, I was intrigued by the article written by Dr. Frank G. Baranowski. Dr. Baranowski said that he had always been able to see the aura, the energy pattern which surrounds a person. He said that the aura surrounding Sathya Sai Baba was not not like any he had ever seen before. Even though he had had opportunities to study the auras of kings, queens, presidents, and popes, he said that none even began to compare with Baba's. Baba's aura extended thirty or forty feet in all directions and was a beautiful pure pink. This color indicates selfless love, according to Dr. Baranowski, and he went on to report Baba's miraculous healing of his infant grandson who had been born with a heart defect and weighed slightly less than seven pounds when one year of age.

I read *The Holy Man and the Psychiatrist* by Dr. Samuel Sandweiss, and I found it to be an excellent introduction to Sai Baba. The experiences of Dr. Sandweiss were such that many of us can relate to them and apply them to ourselves. But I realized that Baba Himself gave the clearest statement of the way to understand Him—the only way to understand Him. He said, "You cannot understand Me and My secret without first

Chapter One

understanding yourselves. For, if you are too weak to grasp your own reality, how can you hope to fathom the much grander reality of My advent? To grasp My meaning, you have to tear into tatters the doubts and theories you now have and cultivate Love, for the Embodiment of Love can be understood only through Love. The Lord (Krishna in the *Bhagavad Gita*) announced that He would come down for the restoration of dharma and that He would assume human form so that all might gather around Him and feel the thrill of His companionship and conversation. And the Lord has come, as announced."

To understand Him, I would have to understand myself. To understand myself, I would have to find the key to the code, the solution to the puzzle of life. I felt sure that, with His help, I could do that. In the succeeding pages I have attempted to relate my first stumbling steps in that direction. As each of the stories of experiences of other devotees has helped me along the way, it is my hope that the readers of this little volume may be stimulated to increase their personal reflection and introspection, to improve their practical experimentation in the art of living, and to deeply contemplate the words of scripture and spiritually illumined Masters. Through these practices they will find ways in which to better play their own game of life, understand themselves, and hence understand the Embodiment of Love.

******

"The word dharma, which is really bound up with an infinite variety of meanings, is being inadequately described by one word, duty, in the modern age. Duty is something which is connected with an individual, a predicament, or with a particular time or country. On the other hand, dharma is eternal, the same for everyone everywhere. It expresses the significance of the inner voice, the soul or Atma. The birthplace of dharma is the heart. What emanates from the heart as a pure idea, translated into action, is called dharma. If you have to be told in a manner that you can understand, one can say "Do unto others as you want them to do unto you"—that is dharma. Dharma consists of avoiding actions which would hurt others. If anyone causes happiness to you, then you in turn should do such things that will cause happiness to others."

—Baba
Sanathana Sarathi, August, 1986

"Before one's birth, one has no relationship with the world and its material objects. After death, they and all kith and kin disappear. This sojourn is just a game played in the interval."

—Sri Sathya Sai Baba
From *My Baba and I*
By Dr. John Hislop

Chapter One

The
simplest questions
are the most profound.

Where were you born? Where is your home?
Where are you going? What are you doing?

Think about
these once in a while, and
watch your answers
change

From *Illusions*
by Richard Bach

2
"WHERE DID YOU COME FROM?"

We arrived in Prasanthi Nilayam just in time to make afternoon darshan (the time when Sai Baba or any holy person appears to His devotees). We found our assigned rooms, left our luggage, and proceeded to the mandir (temple). I was so busy that I had not had time to wonder whether He would acknowledge my presence, whether I would get a seat, or any of the things that I would think about many, many times at later darshans. I was there. I had managed to get my sari (type of dress worn by Indian ladies) pinned on so that I felt reasonably sure it would not desert me at an inopportune moment. Now all I had to do was watch the door of the veranda where I had been assured Sai Baba would appear sooner or later.

The hundreds of devotees sitting on the sand were very quiet, much quieter than the worshippers before any church service I had ever attended. Suddenly, however, there was a hush, accompanied by a slight rustling, as even the few whispered conversations ceased and everyone sat up to honor the most graceful, the most beautiful person I had ever seen. His hand moved in a delicate upward motion as he stepped off the veranda and moved onto the sand. He was the personification of Grace and Beauty, and I felt love flowing from him that bore no taint of earthly attachment. My mind simply ceased to function because it couldn't keep up with the feelings which were flowing over and through me.

Suddenly He was right there, standing in front of me, smiling like a thousand suns, and asking, "Where did you come from?" My voice had departed for the same realm to which my mind had defected and, try as I might, I simply could not make any words come out. He waited patiently for my answer, finally asking "What happened to your voice?" In a faint squeak, I managed to say, "Oh, it's because I love You so much, Baba." He smiled very much as a mother would at a child who was trying to learn to talk. Then He replied, "And I love you, too." As He glided away, I felt no doubt that I had just looked into the face of God and that He had told me He loved me. Neither the word ecstasy—nor the word bliss—even begins to describe the feeling. Only those who have experienced it can reasonably believe that they know what that moment was like. He had showed me the Divine Mother, an aspect of Him which I needed very much to understand and to emulate, but I was not yet able to benefit from the teaching His words embodied. My heart was singing, "He loves me! He loves me!"

Actually He had given me another experience prior to my seeing Him in person, but I didn't understand that either. Baba has said many times, "If you see Me in a dream, I am there. You cannot dream of Me unless I will it." But my attitude toward dreams had always been that they were just a garbled, rather silly mish-mash of our fears, wishes, and experiences, and that only foolish or superstitious people paid any attention to them. Therefore, when the tour group arrived in New Delhi and spent the night there, and I had a beautiful dream of Baba, I had not given it any credence. It was nice, but meaningless, I thought. I had dreamed that I saw Baba sitting behind a desk. At first I mistook Him for a customs official or an immigration officer. As I drew closer to Him, however, He stood and stretched out his arms. With them opened wide as if to embrace me, He said, "Welcome to India."

Chapter Two

Baba has also said many times, "Every word I utter has meaning. I do not waste words." Although small talk had never appealed to me, I could not imagine a Being able to live in the world and say only meaningful, significant things. How could this be? I didn't exactly reject the idea, I just couldn't take it in. So I did not even decide not to consider His question meaningful, I just did not think of it at all. But Baba, like Life, will not take our rejection of His message. He will repeat it until we hear Him.

And so it was that on my second visit to Prasanthi Nilayam (the Abode of Eternal Peace) in May, 1982, He again greeted me with a question. It was: "Where have you been, Bangalore?" As He had a mischievous twinkle in His eye, I thought He was teasing me a little for returning so soon. I had only gone home on the last day of February. Less than three months later, here I was again. So I answered, "No, Swami, I have been back to the United States."

On the following day He again asked me, "Where did you come from?" I replied, "California, Baba." I was delighted to have His attention, and that was all either of these experiences meant to me at first. On the third day of this visit, however, I was privileged to attend a discourse which Baba was giving in the auditorium of the college. My seat was in the first row. When Swami came down the stairs from the stage to greet those who were seated outside on the ground, He made a slight detour, stopped in front of me, and asked pointedly, "Where did you come from?" He continued on His way, clearly uninterested in any answer I might give. My complacency was thoroughly shaken this time. Though I babbled some response at His retreating back, I knew that He was not asking for geographical information. He was, in fact, educating me in accordance with His own definition of education.

He told those attending the First Conference on Education in Human Values for College Teachers that day: "Education is not so much a matter of problem-solving; it is a matter of problem-posing." The problem He had posed three times in three days became the uppermost thing in my thought. I contemplated it day and night. I brought all of the information I had stored in my brain to bear on it, but I found none of those answers helped at all.

Wordsworth expressed it in beautiful poetic language. He said, "Trailing clouds of glory do we come from God, who is our home." I could recite the words. I believed them. But believing was not what Baba was talking about. By definition, to believe is not to know. He was asking me to be so sure of where I came from that I didn't need to believe or understand. Does it ever occur to anyone to say: "Well, I think I came from California. To the best of my understanding, I have come from the United States. I genuinely believe I came here from the Western hemisphere." Of course not. When we reply to such a question we reply with conviction, with an unshakable knowing. I had recited the words "Man is not material; he is spiritual" thousands of times, but knowing does not necessarily follow saying. How to know, I didn't know!

Little by little, as I searched deeper and deeper within myself for the answer to this simple little question, all of the booklearning I had gained in fifty years of studying was seen to be just that—booklearning. Nothing more. Finally empty of theories, beliefs, understanding, and dependence on brainpower, I asked Baba in prayerful surrender to give me the answer. This request was a silent yearning which left no room for anything else. I waited some time in the quiet darkness, hoping for clear insight to come, but finally fell asleep still unknowing.

At an early morning hour, before daylight, I awakened to a light brighter than the sun. It filled my heart "as when a lion roareth." The words which filtered out of the light were: "You have emerged from Me and you will merge with Me again." Knowing flooded in. I not only knew where I had come from, I knew where I was going. I knew what it meant to have "peace that

Chapter Two

passeth all understanding." I knew that Baba was in my heart and that He would always be there. It almost seemed to me at that moment that I knew everything, but that was far from the fact. A breakthrough had come, and it was wonderful, but when daylight came the world and its waking experiences came with it.

I would gradually come to realize that the value of knowing where I came from and where I am going is that this knowledge enables me to carry out my earthly duties with greater equanimity and purer love. Spiritual enlightenment is measured in units of service to mankind.

******

"Service is the most difficult of the nine steps to Inner Reality.....It is basically action arising out of the yearning to win the grace of God.....It is the most important step to erase the ego.....Through service alone can man attain mastery of the senses, the passions and the predilections, and through that reach Divinity itself.....I have come to teach you the proper attitude of service—for Love expresses as service, and God is Love.....Service of man leads to the discovery of man as God."

—Baba

OH, PLEASE, BABA, DISSOLVE THIS I

I, I, I, myself, I
individualized ignorance,
Asking who, what, and why.
Not Self at all—
The ego we call
I, I, I, myself, I.

I saw it, I did it,
I lost or I won.
I'm attached to my mother,
my daughter, my son.

I'm elated, dejected,
Loved or rejected.
I'm so incomplete!
Oh, please, Baba, dissolve this I
At your lotus feet.
Let it merge with you
And blissfully be
Sai, Sai, Sai, the Self, Sai

—Joy Thomas
Sanathana Sarathi, August 1986

3

"I AM PREPARED TO GIVE YOU WHATEVER YOU WANT"

On December 16, 1981, Baba took our group into His room for an interview. As soon as all thirty-four of us had managed to be seated, Baba looked around the room and said emphatically: "I am prepared to give you whatever you want." Then He asked several of us individually what we wanted. When He asked me, I responded with that which was my whole heart's desire. "I want to be your instrument, Swami," I said. He looked at me searchingly, I felt that He was looking deep inside my consciousness to see whether or not I was sincere—or perhaps whether or not I was worthy. Whatever it was, after a few moments He seemed to signal acquiescence, and He turned to someone else.

The first evidence of His response to my request came several months later. In the excitement and thrill of discovery that there was an Avatar (descended Being) on the planet and that anyone could see Him, I was trying to spread the news. At that time, He had asked that no one do that, but I was not aware of those instructions. After I had spoken to several groups in the area and shown slides which we took of Baba and Prasanthi Nilayam, several people expressed an interest in meeting to sing devotional songs and to study the teachings of Sathya Sai Baba. We gratefully opened our home and began regular meetings.

Six months later, the group was accredited as the Sathya Sai Baba Center of Cherry Valley. I was elected president, and it was my greatest joy to serve in this capacity. Raye was elected vice-president, after declining the presidency, and he fulfilled his behind-the-scene duties faithfully and regularly with gratitude to Baba for the opportunity to serve.

When I learned that I was not supposed to be showing slides and giving lectures about Baba, I stopped doing so. However, I just couldn't maintain my interest in the type of presentations I had been making before meeting Baba. That left me with time on my hands even after giving my full attention to all Center duties. When Barbara Bozzani mentioned that she needed help on the *Sathya Sai Newsletter*, I promptly volunteered. Once more I felt that Baba had responded to my request to be His instrument, and I pray every day to be worthy of that grace.

Quite recently, when the plan for this book appeared to me early one morning, I felt such a sense of wonder at the extent of His giving. I recalled that, when in high school, after a full semester devoted to soul-searching as well as some more mundane research into vocational opportunities, I had stated that the two things I would most like to do in my life were to be a florist and to write a book. It seemed as if one of those desires might be fulfilled now—if, in fact, the book became a reality. Of course, the other never would be, but that didn't seem to be a vital matter. A few days later, however, as I was sitting patiently and painstakingly editing the English translation of one of Baba's discourses, a devotee who was reading Baba's writings exclaimed, "Oh, every one of Baba's words is a perfect flower!" Again I was filled with awe at the variety of ways He uses to fulfill His promises. If you think He hasn't answered your prayer, just wait! He has or He will. Even retroactively! Our limited perceptions don't always recognize that our desire to be a florist has been fulfilled by the privilege of arranging the beautiful bouquet of words in a Divine discourse. His creativity is

Chapter Three

unlimited, and His joy in granting our desires is unlimited also. Our bliss is His food, as He has told us many times.

Other desires, which were abandoned long ago and almost lost to memory, are coming to fruition now. In my first two years of college, I majored in journalism. The thrill of "putting the paper to bed" was greater to me than winning a gold medal at the Olympics or being elected to a high office. But after marriage and the births of two children, I changed my major to education, feeling teaching to be a more practical career for a wife and mother. Now, with Swami's grace, I experience the pure joy of fulfillment each time we send an issue of the **Sathya Sai Newsletter** to the printer. Not only has He given me the privilege of serving Him, but He took those two years of preparation in journalism and put them to use, that not a fragment should be wasted!

The same thing has happened to my preparation in the field of counseling. During the years that I served in the public schools, I spent only two as a counselor. I never felt that the many hours spent in studying to earn the counseling credential were wasted, because I have had many opportunities to put the knowledge to use in situations other than in the public schools. However, recently Baba has brought all of my previous training in psychology, counseling, regression therapy, and Patricia Allen's Want Therapy (transactional analysis) into fulfillment. Utilizing Phyllis Krystal's **Cutting the Ties That Bind**, which is a perfect blend of Western psychology and Eastern mysticism, I have been able to be of greater service to others than I ever imagined would be possible.

Phyllis Krystal had been involved in her own inner search for the meaning of life for over twenty-five years, using a meditation technique which she calls a waking dream or reverie. During this time a series of visualization exercises and symbols were revealed to her, which she ultimately described in the aforementioned book. She has been making regular visits to see

Sai Baba since 1972. He not only gave his blessings and approval to the book in which she outlined her counseling techniques, but He also instructed her to write a book about Him. In this book, *Sai Baba: The Ultimate Experience*, she states that Baba has been her supreme Zen master, and continues: "There are many different paths from which a Master selects the appropriate one according to the individual requirements of each aspirant. Even though many thousands of people throng to visit Baba to obtain His blessing, He can not only tell exactly which ones are ready to tread the inner path back to union with the God within, but just which path is best suited to each one for the attainment of that goal. He recommends the path of bhakti or devotion for the majority of people living in this present age, as it is the safest method for everyone. However, even when many people happen to be taking a similar path, the actual steps along the way are very different, as are the various tests which determine the progress and understanding of each individual devotee." As my Master, Baba not only has directed me to the path of devotion, but He has also blessed me with the benefits of Phyllis Krystal's work for myself and to use in counseling others.

It was in just such a counseling situation recently that we saw another example of the way Baba gives us everything we want. A couple who had come for help with marital problems were asked to visualize themselves joined with each other and with me in the triangle or maypole[1], symbolizing our oneness with each other and our connection to Baba. As we asked Swami for His assistance and guidance for this couple, a vision appeared clearly to me at the apex of the triangle. I saw Baba sitting in a tall chair, upholstered in red velvet. He was holding a golden wedding ring in each hand. He held them out, as if offering them to us, and in doing so brought them together until they just touched each other, forming a figure eight. I was so grateful for the clear direction. The figure eight [2] is one of the basic symbols

Chapter Three

used in *Cutting the Ties That Bind* and I felt confident that we would be doing exactly the right thing by beginning that exercise. For the husband, however, the vision had even more meaning. He had written a letter to Baba two weeks earlier, asking for two golden wedding rings. He knew that he had just been given the gift he wanted. I had not known of his request, and he had certainly not expected his wish to be granted in this way; but when it happened, we both knew without a doubt that Baba was right there with us, counseling and guiding us every step along the way.

Sometimes the little gifts are the most precious. A number of these have occurred in connection with Phyllis Krystal's work. When I was with her in her office one day, she pointed out a nondescript little bird sitting on the fence just outside her office window. She said that it often came there and perched on the corner of the fence when she was with someone who had come for her help, usually just before they would enter the reverie state to ask for guidance. She felt it to be another of the assurances that Baba gives us of His presence. The next day, just as I sat down to begin writing the material for this book, the same type of nondescript little bird flew under our patio roof to come and perch on the door sill just beside the chair in which I was sitting. Coincidence? Perhaps. but in the nine years we have lived here, no bird has ever before flown under our patio roof to perch on the door sill beside my chair.

A similar incident occurred at the home of the Drs. Naren and Hyma Reddy recently. As I sat writing a little note to Baba, thanking Him for His grace, a hibiscus blossom which had been placed on the picture frame above me came tumbling down into my lap. This is considered in India to be a clear sign of His grace, and it seemed that way to me, too, as the timing was so perfect. I was just finishing the letter "e" on the word "grace" as the flower fell.

My continuing prayer to be His instrument and a worthy recipient of His grace was expressed so beautifully by Professor Kasturi. The inscription he wrote in my copy of his inspired book **Prasanthi** was this: "Prasanthi is achieved when we are accepted as His instrument, say, the **Pen** He holds to inscribe His love. N. Kasturi. 23.11.85."

******

[1] The triangle exercise is the foundation from which all of the other visualizations begin. It is used to link two people working together as partners with the Higher Self in order to obtain guidance from the wisdom within each of the participants. The partners visualize a line of light connecting them at ground level. They then imagine a line of light going up each spine and out through the top of each of their heads, continuing up to meet at the apex of the triangle. The meeting point is termed "the Hi C" for High Consciousness. Each session is given over to the Hi C, asking that the partners be given whatever guidance they need or are ready for at that particular time. The maypole exercise is basically the same as the triangle except that it is used when more than two people are working together seeking guidance from the Hi C.

[2]"A simple visualization exercise, using a symbol in the form of a figure eight, is a great help in reducing domination, either by another person or by our own desire for something. During a visit to Baba I was wearing a ring in the form of a figure eight made of gold wire. He noticed it and leaned over to touch it, saying with an approving smile, 'Good. Figure eight is also the letter "S" for Sai.'

"The first step in using it is to visualize, imagine, or think of a circle of gold light. To establish the size of the circle, imagine it to have the radius of your extended arm, with a straight line falling from the fully-extended fingertips. It is important to think of this circle on the ground around your feet. Immediately in front of you, visualize a similar gold circle just touching your own, the two forming a figure eight. Place the person or thing which seems to control you in the middle of the second circle.

"Starting at the point where the two circles touch, imagine a pale, neon blue light flowing around the second circle in front of you in a clockwise direction, from your left around the outside and back to where the two circles meet. Let the blue light continue on around the left side of your own circle, behind your back, around your right side and back to where they meet. Continue to visualize this flow around the figure eight for two minutes and repeat it whenever you think of the dominating person or thing during the day.

"This exercise will greatly lessen the control over you by either another person's will, or your own attachment to something you desire. You will then be free to follow Baba's will instead of your own or someone else's."

—Phyllis Krystal
Sathya Sai Newsletter
Spring 1985

"Trying to learn from the scriptures is difficult. One scripture often seems to contradict another. For example, I have told you that the daily experience of a man is different from the Truth itself. Now I'm telling you that only that person who bases his conclusions on daily experience can reach the goal. Nothing experienced through the medium of the body is true, but daily experiences, in spite of the fact that they are of a transient nature, are based on something which is permanent. When a car moves along the road, the road itself does not move. At least we think that the road is not moving. Of course, in a way it is. The whole earth is moving very fast, just as the other planets are. The atoms inside us are also moving. Whatever we see externally is a reflection of our inner being. Our experiences, then, are only reflections. When we develop an inner search, our outer experiences become sacred."

—Sathya Sai Baba
Yugadi Discourse, March 22, 1985

4
"LIFE IS A TEACHER"

One Thursday morning I had been asked to lead a study group. The chairman was unable to attend that day and several of those who regularly participated were absent also. We were studying Baba's teachings, and I always enjoyed the time spent with like-minded others, discussing the Avatar's* words of wisdom. On this particular morning, a new person came in, sat down, and began asking questions which, at first, seemed logical and sincere for a newcomer. Gradually, however, I began to realize that all was not quite as it should be. The questions became farther and farther afield, and a personal story began to unfold. It was a story of persecution that was considerably out of the normal range of experience.

Later that day, in a discussion with another devotee of Baba, I asked the question: "Why do you suppose that I had that experience this morning?" Though I had spent two hours in an earnest effort to answer questions as asked and to be the instrument with which Baba could heal and teach all who came, I ended up with the feeling that there was a message meant for me and that I had not yet accepted it. Again I asked, "Why, on a day when I had been asked to lead the group, did a classic paranoid appear and require my entire attention?" I could neither answer the question nor stop asking it.

The next morning when Raye was ready to go to his office, he found that the car would not start. An annoying electrical problem had been recurring for months. The car would refuse to start and refuse to respond to the ministrations of any of our local mechanics, but by the time we would have it towed thirty-five miles to the nearest dealer, it would fire at the first touch of the starter. So here it was again. Raye tried several different things that came to him to do and finally got the engine going. He asked me to call the dealer and tell the service manager what had happened and that he was on his way to see again if they could find the problem. I did as he asked, and I reminded the service manager that we had been having this same problem for almost a year and that we were hoping for a solution soon.

Having taken care of this quite-necessary duty, I settled down to my inquiry of the previous day. Baba has told us that others are our mirror. I searched myself diligently, looking for fear of persecution or fear of any kind, and I just didn't find any. It seemed to me that I was unusually fearless. I have traveled alone by car, by plane, by train, and by bus; I have addressed large audiences (public speaking is supposed to be the number-one fear today); I have dental work done without anesthesia; I don't panic during hurricanes or earthquakes. Why would I meet a person who was abnormally fearful? There seemed to be no answer, so I went on with the tasks of the day.

When Raye arrived home that evening, I asked him about his experience at the car dealership. I specifically asked whether or not the service manager had told him that I called. He said, "Yes, he did. He said, 'Man! Your wife is sure paranoid about this car, isn't she?'" Recognition came instantly. He was exactly right. I was unduly afraid of having mechanical problems. I was especially paranoid about hidden ones—those that caused inconvenience and expense over and over but could not be located. I had been persecuted by such problems on several occasions. I recalled a beautiful yellow Studebaker convertible,

Chapter Four

a cute little bright-red Nash Metropolitan, and a favorite Chevy station wagon, all of which were finally sold because of mechanical problems which could not be located. I was fascinated by the way this situation had been brought to the level of awareness, and I recognized it as another major breakthrough in learning to play the game of life, but I wasn't yet quite clear as to how all of the pieces would fit together.

One thing I did note, however, was that within a very few days after I saw what the message was that these two experiences seemed to have been designed and coordinated to bring, the mechanic found that by replacing a simple part, costing less than five dollars, the car's will-o'-the-wisp problem was solved and has not recurred. Life seemed to be saying: "Message received; messenger no longer necessary!"

In the meantime, Raye had been having an experience which was too pointed to ignore. In his work as a realtor, he had listed a house for sale for a gentleman whose wife was deceased. The client, whom we will call Mr. Jahn, seemed to be unusually difficult to work with. He would become extremely agitated about matters involving very small sums of money, become threatening and angry without provocation, and generally behave in a very unstable manner.

One evening, after Raye had gone to visit him to take care of some necessary paper work in regard to the sale of his house, we were surprised to realize that Raye's pager was missing. This little electronic device was necessary to his serving his clients promptly and efficiently, so he got back into the car and returned to Mr. Jahn's house to retrieve it. Mr. Jahn said that he had not seen it, but that if he did he would call. Raye then retraced his steps to several other places he had been, but the pager could not be found.

Several days passed and there were occasions on which he was needed by his office while he was out showing property. The loss of the pager seemed quite a major inconvenience. We asked Baba for His help and waited. Almost a week had passed without any clues having turned up. Then early one morning, as I again beseeched Baba for clear direction as to what to do about the pager, words not preceded by thought came into my consciousness. They were: "Accept this loss as My gift to you, and be at peace." This was certainly not the message either of us had been expecting, but we recognized it as authentic guidance and so made every effort to maintain our peace of mind.

The next day Mr. Jahn called and said that he had the pager and that he wanted a reward for returning it. Again, it seemed that once the message had been received, the messenger was no longer necessary.

The pager was back on the job now, but so was Mr. Jahn! One day when I had offered to answer the telephones in the office while everyone else was out in the field, Mr. Jahn walked in. As fate would have it, the file on his property was lying out on the desk. Before I could realize what was happening, he had seen it, picked it up, and was holding it against his chest with both hands, saying, "This is mine!" I was alone, and I realized he was going to remove all of the office records relating to the sale of his house if I didn't act fast.

Silently, I called for Baba's help, while speaking as soothingly as I could aloud. I assured Mr. Jahn that he had been given copies of everything in the file, but he denied that vehemently. I asked him to wait until Raye returned, but he insisted he needed the papers right that minute. Then I offered to make copies of everything for him, and he said "You're not kidding me? You'll really make the copies? You won't just take my file away and not come back?" I assured him that I would really make copies for him. Finally he very reluctantly gave up the file, and I made the copies and gave them to him.

At last the house was sold. Mr. Jahn contested every item on the cost sheet, sometimes going to a dozen or more escrow offices in nearby towns before finding one that offered some

Chapter Four

service for a few dollars less than the one where his escrow was being handled. After ninety days, very few of which were without some contact with Mr. Jahn, the escrow was scheduled to close. Bypassing Raye and the people in his office, Mr. Jahn went to the escrow company and cancelled the escrow. He told them that his children were coming to live with him and so he had changed his mind about selling.

We thought that was the end of the story. We heard that no children ever came to live with him, but we didn't give it much thought beyond a sigh of relief that it was all behind us. We were quite surprised, then, when, about six months later, a call came to our home one evening. When Raye hung up the receiver, he said to me, "You won't believe who that was! It was Mr. Jahn! He said he'd like to relist his house in a couple of weeks."

"What did you tell him?" I asked. He replied, "I just told him to call me when he was ready and we would make an appointment to get together."

Raye has always said that he is in the business to serve, but it seemed to me that this was almost more than could be expected. We discussed it at some length. We have both leaned heavily on Baba's teachings: "Act, without being attached to the results of the action" and "Serve all, without judgment as to their worthiness or unworthiness," and also on the Biblical quotation: "All that the Father giveth me shall come to me, and him that cometh to me I shall in no wise cast out." No matter how we tried, we could not come up with a valid excuse for not relisting the property if the call came to do so.

So, two weeks later, Mr. Jahn called again, and Raye relisted the property. The entire scenario began again. It was almost an instant replay. If anything, the problems were greater the second time. Raye sold the house again, this time to a Christian minister and his wife. Ninety more days in escrow, almost every day of which Mr. Jahn threatened to cancel the escrow. He quibbled over every word, every penny, and began being even more belligerent than before. It did not seem possible that the escrow would ever close. With the minister and his wife sleeping on the floor of the church and Mr. Jahn really needing to be free of a house that was much too large for one person alone, it seemed so right for the sale to be consummated. We prayed for Baba's help, but the situation only seemed to grow more hopeless.

Finally, one morning Raye said, "I had the strangest dream last night. I dreamed that the reason Mr. Jahn is so attached to his house is because he loved his wife so much and he has her buried in the back yard." That did not seem to be too wild a dream, as dreams go. We did know that he missed his wife very much. At first I didn't give the dream any more than passing interest, but it stayed close to the surface of my thought all day. Upon retiring, I asked Baba again for His help to get the escrow closed and to learn the needed lesson.

The next day, as I awoke, I saw the whole picture quite clearly. The first thing I realized was that Mr. Jahn was playing an essential role in our lives and that he was playing it well. He had a lesson to teach us, and he had come back to try again since we had not been receptive the first time. Raye's dream was the key to the whole experience. Mr. Jahn was Raye's mirror, and we had both been unable to see into the mirror clearly. Now it was plain. Raye's first marriage had ended in divorce, much to his sorrow. He had loved his wife and children very much, and the pain of that separation was buried deep in his consciousness. His efforts now to move into a new house, or higher state of consciousness, were being thwarted by this subconscious attachment.

From the moment we realized the message that this whole experience entailed, Mr. Jahn became as meek and mild as a lamb. He signd papers that he had said he would never sign, the escrow closed without a hitch, and we have never heard of him since. Wherever he is, we hope he has been as blessed by the experience as we have.

Chapter Four

*"The Avatar is the Lord, majestic, poweful and all-perfect, formless and without name, who descends to the plane of earthly existence in full awareness of His higher reality. He acts as the exemplar of the virtues man must cultivate and as a channel of grace to help human beings to become perfect in their nature and to raise human life to a higher plane. The ***Bhagavad Gita*** offers the clearest statement of the nature and purpose of the Avatar. Krishna says that he has taken human birth to restore to humanity ancient knowledge and tradition which had been lost through the passing of time and that He does so from age to age. He restates those ancient and unchanging truths: for the born, death is certain; the body is but the Soul's clothing, and its loss is not to be grieved; the Self, the Lord's image in man, is indestructible. Man must perform his duty fearlessly; he has the right to action alone and the highest action (karma) is free from selfishness and the desire for reward. Renunciation, devotion to and refuge in the Lord lead man to union with Him. Krishna describes His larger social purpose as the protection of the virtuous, the destruction of the wicked, and the restablishment of righteousness in the affairs of men. To reinforce Arjuna's faith, He reveals to him His transcendent form—majestic, awesome, omnipresent, and omnipotent. But the God of the ***Gita*** is no abstract, forbidding spirit. He is a God deeply concerned with the well-being of men. He is desirous and capable of forging relations with them. His is teacher, elder statesman, consummate diplomatist, charioteer, companion, guide, guardian, and friend. He has taken human birth precisely to be able to forge personal bonds with human beings. The Avatar is everyman's personal God."

—Maharajakrishna Rasgotra
Golden Age 1980

"Use the world as a training ground for sacrifice, service, expansion of the heart, cleansing of the emotions. That is the only value it has."

—Baba
Words of Jesus and Sathya Sai Baba

"Wisdom is ofttimes nearer when we stoop than when we soar."

—William Wordsworth

5

"BRING ME YOUR GARBAGE"

Having become aware of the lessons in our daily experiences, hardly a day passed without one really pointing out something we needed to know. There was the day, for instance, when I had joined Raye for lunch at a restaurant near his office. I mentioned to him that one of the cars had two tires which seemed rather worn. I asked him if I might change cars with him, since I would feel more secure in the one which had four new tires. He concurred, and I got into the car to drive to our home three miles away. I had driven only about two miles when a sudden noise and bump indicated that a tire had gone quite flat. I began to laugh. I should have known that my security was not to be found in things.

Getting out of the car, I found that it had run over a broken bottle, slicing a six-inch hole in one tire and rendering it completely useless, of course. At that moment, a shiny black Trans Am pulled to a stop on the other side of the road. A handsome dark-skinned young man, dressed in immaculate, expensive clothing, stepped out. He crossed the street and offered to change the tire, speaking with a delightful foreign accent. Not wishing to cause him any inconvenience, I asked if he would just call my husband for me. He replied that it would be quicker and easier for him to change the tire than to make the telephone call. Indeed, he changed the tire in what seemed to me to be an incredibly short time. As I had felt some concern about his clothing, I was pleased to see that he was as clean and well-pressed when he finished as when he had alighted from his car. Not even his hands were soiled.

It had occurred to me to offer him money, but, upon reflection, that seemed inappropriate. So I asked him if he lived in the Village, thinking that he might be a neighbor. He replied, "No, I'm your garbageman." The lesson seemed to be in regard to security—one which I recognized as having been an excellent reminder that security was always to be found in our inner Divinity—not in any outer circumstances. I renewed my efforts to always rely on Baba for security, and I gave some casual thought to the role the garbage man played in this little drama, but it was not until several months later that a deeper significance of the entire incident was revealed.

This time the key was located in the dream of a friend. Patricia Bradley had led the study group in Baba's teachings which I had attended as a wide-eyed beginner, and in which I had learned the pleasures and benefits of satsang (association with other spiritual aspirants) as well as gaining a grasp of the philosophy which Baba expounded. And it was in this class one Thursday morning that Patricia shared with all of us a dream which she had had the night before. She said that Baba had appeared in her dream, standing outside her house. She went outside to join Him and they stood shoulder-to-shoulder, watching the mountains which surround the house. She said that the mountains were moving, either rising off the earth or just growing taller, she wasn't quite sure which. She and Baba enjoyed this glorious sight together for a few moments. Then he turned to her and said, "Now go back in the house and bring me your garbage."

I saw now why it had been so important that the handsome young man who had changed my tire recite the line: "I'm your garbage man." He had come to collect the garbage of my insecurities and to dispose of them. That was an important part of the message he had come to deliver. Just as Mr. Jahn had played the role of a villain to deliver a vital message, our garbage man had played the role of a hero. In both cases, however, the important part of the experience was the message.

When I began to get a glimmer of understanding of the necessity to decode every part of the experience, another friend stepped in to provide the inpetus to go further with the interpretation of this one. Karl Trisler asked me if I had any idea why the car had been a Trans Am. I hadn't, but I knew instantly that it could easily be another part of the message, and I didn't want to miss a word. Looking up the words "trans" and "am" in **Webster's New World Dictionary,** I found the following: "trans: above and beyond" and "am: the first person singular present indicative of BE." I felt that the message for me was that this entire experience was above and beyond the first person singular, but that its presence in my life was indicative of Being. It was as Baba has said: "When we develop an inner search, all of our outer experiences become sacred." This was a sacred experience, indicative of Being, and it became the first of a series of such experiences which followed.

The most important messages are frequently delivered through the least desirable experiences. We don't prefer to have flat tires or plumbing problems, we don't choose to lose items that seem necessary to our smooth functioning in the carrying out of our earthly duties, but gradually we can come to recognize that these experiences are among the most valuable gifts that Life has to offer us. Unfortunately, at the time of the incident I am about to relate, I had not yet reached this level of awareness.

It was on a Sunday morning that the water simply refused to go down the drain in the kitchen sink. Raye had removed the trap under the sink and tried all of the known home remedies to no avail. It was evident that this was a job for a professional plumber. We decided that, since we would be gone most of the day anyway, we would not call the plumber until the following morning. We were attending a satsang that afternoon, and I had planned to bake a cake. After debating the pros and cons of attempting the cake with a stopped-up drain or of buying one at the bakery, I decided to go ahead with the project at home.

Raye had used an aluminum pie tin to catch the drips under the sink when he had removed the pipe and I noticed that the pie tin was sitting on the kitchen counter. Wanting to be sure that there would be no possibility of contamination, I picked up the pie tin with the intention of taking it to the bathroom to empty it there. Somehow, in the process of this maneuver, I moved too quickly and the water sloshed over the side of the pie tin and into the back of the television set. I was aghast at what I had done. Berating myself for clumsiness and stupidity, I dried the outside of the set and got the hair dryer from the bedroom. I aimed the hair dryer at the back of the television in the wild hope that the warm air would dry up the water quickly enough to prevent damage.

Although I am not the least bit secretive, as a rule, I found myself unable to tell Raye what I had done. I didn't even try the set to see whether or not it would work. It was not until we returned home that evening and Raye turned it on that my worst fears were confirmed. What had been a nice sharp picture at our last viewing, now looked like a Maine snowstorm. Raye commented that the set was over ten years old and he guessed it was time to have it overhauled. I meekly agreed, still unable to confess the part I had played in the situation.

The next morning, after Raye had left, taking the television set with him to leave at the repair shop, I decided I would move a small black-and-white set from our bedroom into the family room where the other set had been. I did so and turned it on. To my surprise, its screen showed the same snowstorm. Knowing that there was nothing wrong with that set, I began to check to

Chapter Five

see what could be interfering with the reception. It took only a glance to realize what had happened. In my desire to make sure that I was baking the cake under the most sanitary conditions, I had mixed it on the breakfast bar. In order to plug in the mixer, I had unplugged the video cassette recorder (VCR). Without the VCR plugged in, the television was not receiving input from the cable and so naturally could not produce a clear picture. I plugged the VCR into the electrical outlet and the picture on the television became sharp and clear. I realized then that there had been nothing wrong with the other set either. The problem had arisen only because my guilt feelings were so great that they blinded me to any other possibility.

    I called Raye, then, and asked him if he could have the local shop check the television on their cable or antenna before they sent it out. I told him that there was a possibility that it had been only because of the unplugged VCR that it wasn't working. Such was found to be the case, and the part the television set had played in this little drama was over. I reviewed my own history and could recall numerous occasions on which, as a child, I had been punished for breaking or ruining things. There was no reasonable or logical explanation for my still reacting in this manner, however. Raye would not have been angry or critical. These guilt feelings had been brought to the level of awareness, but I still was not quite clear on just how to "go back into the house" to give them to Baba.

    The next incident in this series began one afternoon as two other devotees and I were preparing to leave the room in which we had been working. Vidya Alekal asked Barbara Bozzani and me whether or not we smelled vibhuti*. Barbara immediately responded, "Yes, I do." I sniffed the air expectantly but smelled nothing. I felt quite disappointed and immediately began to search for the error in my thinking or behavior.

    For more than an hour, as I was driving home, I prayed to Baba to reveal to me what I had done wrong and to help me to avoid making the same mistake again. In spite of repeated entreaties and earnest self-inquiry, thirty-six hours passed without my having received an answer. On awaking the second morning, with the question still unresolved, I felt totally off-center. I tried not to be out of sorts but was not able to disguise my irritability. Raye left for his office saying that he hoped I'd feel better soon.

Closing my eyes for another period of meditation, I was suddenly aware of the heavenly fragrance of vibhuti. I reveled in the joy of the scent for a few moments, then another question jolted me out of my reverie. "Why now, Baba?" I asked. "The other afternoon I was centered, peaceful, and working on Your Newsletter, and You showed me no grace. This morning I awoke lazy, disgruntled, cross with my husband, and the fragrance of Your presence enfolds me. Why?"

Listening patiently for the answer, I relaxed into reverie again and these words appeared clearly on the screen of my heart: "In this way I bring to your remembrance that you are guiltless. I love you because of who you are, not because of what you do. I am your very Self. You are My very Self. I created you in the pure joy of Self-expression. When you judge yourself, you imagine yourself to be separate from Me. Surrender now, and just be what We are—Love incarnate."

---

*Vibhuti is the sacred ash which Sai Baba frequently materializes for His devotees. It is symbolic of the ultimate reality which remains when the dross of ego is burned away by the fire of illumination.

Chapter Five

"Verily it is not for the sake of the husband
that the husband is dear,
but for the sake of the Self.

And it is not for the sake of the wife
that the wife is dear,
but for the sake of the Self."

The Brihadaranyaka Upanishad 4.V.2

6

"WHERE IS YOUR HUSBAND"

The first time Baba asked me "Where is your husband?" I pointed to the men's side of the darshan area, and He seemed satisfied with my answer. The second time He asked, we were in His interview room and I pointed to Raye sitting in the back corner of the room. This time He smiled but followed His first question with another: "And what is his name?" I replied, "Raye, Swami." He looked puzzled, as if He had not heard me, and asked, "What?" I responded more clearly, then, and added some helpful information: "Raye, Swami. His name is Raye, like a ray of sunshine." This time He smiled in obvious approval of my answer. Why did such a simple response to a simple question elicit such a vigorous approval, I wondered. It took me a number of months, greater familiarity with Baba's frequent use of the pun or play on words, and deeper understanding of His teachings before I was able to understand this particular incident.

The question itself is not one which is quickly or easily answered. For me, the answer was buried under layers of habitual thought patterns that would yield only slowly to the impetus of Baba's love. Just as He had done with the question "Where did you come from?" He persisted in asking "Where is your husband?" until He was certain that I would not just put the question aside and forget it. One day at Brindavan (Baba's college at Whitefield), He stopped in front of me, and I asked to be allowed to kiss His feet, saying, "Padnamaskar, Swami?" I was so confident that He would grant my request that I leaned forward on my knees, preparing to put my lips on His soft little brown feet. However, much to my surprise, He said, "Sit down!"

Unwilling to believe what I had heard, I repeated the words "Padnamaskar, Swami?" Again He replied, "Sit down," and began to move away. He took eight or nine steps, then turned back to face me and asked quite sternly, "Where is your husband?"

After that experience, I desperately wanted to know the answer. I wanted more than anything to recapture the feeling of Mother Love and escape the Father Discipline, both of whom Swami personifies so well. One of the ladies sitting near me had heard the interchange and wanted to be helpful. She said, "The right answer is: "You're my Husband, Swami!" Of course. How could I have been so dense? My mind began presenting stored data to confirm this conclusion. I knew the Bible verse "Thy maker is thy husband." In my study of Christian Science I had memorized Mary Baker Eddy's teaching: "God is our only real relative on earth or in heaven." I wouldn't make the same mistake again. The next time He asked, I would be ready.

I had joined the Drs. Benito and Dominga Reyes and a few friends who had traveled with them, and so had been invited in for an interview with their group. Baba looked around the room as if taking roll call, and then He looked at me and asked, "Where is your husband?" Without hesitation, I replied, "You're my Husband, Swami." But instead of seeming delighted, as I had thought He might, He frowned and asked again, "Where?" I repeated the answer I had given Him, this time a little louder and with an effort to sound more convincing. He looked at me as if I were somewhat simple minded, turned to Benito Reyes, and asked, "Where is her husband?" Dr. Reyes responded, "He is in California, Swami." Baba nodded, then, and appeared quite satisfied with the answer.

It seems to me now that I should have known better than to try to give Baba a right answer. He doesn't listen to our words; He listens to the feelings we have in our hearts. Because He knew me better than I knew myself, He was giving me push after push toward self-inquiry. He was bringing my days of depending on textbooks and teachers for my answers to an end. I felt very humble and genuinely willing to begin my self-search. Baba must have recognized the effect His little play had had on me because He granted padnamaskar at the end of the interview. Being a symbol of humility and surrender, as well as devotion, kissing Baba's feet was the perfect end to that part of the lesson. It also illustrated a pattern of Baba's behavior that I would come to know well. Even though He found it necessary to be stern with me to wake me up to what I needed to know, the moment I showed the slightest sign of becoming aware of what He was trying to do, He would then shower me with Love.

As I reviewed the incidents, I saw that He first pointed out that my husband's name was Raye, putting the words "like a ray of sunshine" in my mouth. Then He made it clear that I felt no genuine surrender to either my husband or to Him by not allowing me to just go through the motions of kissing His feet. Finally, He had refused to accept my verbal statement of devotion, knowing it was not yet heart-felt. But when I was genuinely feeling humble, even though the situation was still a long way from being corrected, He showed His Love, compassion, and support by granting padnamaskar.

I didn't feel that I was completely lacking in humility. Isn't it strange that we can be so totally blind to our shortcomings? As I looked searchingly within to find this blemish, I remembered that this was not the first time I had been given the message that I needed more humility. The body had been giving out signals for a long time, but I hadn't known what to do about them.

I had a history of knee problems. They began, my mother has told me, before I could either walk or talk. They were diagnosed as "growing pains." Every known remedy was applied, including removing my tonsils and adenoids, in an effort to correct the aching knees, but nothing seemed to have any effect at all. The pain continued unabated through my teen years and has recurred at intervals up to the present time. Several years ago one doctor recommended replacement of the knee joint with an artificial one, but that seemed to be too drastic a measure to take. Now it seemed that life was intensifying its efforts to get a message through to me from more than one source.

As I studied Baba's teachings regarding the husband-wife relationship, I found them quite difficult to accept. He says that the husband should be revered by the wife. One statement stood out to me especially: "The wife should follow the husband's desires." I began to try to be obedient to Baba's instructions and found it to be one of the most difficult things I had ever tried to do. Every time I thought I was being truly obedient and submissive, the old self-will would resurface where I least expected it. Raye was patient and supportive most of the time, but occasionally his patience would wear thin and we would find ourselves in a clash of wills. By this time, though, we both knew such incidents were only signs that more inner work was needed, and we would quickly recover and renew our efforts to bring our lives into better balance.

The situation was gradually improving in our outer experience, but my understanding of the inner significance was superficial. One day, while actively engaged in chores related to the Sathya Sai Baba Center, I tripped, fell, and broke my shoulder. The immediate results were that I could do virtually nothing for myself. The doctor's prediction was that my right arm could never regain a full range of motion and that I should

Chapter Six

have surgery immediately to replace the shattered bone with an artificial one. That seemed to be a repetition of the recommendation in regard to the knees. Knees were used for bowing down, kneeling, expressing submissiveness. What were shoulders for?

The shoulder is the bearer of burdens, the worker, the ego of the body. With it we shoulder others out of our way, we put our shoulder to the wheel, we shoulder the whole load. Could it be that I take on too much responsibility? It was beautiful to see how husband and friends took over all the responsibilities of our home and the Center and everything ran just as well or better than when I felt I had to do it all. This period was a peaceful interlude from my outer duties, so I pursued the answer to Baba's question more diligently than ever. Where was my husband?

This time, when the light came, I was not alone praying in the dark in Prasanthi Nilayam. I was with other devotees in a daytime study circle, reading **Sathya Sai Vahini** aloud. But the words, which seemed to come from within simultaneously with their outer utterance, struck with an impact similar to the one I had received in answer to the first question Baba had posed. One of the circle members read on pages 87 and 88 the words: "'The truth about duality—the jivatma (individual soul) and the Paramatma (Oversoul) relationship—is as the wife-husband relationship. The full, free Supreme Vishnu (protector and preserver) is the husband, the master, the lord, the ruler, the provider; the individual is the ruled, the dependent, the wife."

The inner sight which I experienced at that moment could not be put into words. The mind, however, requires words, and so gradually the words came with which to partly describe what occurred. I realized that my marriage on this earth plane was only a parable—a reflection of the state of my relationship with God. My unwillingness to kneel, to be ruled or dependent, expressed the ego's resistance to submitting or joining its will to the will of the Inner Wisdom. The ego was shouldering responsibility that rightfully belonged to my Husband, Master, and Lord. This is what Baba means when He tells us that He is the Doer. He accepts the role of the Husband in order to help us. Our ability to realize abstractions is so limited that Baba has given Himself to be a living symbol of Love, Life, Infinite Wisdom, and Our Higher Self. To submit ourselves to Him in complete devotion is to submit the will of the ego to the will of our own Divinity.

I now see quite clearly that by Baba's emphasis on Raye's name, He was telling me that the role that Raye was playing in my life was that of a ray or emanation from the Infinite. By being a dutiful and obedient wife to Raye, I would be expressing the ego's subservience to the will of God. As the sun without its rays would be useless in our present experience, so Raye makes the love and provider aspects of God appreciable to me in my role of wife. If I can't love, trust, and depend on my husband, whom I see every day, how can I possibly submit to the inner Me, whom I know hardly at all?

At about this time, I had a beautiful vision. I saw Baba's face looking directly at me and smiling happily. As I looked into His eyes, His features gradually faded and the face became Raye's. I realized that the message was that He and Raye are One. Knowing that, it becomes ever easier to be the ruled, the dependent, the wife.

As if in validation of the inner experience, X-rays taken three weeks after the shoulder injury revealed a perfectly knit bone. All of the many small pieces had come together and the X-ray looked like a completed jigsaw puzzle. The arm regained its full range of motion within a very short time.

As a natural consequence of Swami's teaching in regard to the wife-husband relationship, Raye and I are having a happier, more fulfilling daily experience than either of us ever dreamed

Chapter Six

would be possible. Our marriage has become the screen on which we view our progress toward union with God. Baba has told us in **Sathya Sai Vahini** that "The universe is for each jivi (individual) its own mental picture and nothing else, fundamentally," but that when reflected in the maya mirror "the image is distorted and defaced.....and the object itself is usually condemned on the basis of its reflection." He also says: "The quality named Sathwa is a clear mirror; it gives a correct picture of things and events that happen before it."

Sathwa is the quality of peace, surrender, trust, and acceptance. Distrust, resistance, agitation, and rejection are illusions arising from maya (mist). While the husband carries out his functions as provider and decision-maker, he must constantly turn within to seek guidance, hearing and trusting the Higher Wisdom that is within himself. The wife, in her role as dependent, must place her faith in the Husband behind the husband, recognizing God in him as well as in herself. Ultimately the sense of separation or twoness will completely dissolve, and Oneness will become the reality. The words which filtered out of this experience seemed to come directly from the Higher self:

"When you look at your husband, see Me. Trust Me to provide your every need through your husband. Consider your husband as God. Worship him, minister to him, and follow his desires for the fulfillment of your duty. Nourish and increase your humility and your adoration of your husband. This is the reason you incarnated as a woman. Your accomplishment of this task will bring you much nearer your goal of liberation."

In a discussion recently with another devotee, I was asked, "But what if the wife is mistreated, asked to do foolish or demeaning things, and never allowed to do the things which seem right to her?" This is, of course, a very legitimate question and one which concerns a large percentage of the women on earth today. The answer to this is one which I have had to wrestle with many times in working on myself.

If a woman has not developed her own self-esteem, has not appreciated her value as an individual expression of God, then she will need to begin there. To be submissive does not mean to be terrorized. It does not mean to do anything which is physically harmful to oneself or to anyone else, or is illegal. To be obedient does not mean to be a doormat. The response of the jiva to the will of the paramatma is based on Love—not on fear. In order for the subservience of the wife to the Husband to effectively bring about freedom from domination by the ego, the wife must be constantly aware that her behavior at the action level is a symbol of her relationship with her God Self. Without that consciousness, there will probably be little or no benefit from her behavior in either direction.

It is worthwhile to note that one of the major themes of the ego is: "If I were doing it, I wouldn't do it that way!" or "I want to do it my way!" Therefore, when anyone can freely surrender the ego desire to do his own thing his own way, recognizing that he is not surrendering his will to the will of another ego, but that he is surrendering to God, he will have made huge strides along the path. *A Course in Miracles* teaches that if our brother asks us to do any outrageous thing, we do it simply because it does not matter. Again, however, this instruction must be followed by a person who has reached the level of awareness at which he recognizes the illusory nature of external experience and the goal of life to be union with God.

It is precisely because of these differences of awareness that we find Swami's teachings to vary from person to person—or to vary according to the group He is addressing. Each person must be his own guru, progress along his own path, and listen to the guidance coming from within himself. If we attempt to follow someone else's guidance or direction, we may find ourselves temporarily frustrated. However, we cannot lose the game entirely. Sooner or later, no matter how far afield we go, we shall all reach the goal. How do I know? Swami has promised that not one of His little ones will fail.

Chapter Six

******

"Every being that is in the universe has the potentiality of transcending the senses. Even the little worm will one day transcend the senses and reach God. No life will be a failure."

—Baba
My Baba and I
by Dr. John Hislop

"I must tell you of the paramount importance of Love. Love is God, live in Love. God is the embodiment of perfect Love; so He can be known and realized, reached and won, only through Love. You can see the moon only with the help of moonlight. You can see God only through the rays of Love."

—Baba
Words of Jesus and Sathya Sai Baba

"Falsely identifying oneself with the body, man suffers in the coil of attachment towards mother, father, wife, children, relatives, and friends. He does not realize that he has neither the body nor the senses, but that he is Brahman Itself."

—Baba

7

"I HAVE TO MOTHER MY WESTERN DEVOTEES"

Mothers become the fall guys for every problem known to the human race—at least in the Western world they do. As a mother myself, I can vouch for the fact that most mothers, do the very best they possibly can to raise healthy, happy, successful children. The trouble is inherent in humanity. Their mothers did the best they could, too, but nowhere was there offered a definitive course in how to be a good parent. So somewhere along the path this deficiency has to be corrected.

During my third visit to Prasanthi Nilayam, Swami emphasized the importance of this aspect of each soul's development. While He answered questions and discussed matters with various individuals whom He had called in for interview, He took one of my hands in between His and held it gently, occasionally stroking it lovingly. When He put it down after several minutes, He placed one hand on my head. Evidently sensing unasked questions in the group, He spoke to all assembled, saying: "I have to mother my Western devotees because most of them have never been properly parented."

In my own situation, my mother had been only seventeen years old when I was born. She and my father separated five years later, and I stayed with my father. After my father died and I went to live with my mother and stepfather, I never found the total fulfillment in my mother's love that I had always imagined I would. My mother refrained from praise but offered generous amounts of criticism. At that time, this behavior was considered to be essential to keep children from becoming lazy or conceited. Perhaps it was. I realize now that the fault in communication was in the receiver rather than in the sender. Nevertheless, the decisions I made and the reactions I experienced have caused pain over and over again—many times without my being aware of the source of the difficulty.

During the celebration of Swami's Sixtieth Birthday in Prasanthi Nilayam, a very rapid purification process was experienced by all in attendance. All of the negativity buried in the subconscious mind seemed to be trying to surface at once. I was no exception. I found myself feeling that I was being subjected to unwarranted criticism, and I began to behave in irrational ways in an effort to avoid the criticism and to win the love of those around me.

Caught up in the throes of this old thought pattern, I behaved in a way which I thought was loving but which turned out to be very inhospitable to some other visitors. I was aghast at what I had done, but there seemed to be no way to rectify it. Not understanding my reason for having behaved in such an unkind way, I prayed for Swami to heal the hurt I had inflicted, to show me what needed correcting in my thinking, and to forgive me. It was not until two months later, back in California, that I finally realized what had happened. I was still trying to win a special kind of mother love. Criticism had triggered the old unsatisfied desire of my childhood and I had responded in the way I had responded then. This habitual thought pattern was controlling me, even though my deepest desire now was to surrender to Baba, to turn the control over to this living symbol of my Higher Self.

I loved Baba deeply. Recognizing my need, He had made a special effort to assure me of His love. I desired to surrender to Him more than I wanted anything else. Yet something was in the

Chapter Seven

way. I was willing to take all of my worldliness to Him, but I couldn't seem to let go of it. I asked Him over and over again to show me a process by which I could do that. One day, as I entered the darshan area, I felt impelled to introduce myself to Phyllis Krystal. I had never met her, heard her speak, or read one of her books. As an editor of the *Sathya Sai Newsletter*, I had proofread her articles on "Ceiling on Desires" but that was all. I was quite pleased to see that she was a gracious, friendly lady, who did not appear to be overcome by self-importance, even though everyone knew that she received generous amounts of Baba's time and grace. Later, after we had both returned to California, I asked her to speak at the Cherry Valley Center. She agreed without reservation. We compared calendars until we found an appropriate date and the appointment was made. No mention was made of the distance (a three-hour drive for her each way) or the size of the group. We agreed that she would speak about her experiences with Baba over the past twelve years, many of which she had related in her book *Sai Baba: The Ultimate Experience.*

Between the time of my first conversation with her and the date we had made for her to speak at the Center, I began to feel a mild curiosity about her first book, *Cutting the Ties That Bind*. At least I thought it was curiosity. Actually it may have been Baba's nudging me to find the answer to the questions I had asked Him and His way of providing solutions to the problems of deeply ingrained thought patterns, behavior motivated by hidden causes. Thus, I embarked on the next phase of my search, not only uncovering monsters but disposing of them with dispatch.

As soon as I had finished reading Phyllis's book, I realized the purpose of each experience and impulse I have related thus far in this chapter. These were not random or unrelated incidents, they were carefully designed plays in the game-plan. The exercises outlined in *Cutting the Ties That Bind* were developed by Phyllis Krystal and another lady during twenty years of searching for answers to serious questions about the meaning of life. Phyllis relates how the exercises have been corroborated and augmented by Baba, and I felt guided to them as directly as if He had told me to use them. I immediately began one of the basic exercises, the figure eight, visualizing myself in one circle and my mother in the other circle. Since Baba was supplying perfect mother love in my experience, I no longer needed to behave irrationally to try to free myself from criticism or to win the approval of any other ego. I felt confident that this simple process of cutting the ties to my mother would leave me more open and available to accept the Love which constantly flows from Baba to everyone, and to receive the direction which is readily available to all from the inner Divinity.

The very first night after I had spent two minutes in the morning and two minutes in the evening visualizing the figure eight, I had three vivid dreams. In the first I was in a room with my mother. She left the room, and as soon as I finished what I was doing, I decided to leave also. When I turned the corner to pass the closet and could see the door, I saw my mother's body hanging by a rope in the center of the door. It was not possible for me to proceed without cutting the rope and removing the body of my mother.

This dream clearly presented the message that I would be unable to move into the next room or level of consciousness, until I had cut the rope or binding and removed the dead body of parental thinking from my consciousness. It is important to emphasize that this dream did not indicate a need for any change in my present relationship with my mother, which is warm and loving. The change that is required is the removal of all decisions, reactions, and misunderstandings which had been stored in my mind below the level of awareness and still survived as controlling factors in my experience.

The second dream which I had that night was of having an overhead fan installed. I had been told by the technician that the cost for the fan and its installation would be $300. However, upon completion of the project, he brought me a bill for only $200. On relating this dream to a friend, Dave Davidson, I was surprised to hear him say that he had just installed an overhead fan. He said that the biggest problem was to get it properly balanced. Since research into the accumulated body of knowledge regarding symbols had revealed to me that the fan itself is a feminine symbol, and the rotation, a masculine symbol, the message of this dream seemed to be that balancing the masculine and feminine qualities within myself would not be as costly as I suspected. After cutting the ties with the female authority figure, my own feminine qualities would be free to grow and develop, thus bringing about greater balance.

In my work with others, I have found that one of the fears which many people feel in regard to cutting the ties to relatives is that they will in some way lose something valuable in the process. I have, therefore, related this dream many times, reassuring others that they will be enabled to bring about a balance in their own masculine and feminine qualities, once the ties are cut to external relationships, and that they will find this process much less costly than they think. As a matter of fact, they may even find it to be one of the most valuable steps they have ever taken.

The third dream was of a young girl. I saw her holding a beautiful gift which she had just been given. It was made of gem-cut crystals, clear, sparkling, and beautifully designed. She appeared to be very happy. The item was not wearable. She held it in her hand by a stem. It was shaped like a tree, with a crystal at the end of each branch. One of the interesting things I learned about dreams, as I delved into the literature, was that the dreamer tends to dream in symbols which are specific to the therapy or discipline which is meaningful to him at the time. This dream was directly related to the therapy developed by Phyllis Krystal. It contained instruction for the next stage of the work, as well as encouragement for the effectiveness of the present activity. The young girl was my true feminine psyche, now being given the gift of freedom from suppression by the old ties. She was expressing her joy over this fact, meanwhile exhibiting a tree of crystals.

The tree meditation, described in Phyllis's book is designed to balance the masculine and feminine qualities. The crystal also, being polarized, is often held in the hands during the tree meditation to further enhance the balance. Could "crystal" also be a play on words, I wondered?

These three dreams opened a whole new aspect of the game of life to me. In order to unlock their meanings, it was necessary for me to learn an entirely new language—the language of symbols. I found that, even though there was enough commonality of experience to warrant the publication and use of dictionaries of symbols, the ultimate meaning of each symbol was highly individual.

It quickly became evident that no one else could interpret my dreams for me. Others can be very helpful—especially those who have had years of experience in the field—but the final feeling of rightness must come from the one to whom the dream appeared. The message is not a news release; it is an interoffice memo. It is from part of the self which has been temporarily separated from the whole, and the messages I have received seem to be always toward the reestablishment of that wholeness. Once I realized that the dream-messages were from myself, to myself, and about myself, and that the objective for interpreting them was to know myself, it became possible to take up the task with enthusiasm.

I pondered, prayed, consulted books and dictionaries, discussed some of the symbols with others, and occasionally asked Phyllis to contribute to my interpretation. But the presentation of these three dreams in such an orderly fashion, much like chapters in a book, was truly amazing to me. It

Chapter Seven

rekindled in the newest and most meaningful way my old fascination with puzzles and games.

In a very short time, I became aware that every dream, every experience, and every ailment of the body contained a message and that each of these messages could be decoded once the key was located. The key might be anywhere—in a book, a saying, my own experience or someone else's, a dream, a pun—anywhere at all. Finding the key was half the fun!

Sometimes it could be found quickly in a standard source, such as the ones listed in the bibliography of this book. At other times it might be months before some happening triggered the "aha!" experience and all of the pieces of the message fell into place. Taking the message to heart in a way which is positive and beneficial enables one to move through the game faster. And all along the way the player receives feedback which lets him know how he is doing. Naturally there are obstacles to be overcome. Who ever heard of a game with no challenges? But when we become aware of the game, the obstacles seem less and less threatening, and the rewards for overcoming them become greater and greater.

The experiences which people have when cutting family ties are quite unusual and frequently unexpected. My relationship with my father was not one which had ever seemed to be of great concern to me. I knew that he had been disappointed that I had not been a boy and had named me "Jo" after his father. He was always very generous with gifts, but he could also be a harsh disciplinarian. When he died, I had been whisked away to Florida (from Tennessee) within a few hours following the funeral. I never recall having mourned him or missed him or felt any concern at all about the relationship. Therefore, when I began visualizing him in the figure eight, I was quite surprised to see that he appeared to me as a smiling, animated, and loving figure. After the ties which had bound me to the old memories and kept me dependent on the paternal authority figure had been cut, I found that I had a warm, loving, happy, and positive feeling about my dad that I had never before felt.

Baba has said that we should be extremely grateful to our parents for having given us the opportunity to be born—to have this body and the learning experiences which go with our earthly sojourn. I now find this a natural state of mind in relation to my earthly parents. Not only do I now have a comfortable, blessed relationship with my human parents, but by removing the old parental tape recordings from my subconscious mind, I have also expanded my heart. I am more aware of Baba's presence there than I was capable of previously. Memories of my youth frequently relate to the many valuable teachings transmitted to me by my mother and the generosity and boyish enthusiasm for adventure displayed by my father. The negative, painful memories which persisted for so long now have less reality than a dream.

Dreams give me wonderful assurance and validation of my progress as I do the very best I can, leaving the outcome to the Lord. After cutting the ties to my parents, I had an experience very early one morning, which was a vivid illustration that I had not left mother love behind me. Raye is an early riser. When he gets out of bed, I may still be dozing. Frequently he walks around the end of the bed brushing by my feet as he does so. On this particular morning I was still asleep. As I felt the familiar touch on my feet I was aware but still too drowsy to open my eyes. I felt someone sit down on the bed beside me and pull the comforter up around my shoulders. I was thinking that it was such a cold morning and that it felt so good to be tucked in that I wanted to look up and say "Thank you." I opened my eyes and looked up. The face I saw was not Raye's but Swami's. He sat there smiling down at me. His hands were still holding the comforter up around my shoulders. I "blissed out." When I became aware of the room again, there was no one with me, but I was not alone. For a few wonderful moments, at least, I was quite consciously All One.

Chapter Seven

******

"The question arises—how can you be content, living in this illusory would, gathering and relying on illusory knowledge? Realize the Person beyond all illusion, who is the Creator of this illusion, who is revealed in and through this illusion. Worldly knowledge is of the temporary, the particular, the finite, the individual; how can it reveal the Eternal, the Universal, the Infinite, the Absolute? The Vedas have the answer. They ask us to analyze our dream experience. Dreams are unreal; they are illusory. Yet, for the time we are dreaming, the experience is real and valid. Often, in these dreams, as a result of the illusory experience itself, such extreme awareness is created...that the person dreaming awakens. What caused the awakening? The dream itself helped in the destruction of the dream. So, too, in this wakeful dream—in the illusory world where every experience is deemed true and valid—some experience or divine axiom will awaken man into the Higher Awareness."

—Baba
Sathya Sai Speaks, Vol. VII

Chapter Seven

TEACH ME TO LOVE

In my youth I prayed for houses with broad lawns,
  swimming pools, fancy cars, fame, security,
  and knowledge enviable by all.

As I matured, I asked for peace and joy and the
  privilege of helping others in their
  search for Truth.

Today I have but one petition, Lord: Teach me
  to love.

Indeed it is my greatest and my only need.

Not that love which I once deemed most fair—
  the love that sees a sufferer and longs
  to teach him to walk my own tried path.

Now I ask for wider vision and the gift to know
  that Your grace is love beyond compare,

That suffering is only a word we use to describe the
  tug-of-war between Your will and ours.

Teach me, precious Baba, to love you with such un-
   adulterated faith that all temptation
   to help You do Your work is washed away.

Teach me the love that neither likes nor
   dislikes anything in all Your universe,

That love which feels no pride nor shame,
   which does not waver when assailed by
     praise or blame,

That love which, though receiving no appreciation
   nor cooperation, still humbly serves,

The love which casts out fear and asks for
   nothing, knowing You are Here.

Oh, Swamiji, free me from all desire save one:

Teach me to love . . .

                              —Joy Thomas
                             Sanathana Sarathi
                              October 1983

8

"YOU HAVE SEVEN CHILDREN"

Like most parents, on my first meeting with Baba I was eager to discuss the children. I told him that my daughter was very active in the Transcendental Meditation program, and He responded that He was blessing her. I told Him that my son, being a born-again Christian, was not at all pleased with the direction my life was taking and had ceased to communicate with me at all. He looked at me with the utmost compassion and replied, "I know it makes you sad. It will eventually come right. In the meantime, just put all of your attention on your Center duties."

I had followed Baba's directions to the best of my ability and had ceased to actively mourn the loss of my son, daughter-in-law, and grandchildren. However, I was aware that I could still become attached very quickly to anyone who reminded me of them or represented them in any way. Therefore, I had some interest in cutting the ties to the children for my own sake. More than anything, though, I quickly became aware of what a blessing it would be to them when this ritual had been carried out.

It was about 1977 or '78, prior to my first becoming aware of Baba's presence on the planet, that I had gone to visit my daughter one evening. She and I were earnestly engaged in conversation and I was leaning forward in my chair, speaking. When I had finished what I was saying, I leaned back against the back of the chair again. As I did, Kathi said, "Mom, did you feel that?" I replied, "No, what?"

She said, "As you sat back in your chair I felt a tug on me (and she indicated the area of the heart chakra) as if we were tied together by a strong rope." We both felt it to be a positive indication of our love, and the thought that it could in any way be detrimental to either of us did not occur to me at all. Now, however, Baba has made me very aware of the counterproductive—even destructive—effects of attachment to family, friends, and worldly possessions. During our first interview, He had asked me how many children I had. I had replied, "Two, Swami." He corrected me. "You have seven children!" I asked Him for clarification of His statement, but He just smiled sweetly and declined to answer my question. Over the five years that I pondered this statement, I entertained different theories at different times as to its meaning. Occasionally I was close to solving the riddle, but the solution was only a mental one and did not bring about the transformation of character—that deep sea change—that occurs when Baba's words have been followed to their source.

In thinking about children and what they had meant in my life, I remembered the experience of becoming a mother (as I thought then) for the first time. My son was born when I was twenty-two years of age. The intensity of feeling which came over me when I saw him was something I had never felt before. It was something entirely different from the love I had felt for parents, friends, or other relatives. It was the closest thing to selfless love that I had ever experienced. I wanted to care for, protect, and provide every advantage for this tiny being that I held in my arms so tenderly. He could never lose my love or leave my heart regardless of his behavior, location, situation, or reciprocation. The love that I felt for him was then and is now

Chapter Eight

completely unconditional. The joy of that love was so great that I looked forward to expanding it to include another child, and the birth of my daughter fulfilled this expectation. There were two beings now alive that I loved totally. I have thought many times of Shakespeare's definition of love: "Love is not love which alters when it alteration finds, or bends with the remover to remove. Oh, no, it is an ever-fixed mark, which looks on tempests and is never shaken." That definition, for most of my life, has been applicable only to my children—and they were just two in number.

Swami had become the third being whom I loved unconditionally, and through His patient teaching He had helped me to add my parents and my husband to the list. Now, however, He was expecting me to love seven children. What did that mean? The definitive answer—the one that brought about the knowing that permeates the heart—came in an unspectacular "accidental" occurrence. In glancing through a book belonging to a friend, I came across a reference to the definition of "seven" given in *The Aquarian Gospel of Jesus the Christ*. It said, "Seven [is] the number of the all, including every man." As I read those words I felt the shift in consciousness for which I had been looking. The discovery was complete; the puzzle, solved.

The information itself was not new. Virginia Rinehart had related her experience to me. When Baba asked her how many children she had, she had replied with the number in her family. He had gently rebuked her, saying, "Wrong answer! All are your children." So my head knew the answer, but I had learned to persist in my search until the answer became engraved on my heart. Now it was. Baba was teaching me to love, just as I had asked him to do. It was not something that could be accomplished instantly, but progress was being made. And how clear His directions were! He might have said, "Love everybody," and I might have responded, "Yes, Swami, I will," and not much would have happened beyond that. Now I knew **how** I had to love everybody—unconditionally, wholeheartedly—**the same way** I loved my children.

The influx of knowing brought with it an understanding of why it is so necessary to break the attachment to our children. The unconditional, unchanging love is contaminated by being limited to only those with whom our ego identifies. Attachment causes us to be either proud or ashamed, controlling or indulgent, fearful or overconfident, and a long list of other opposites. Children need to be free from the emotional demands of their parents, which are felt from below the level of conscious awareness whether parents ever voice them or not. Parents need to be free from the criticism, judgment, and blame which has been heaped upon them for every problem a child experiences throughout his or her life. Each needs to be free from responsibility for the other—not free from compassion and caring but aware that each is a child of God and that the responsibility belongs to God.

For the first thirteen years of a child's life, he is dependent on his parents. The bonding which was formed at his birth is necessary to his proper development. Unless a clear separation is made at some point, however, the child is unable to take his place in the world as a fully functioning, independent adult. The puberty rites, which have largely been given up by modern society, are an extremely effective way to sever the emotional attachment and interdependency of parent and child, leaving the love between them even purer than before. The love, which has been limited to just a few special relationships, becomes free to embrace all mankind.

I knew that Swamiji was telling me that I must love those who did not love me, who were unkind and critical, just as much as I loved those children to whom I had given birth. I must love the terrorists, criminals, and other violent members of society. I must love those who disagree with me just as much as I love those who agree with me. A limited love is not love at all. This all

Chapter Eight

seemed to be a revelation, but the teaching itself was certainly not new. I had memorized Mrs. Eddy's words when I was a teenager in the Christian Science Sunday School: "Love cannot exist alone but requires all mankind to share it." At an even earlier age, I had memorized Jesus' words in Matthew: "Love your enemies, bless them that curse you, do good to them that hate you, and pray for them which despitefully use you, and persecute you; that you may be the children of your Father which is in heaven."

The apostle Paul had realized the need for the heart to expand and to include all mankind in one universal, unconditional love. His definition of love has become the standard by which Christian love is measured, and it stirs the heart as much today as it did two thousand years ago. Baba's words are equally beautiful, inspiring, and eloquent when He speaks of the power and importance of love. But it was neither Paul's letters nor Baba's discourses which brought the message to me. It was Baba's grace and his four simple words: "You have seven children."

******

"Though I speak with the tongues of men and of angels, and have not love, I am become as sounding brass or a tinkling cymbal. And though I have the gift of prophecy, and understand all mysteries, and all knowledge; and though I have all faith, so that I could remove mountains, and have not love, I am nothing. And though I bestow all my goods to feed the poor, and though I give my body to be burned, and have not love, it profiteth me nothing.

"Love suffereth long and is kind; love envieth not; vaunteth not itself, is not puffed up; doth not behave itself unseemly, seeketh not her own, is not easily provoked, thinketh no evil; rejoiceth not in iniquity, but rejoiceth in the truth; beareth all things, believeth all things, hopeth all things, endureth all things. Love never faileth: but whether there be tongues, they shall cease; whether there be knowledge, it shall vanish away.

"For we know in part, and we prophesy in part. But when that which is perfect shall come, then that which is in part shall be done away. When I was a child, I spake as a child, I understood as a child, I thought as a child; but when I became a man I put away childish things. For now we see through a glass darkly, but then face to face: now I know in part; but then shall I know even as also I am known. And now abideth faith, hope, love, these three; but the greatest of these is love."

I Corinthians, Chapter 13

Chapter Eight

Dr. John Hislop: "Swami, people of one religion kill people of another religion...because their conscience tells them it is right to do it."

Sathya Sai Baba: "It is not that way. When such things occur, it is because the individual has surrendered his judgment to someone else, or to an idea propagated by someone else. If the person were to reject ideas and rely upon himself, his conscience—even though deeply buried—would be there to prompt him; for conscience is God resident in the person."

—Baba
My Baba and I
By Dr. John Hislop

"Whatever you experience depends upon the commands, yearnings, promptings, and demands of the mind, your thoughts or sankalpas. Every decision the mind makes, whether to commit a thought to memory, to act upon it, or to dismiss it altogether, has a tremendous impact on the individual, for creation and all of its varied contents result from sankalpas. The thought (sankalpa) bears fruit which conforms to the seed from which it springs. To harvest good fruit, cultivate good sankalpas. You can easily indulge in bad sankalpas about others, but remember that you yourself must bear the consequences of such evil thoughts. Nobody can escape the fruits of sankalpas—either good or bad. For example, one might entertain a desire to harm or injure someone else, and it might fructify as harm or injury to that other person. But it is certain that the sankalpa will rebound against the person who originally welcomed it into his mind, bringing with it a hundredfold more harm and injury. A bad sankalpa hurts both the sender and his target. It is vitally important that you realize this fact about thoughts."

—Baba
Discourse, July 10, 1986

9

"YOUR GUIDANCE IS AS GOOD AS MINE"

There are many rewards of becoming a good game player. One of them is the advantage of having obstacles brought to the level of awareness through dreams rather than through our everyday experiences. In my own game of life, I have never experienced a dream which contained a warning or which required any drastic action. However, my dreams have been extremely useful in bringing needed lessons to my attention without my having to go through the daytime experience which would be required to teach the same lesson. In other words, when I learn the needed lesson from the dream, I do not require the daytime experience. When the message has been heard, no additional messages are needed.

I had a dream which began to bring me into new awareness of information which was readily available to me intellectually but had not been functioning as effectively as it might have been in my daily experience. In the dream, I saw my son trudging home in his football uniform. He had on the huge shoulder pads, helmet, hip-pads, knee-pads, and all of the protection from physical harm that is provided for one participating in rough contact sports. Then I saw that he was being accosted by several persons. They were quite indistinct. I was unable to see them clearly or identify them. They sat him down facing me, and I saw that his face was covered with blood which was coming out from underneath the helmet he was wearing. He put up no resistance at all, not even making a sound, but the expression of pain in his eyes seemed to call out to me for help.

I asked Baba for assistance to find the key which would unlock this message. Two days passed without any clues to its meaning appearing. On the third day, I had gone into the kitchen without turning off the television set in the bedroom. This was unusual behavior, but what was even more unusual was that I heard something on a talk show that attracted my attention. Even though I was far from understanding why, I felt so impelled to listen to the interview which was going on that I gave in to the impulse and turned on the set in the kitchen. The host was interviewing a husband and wife in regard to their separation and remarriage.

The story unfolded that he had left her several years previously. Her efforts to prevent the marriage from being dissolved were unsuccessful, and they were legally divorced. However, she did not give up. She heard of a group which was organized for the specific purpose of praying for straying husbands to be returned to their wives. She joined the group and asked the worldwide network of members to pray that her husband return to her and marry her again. The husband took up the story at this point. He told how he had felt an uncontrollable impulse to go back to her. He had done so, and they were now remarried. This was presented as a love story with a happy ending, but there were signs which made me feel strongly that there was more to it than that.

During the time the wife had told her story, she gave not the least indication of having any feelings of love or tenderness toward him. Her words were: "I did not want him to go," "I wanted him back," and "I was determined to never give up until I got him back." During the husband's portion of the interview, he said all of the right words, but the look in his eyes was exactly

Chapter Nine

the same look of pain, hopelessness, and helplessness which I had seen on my son's face in my dream. I knew that I had found the key which was needed to decode the message. The decoding process may not be instant, however, even after the key has been found. To unlock this particular dream, I also needed Baba's frequent statement that wisdom is our son. Then it all began to come clear.

My son (wisdom) in his football uniform (external knowledge or booklearning) was being attacked by indistinct persons (hidden forces). This attack was not physical but mental, as signified by the blood coming from beneath the helmet. The victim was apathetic, even though obviously suffering. Our wisdom or lack of it can only be seen on this plane by the choices we make. Just as the husband on the talk show had been influenced by mental forces, of which he was not aware, to return to his wife, so my right of choice can be attacked or taken away by the thoughts or opinions of others unless I become alert to actively protect myself. The wife and those who helped her in her efforts to get her husband to return home were quite sincere in their belief that they were doing the right thing. They believe that marriage is sacred, supported by God and the church, and that there is nothing wrong with praying for something which is obviously the will of God.

Baba has shown me the importance of marriage also. I now firmly believe in the sanctity of the marriage contract and that it would not be in my best interests to abrogate my obligations to that contract. However, I would not attempt to persuade anyone else either mentally or audibly to marry, stay married, divorce, or separate. In doing so I would be infringing on his right of choice. Taking it upon myself to be another's guide would be to assume the role of his own Inner Voice, and I would thus teach him by my action that I had no faith in the God in his heart.

As I contemplated the dream and its unfolding experience, two of the quotations from my early religious teachings became quite prominent in my thought. One was from St. John, Jesus' beloved apostle: "Love not the world, neither the things that are in the world. If any man love the world, the love of the Father is not in him. For all that is in the world, the lust of the flesh, and the lust of the eyes, and the pride of life, is not of the Father, but is of the world. And the world passeth away and the lust thereof, but he that doeth the will of God abideth forever. Little children, it is the last time; and as you have heard that anti-Christ shall come, even now are there many anti-Christs; whereby we know that it is the last time." (I John 2:15-17)

The other quotation that came to the surface of my thinking was from Mary Baker Eddy's writings. She said: "The mild forms of animal magnetism are disappearing and its aggressive features are coming to the front. The looms of crime, hidden in the dark recesses of mortal thought, are every hour weaving webs more complicated and subtle. So secret are the present methods of animal magnetism that they ensnare the age into indolence and produce the very apathy on the subject which the criminal desires." I had particularly noted the apathy of the son in my dream. The mild forms of mental influence are worrying about another, wishing he would change, judging his thinking or behavior to be wrong, feeling critical toward him, or condemning him. The aggressive features are to make specific declarations designed to change him or to remove his right of choice. And those enemies which are hidden in the dark recesses of mortal thought are the subconscious fears, attachments, and lusts (appetites) which Baba is helping us bring to the surface to destroy.

A friend recently told me about a dream which came to her. In it, she had on a pair of new shoes. Looking down at her feet, expecting to see them attractively displaying the new shoes, she saw, to her dismay, that she was standing ankle-deep in a cesspool. Looking up, she noted that there was an antenna on her head.

Chapter Nine

New shoes, symbolizing beneficial changes, were a representation of her walking a spiritual path. The cesspool obviously indicated a contamination of that new direction. I was reminded of the story of Walter Cowan, a gentleman from Orange County, California, who was restored to life by Sathya Sai Baba. After his restoration, he said, "The hardest thing for me to do was to crawl back into this sewer (referring to his body). It seemed to me, then, that a logical interpretation of the cesspool in my friend's dream was "body consciousness." Our spiritual progress is always in danger of being contaminated by body consciousness (ego).

The antenna on the head represents the mind's willingness to receive thoughts. Just like a radio or television antenna, the mind pulls in whatever is being broadcast. The mental atmosphere includes thoughts of all kinds, including fear, greed, anger, violence, and limitation. Unless we have our attention tuned in to station GOD, we are subject to receiving programs originating from opposing forces—those portraying the lower emotions. Even though the thought did not originate with us, and we did not consciously tune in to it, the mind plays it out as if it were our very own. Each of us becomes aware at some point in our spiritual journey that we must defend ourselves against such random negative thoughts. Ultimately, we can leave this need for defense behind us and rise unto a purer, more rarefied atmosphere. But beware of trying to assume a position which has not been legitimately won. Until you are totally free from negative thoughts and lower emotions, defend yourself constantly by repeating the name of God, singing devotional songs, keeping company with like-minded people, and studying scriptural writings.

Baba's teachings in regard to accepting others, refraining from criticism, and becoming detached from psychological and emotional entanglements, are clearly instrumental in rooting out the opposing beliefs and behaviors. We must arrive at the point of Oneness, in which there are no opposing beliefs. Baba is teaching us vividly and directly now that all there is, is God. Why, then, do we need to do all of these other things? It is so that we won't forget who we are. The only real protection we have from attacks of worldly thinking is remembering who we are. It makes no difference whether that thinking is of others, of our conscious mind, or of our subconscious mind.

Baba has said, "If you see the world as the world, there is going to be misery, but if you see the world as it truly is—God—then you will experience only bliss. All there is, is God. It's as simple as that. So why do we repeat the name of God? Why do we use all these different techniques of worship and protection? They are only ways to remember who we are. As soon as we forget who we are, we believe ourselves to be limited, helpless beings, and we get pushed around by the world."

A little analogy which I find helpful is that of the safety match. It is impossible to strike fire with a safety match unless it is applied to a rough surface. By the same token, it is impossible for the negative thoughts of others to find any place to strike fire within us unless we provide the friction. Remembering God smooths away the roughness and protects us from anything which might otherwise create temporary loss of our freedom of choice.

One day as Barbara Bozzani and I were performing the last-minute tasks preparatory to sending the Newsletter copy to the printer, we received a note from Dr. John Hislop, one of our advisors. In it he had questioned the use of a particular word in one of the articles which was to be used in the issue we were preparing. For some reason, I'm not sure why now, I felt that the word was correct and was reluctant to change it. Barbara suggested that I talk to Jack about it since I seemed to feel so strongly. Since Jack is much more qualified than I, it seemed almost ridiculous for me to even consider questioning his judgment. His academic qualifications are more prestigious

Chapter Nine

than mine; his spiritual qualifications are infinitely more mature than mine; his experiences with Baba outnumber mine by hundreds to one; and besides those things, he has been given the authority and the responsibility for maintaining the purity of Baba's teachings in the United States. He is president of the Sathya Sai Baba Council of America.

This was, I see now in retrospect, one of those obligatory scenes that become guiding lights for the rest of our journey. At the time all I could see was that I was a rookie player questioning one of the decisions of a world champion. But I felt compelled to do it. Jack listened patiently to all of the reasons I gave for wanting to retain the word. I finished my argument and braced myself for the wipeout which I felt was inevitable. Then Jack said mildly, "Go ahead and leave the word in, then. Your guidance is as good as mine."

I had been seeing myself as a mortal personality, having qualifications which could be compared to those of another mortal personality. As an ego, we are always either in a one-up or one-down position. But Jack was seeing both of us as embodiments of the divine Atma, equal because of our Oneness in God. His words have saved me many times from making the mistake of thinking that I have the wisdom or authority with which to advise anyone else.

What I have found works effectively for me may not be useful to another in a different set of circumstances—or even in very similar circumstances. On the action level, we are in the becoming mode and our business is to be an individual expression of God. Although certain principles may be applied to all, such as the Eternal Dharma or Golden Rule described at the end of Chapter One, others must be recognized as right and necessary for a particular individual but not at all applicable to others. As long as we are able to discriminate—to "take the cash and let the credit go," as Omar Khayyam said in his great poem "The Rubaiyat"—we can benefit from hearing about the experience of others. They frequently reinforce and validate our own guidance. But to give or accept advice from another is usually only to **add vice** to an already troubled situation. Each of us must learn to discriminate between the voice of Conscience, which is God, and the influence which can be exerted over us by the thoughts of others. The longer we lean on someone else for advice, the longer it will take us to develop this vital discrimination.

Listening for the Inner Voice to sum up this series of experiences, I heard:

> Protect the mind from all that I'm not!
> Let the heart remember all that I am.
> I am your very Self; I am God.

******

Like flowers of various hues, each with its own fragrance, men and women are basically of the same species of the Spirit. Their fragrance arises from the divine Essence, which is the real reason for existence. Everyone has to realize that Essence, thus ending the series of births and deaths. Like a student leaving college, once the degree is awarded—once Truth is realized—human beings have liberation. They can leave behind them their college with all of the study which was entailed in their attendance. But the degree must be earned. Why are you averse to making the effort which is involved? Instead, you run after one teacher or another, hoping to avail yourself of his victory. If he has achieved, of what value will that be to you?

—Baba
Sathya Sai Speaks, Vol. II

Chapter Nine

"Some people say that the *Bhagavad Gita* teaches us devotion (bhakti), some that it teaches right action (dharma), others meditation (dhyana), and so on. All of these commentators, interpreting the *Gita* in the light of their own understanding and intelligence, are losing the real meaning of what Krishna has said. In the process of developing different interpretations, the real meaning is lost. The first word of the first stanza is dharma and the last word of the last stanza is mama. Joined together, the message becomes mama dharma (my duty).

"By reading the *Bhagavad Gita* we can come to recognize our own dharma. One may be a student, an agriculturist, a businessman, or woman. For each there is different dharma. Even among women, one may be married and another not. Thus dharma is not uniform for all. One must recognize not only what state he or she is in, but what stage of evolution as well. It is very difficult to understand one's present condition, the direction of movement, and the limits of boundaries in this process. The easiest thing is to dedicate every act to God. Say: 'God, by Your own grace I can do this, thus I offer it to you.' However, do not stop with just the words coming from the mouth; the heart must be transformed by that which is spoken."

—Bhagavan Sri Sathya Sai Baba
Discourse, October 9, 1986

"No matter what others think about you, no matter how they treat you, don't worry in the least. Follow the divine Person. Follow Jesus Christ. Live for your own evolution. Do not live for what others will say. You have your own life, your own heart, your own opinion, your own ideas, and your own will. There is no need for you to imitate others. Imitation is human; creation is divine. Follow your own path! Let your experience of God be your Master. Follow the Master [within]. Face the devil [temptation]. Fight to the end. Finish the game.

"Carry out these four. Don't go to your grave weakly copying other people. Conduct research. Find your sacred spirit. You won't find God in the outside world. Your own loving heart is God's home. You are God! The true you is God. You are not one person, but three: the one you think you are, the one others think you are, and the one you really are."

—Baba
An Eastern View of Jesus Christ

Chapter Nine

"Individual effort and Divine Grace are interdependent. Without effort, there will be no conferment of Grace. Without Grace, there can be no gain from the effort. To win Grace, you need only have faith and virtue.....Knock, the doors of Grace will open. Open the door, the sun's rays waiting outside will flow in and fill the room with light."

—Baba
Words of Jesus and Sai Baba

"When you begin to see the roots of your problems, you find that they go deep. On the surface you see only innumerable little weeds, which you think can simply be pulled up and thrown out. But as your meditation deepens you will see that what you thought were twenty weeds have actually only ten roots. Then, deeper still, you see that these seemingly ten roots are actually ten shoots off five stout stems, each of which is so strong that you scarcely know how to get at it. At last you get to the taproot, which is self-will. Then the going really gets tough. After this long journey you realize that you have only been trekking across the prison of the ego. There are no doors, no windows, no exits of any kind. There is nowhere to go. When you come face to face with the ego in the basement of consciousness, you have to do something about it."

—Eknath Easwaran
The Bhagavad Gita for Daily Living

10
"DON'T TRY, DO"

After I had completed the series of rituals in which I had cut the ties to my parents, grandparents, and children, I had a dream which defied every attempt I made to interpret it. I dreamed that my son and his father were having an automobile race. I was inside the house. I could hear all of the preparations being made, but I couldn't see anything from where I was. Finally I heard the cars start, and I stepped outside of the house just in time to see the father's car hit a bridge off-center. The son's car had disappeared, and he was standing by the bridge and was struck by his father's car. I saw him take the impact of the blow. He didn't fall, but I could see that he was in great pain. He began running toward me, carrying a large box. Finally, when it seemed the pain had increased to the point where it was unbearable, he put the box down in order to run faster.

The son (wisdom, freedom of choice) and the pain (restriction of or attack on the freedom of choice) were a repetition of the symbols from the football uniform dream, but the rest of it just wouldn't yield. Over two weeks passed without my having found the key to unlock this one, and I had another. I received a business-size envelope in the mail. Upon opening it, I saw that it contained what had been my medical record. It was now blank. Where my name had been erased, a very faint outline remained. However, in the upper left-hand corner was written in bold black letters the word "Kruger." I looked up "Kruger" in the dictionary and found that there was an official in South Africa about the turn of the century by that name, but that information didn't seem to help. I asked Raye and several friends what "Kruger" meant to them, and they all mentioned the Krugerand (gold coin), but that was all any of us could think of.

Finally, my friend Forest Wilcox handed me the key which opened up the meaning of both dreams. He said that Kruger was a Dutchman in South Africa. That rang a bell. My mother had often teased me about some of my physical traits, which she said were due to my Dutch ancestry. The message was clear now. My family history had been erased, barely leaving a trace on the record, but there was a racial tie to be dealt with still.

And that dream was the key to the previous one. It hadn't occurred to me that "race" could be a play on words, but obviously that was the case. The first dream, involving father and son in a race (the human race), both trying to cross a bridge (back to their spiritual home, wholeness, or true identity), the father, being off-center (unbalanced) struck the son (visited his sins upon the son to the third and fourth generations). The son (wisdom) thus found his right of choice restricted (by all of the inherited traits from the father). He was carrying a large box (Pandora's box containing all the ills that flesh is heir to). When the pain became unbearable, he put the box down, in order to get home faster.

The message from both of these dreams seemed to be the same: the family ties are cut, but there is still a racial cloud which needs to be dispelled. The auto race dream added this rather interesting tidbit, as a postscript. When the pain becomes bad enough, you'll let go of all of these ills and attachments, and get on with your return to your original home (God-consciousness). I thoroughly enjoyed solving these two riddles, and besides the fun, there was the reward of being able to follow the insight with action. Forming the triangle to contact the Hi C, my partner, Betty Davidson, and I promptly went to work on a ritual to free ourselves from racial characteristics and conditioning, listening for Baba's guidance each step of the way.

Baba has frequently rebuked us for saying "I'll try" in response to His direction. Although I have never been on the receiving end of this particular correction, I have felt great compassion for those who have. It seemed to me that you had done all you could do when you tried. In studying Swami's teachings and listening for His guidance over the past five years, several things have come to my attention which are easily done and very helpful in situations which require specific action. As a counselor, I had always felt somewhat baffled by conflicts in which only one party was willing to come for counseling. Swami's way of expressing the golden rule solved this problem neatly and effectively. He says, "What you desire from the other person is the measure of your duty to him." That gives us all something to do when we are experiencing an inharmonious relationship. If we want more love, we can **give** more love. If we want more cooperation, we can **give** more cooperation. Whatever it is that we wish the other person would do, we can immediately begin doing it. No trying necessary!

Whatever the problem seems to be, we can always take prompt action by turning it over to Baba. I like to write a letter and actually put it in the mail to Him, asking that He take over. Of course, it is not necessary to do that, but it is a very good way to impress it on our subconscious mind that we have turned it over to God and thus don't have to keep trying to work it out ourselves.

Raye and I have a "God box" on our altar. We place notes to Baba in it or just slips of paper on which we have written the name of a person or situation which we genuinely wish to turn over to Him. We have friends who have added ingenious little twists to this exercise in letting go. One lady disciplines herself to remove the slip of paper from the God box if she finds that she is still worrying about the situation or trying to do anything about it on her ego's behalf. She forces herself to hold the note in her hand and carry it with her everywhere she goes until she becomes fully ready to release it.

Another friend said that she never took her note out of the box once she had put it in, but that each time she caught herself still taking responsibility for or giving anxious thought to the item, she added another note to the original one, symbolizing the letting go of each part of the problem as it presented itself.

There is always something we can do. If we are striving to break an addiction, for example, we may not immediately succeed in giving up the unwanted habit. But we can refuse to indulge in it without first asking for Baba's help, remembering Baba, dedicating it to Him, or performing some specific action which indicates our willingness to be free of the earthly attachment. It is not neessary ever again to just try. Baba says, "All the sacred scriptures of the world conclude with the order to do something positive."

In the process of carrying out appropriate actions, we are sometimes rewarded with unexpected visions or insights. Such an experience came to me one morning as I pondered the automobile race dream. The bridge which father and son could not cross because of their imbalances and attachments, I saw as the bridge between Being and becoming. I felt my becoming self gradually letting go of the myriad earth weights which were holding it back. It appeared to me as a hot air balloon, and one by one the guy ropes which were attached to weights of various shapes and sizes were being cut loose. With each release the balloon shuddered from side to side for a few moments before regaining its equilibrium. Finally, as the last tie dropped away, it became steady and upright and began to rise from the earth, gently floating above the bridge as it traveled over its exact

Chapter Ten

center. My becoming self was of beautiful bright colors and an artistic design. As I approached the far side of the bridge, I saw Swami waiting there. He was smiling, waving, and guiding me in. It was a joyous homecoming. With the bridge behind me now, the becoming self rapidly expanded. Its colors began to run together and blend into a brilliant white. I saw that Swami's robe had changed from orange to white and, as I watched. it too became brighter and brighter. The light became so intense that I could no longer see His face or His hair. Knowing seemed to come from the light that my beloved, my Swamiji, was now and always had been my Being Self. The colors were all gone; the boundaries had disappeared; all separateness ceased; and only the brilliance of blissful Being remained. Being and becoming were not two but One.

******

"While writing on dharma in 1960, Baba emphasized the need for weeding out from the heart the latent instincts and impulses inherited from our primitive savage past."

—N. Kasturi
Sanathana Sarathi
June 1986

"The law of correspondences is the foundation of all symbolism. By virtue of it everything, proceeding essentially from a metaphysical principle which is the source of its reality, translates and expresses this principle in its own way and according to its own level of existence. Thus all things are related and joined together in total, universal harmony which is, in its many guises, a reflection of its own fundamental unity. One result of this is the range of meaning contained in every symbol: any one thing may, indeed, be regarded as an illustration of metaphysical principles and also of higher levels of reality."

—Rene Guenon

11
"DON'T EXHIBIT; EXEMPLIFY"

As mentioned earlier, I had made a number of presentations to groups about Baba before I learned that He had not given His permission for anyone to do that. This restriction has since been removed, but at the time of my return to India, following my over-zealous reaction to meeting Him, it was still in effect. Therefore, you can imagine my dismay when, upon entering His interview room, He pointed His finger at me and said, "You have been making speeches about me!" Shaking in my bare feet, I replied, "Yes, I have, Swami. I hope it's all right." He laughed, and I realized that He had tried to sound severe just to tease me. He said, "Yes, yes! And you will make many more." What a wonderful reprieve. I was so grateful not to be reprimanded that I gave very little thought to the implications of His words.

Several years passed, and one night I had an intriguing dream. I was in a parade, on a float. As the parade moved down the boulevard, I looked out at all of those lining the streets to watch. Suddenly, I noticed that, behind one group of spectators, a man's body was hanging by a rope from a tree. I jumped from the float to see what was going on there. Landing off-balance, I fell against a large dog and got some of his hair in my mouth. He was a beautiful, light tan, friendly dog, and his hair was shiny and clean. He did not react to my bumping against him.

At that time, I did not have any reference books in which to look up the symbols which appear in dreams. I looked at the shelves of books which I did have, wishing I had something which would give me a clue as to how to interpret this one. One title appeared somewhat promising and I opened it. It did relate to dreams, but it had no index or glossary. It was only a narrative. I evidently had obtained it and forgotten about it because it had never been read. I opened it and began scanning the first few pages to see what it was like. I had reached page eleven and was ready to put it down, when suddenly the words leapt from the page: "Dreams use hair to represent thinking." Even though I have experienced "coincidences" of this type many, many times, I haven't yet overcome the feeling of awe which envelops me at the moment they occur. [1]

I looked up "hanged man" and found that one book on the Tarot cards gave the definition "suspended mind." The hanged man also symbolizes a complete change in the way we live—not the world's way, but the inner path back to God. [2] A friend pointed out that a dog symbolizes faithfulness, and it also symbolizes the extrovert or outgoing personality. It appeared that the dream was saying that I had stopped parading or exhibiting my knowledge, that I was attracted to the idea of suspending the mind, and that my outgoing personality should express itself in faithful thinking (words). What was not clear to me at this point was whether this meant that I had done this, that I was doing it, or that I should do it. No one else seemed to know how to make that determination, either.

During a group meditation, the dog dream was in my thought, and I was hoping that I might receive a clue to its placement in the past, present, or future. As I relaxed into the reverie state, suddenly I sensed or felt a clear message. It was: "Speak, for your words are true and faithful." I felt quite certain that these words were of Biblical origin. As soon as I could, I looked them up in a concordance to the King James version

Chapter Eleven

of the Bible. I found that the words: "Write, for these words are true and faithful," were words which John had heard when he was writing the book of Revelation. That was rather interesting. Revelation is a record of the dreams and the visions which John beheld in the reverie state rather than a historical record of everyday events, such as may be found in the gospels, for example. However, it still didn't answer the question of placement in time of this instruction.

Several days later when I woke up after sleeping soundly all night, I found that the outline for this book was complete and quite vivid, as if I had been working on it for some time. I jumped out of bed, went directly to the typewriter, filled a legal-size sheet of paper with chapter headings and content notes, and was quite surprised to realize that I had enough material for a book. The desire to write a book had been with me most of my life, but the follow-through had not seemed imminent when I went to bed the night before. In light of this development, I felt more comfortable with the message which the dream seemed to contain. I was to leave behind me any desire to parade or show off booklearning; suspend the mind; and report those things of which I had true and faithful knowledge, not hesitating to include those things which came through dreams or in the reverie state.

Another dream, which came along about this same time, provided additional instruction. I dreamed that my husband had asked me to help him with a task. It entailed carrying a number of small objects from one side of a street to the other. I had on shiny new shoes and was walking briskly back and forth, carrying the small objects across a smooth surface and placing them on the other side. I seemed to be enjoying the experience very much.

In my attempt to interpret this dream, I consulted a number of different books, finding that there was fairly general agreement in regard to new shoes. They indicate beneficial changes. In light of my previous experience in regard to the husband-wife relationship, I felt that the wife symbolized the jivatma or individual soul, assisting or serving as an instrument for the Paramatma (infinite, Divine Principle). The small objects eluded me for some time. The dream gave no indication at all of what they could be. They were that fuzzy, indistinct sort of thing which appears in dreams only enough that you know something was there without being able to say what it was. Finally, realizing no outside source was going to be useful, I determined to go to the Hi C. Hi C is a term for Higher Consciousness, the point at which the individual merges into oneness with the Self. By visualizing a triangle of light, connecting two individuals at the base and reaching up to the High Consciousness at the apex of the triangle, partners tap into wisdom greater than either individual possesses on his own. Using this technique, the answer to unlock this puzzle came quickly. The small objects were "things," and the job the wife was to perform was to change "things" or material objects of any kind into thoughts or symbols.

As the answer came from the Hi C, symbolized to me as Baba, another memory from Mary Baker Eddy's teachings was triggered. She had said that we must change things into thoughts and exchange the objects of sense for the ideas of Soul. Now I was actually doing this in my daily experience, not just reading about it! I was translating everyday experiences into ideas of Soul (term used in Christian Science for God), and I was exchanging the objects of sense for symbols in order to communicate with the subconscious. Therefore, I was moving back and forth across the street as I performed these tasks, going to the Hi C (superconsciousness) to receive instructions in the form of symbols and carrying these symbols across into the subconscious, making beneficial changes.

I felt extremely grateful for this confirmation that I was serving my Husband—my Higher Self—my Swamiji. Hardly a

Chapter Eleven

day passes that I do not receive a beautiful letter or gift from Him. Let me hasten to say that these do not come in the mail, postmarked in India, and signed with those precious words: "With Love, Baba," They are gifts from Him, nevertheless. He has told us Himself that our experiences are His gifts to us. The message came through Baba in my heart, that the loss of Raye's pager was His gift to us, and the scriptures teach that "Every good gift and every perfect gift is from above, and cometh down from the Father of Light, in whom is no variableness, neither shadow of turning." I find that almost every dream, every experience, when carefully interpreted, can be expressed as one of Baba's teachings. When I check them against Baba's printed words, they serve as a highlighter, directing me to the words of Truth which can be of the greatest benefit to me at my present stage of development.

Dreams are a very controversial topic, and it is natural that they should be so. They are revelatory of the contents of the subconscious mind of the dreamer and, as such, have no relevance at all for anyone else. It is supreme folly to take advice from anyone's conscious mind—much less another's subconscious mind. However, to pay attention to one's own dreams can be very helpful to those who wish to leave both the waking dream and the sleeping dreams behind them.

I find keeping a dream journal useful. Spiritual teachings found in books and discourses are invaluable guides for all of us, but teachings which are pointed out to us by our own inner Wisdom are the ones we are ready and able to put to work in our lives today.

At the Fourth World Conference of the Sri Sathya Sai Organizations held at Prasanthi Nilayam in 1985, Baba's gift for the delegates was a spiritual journal. Each page begins with a short quotation from Swami's teachings, but most of the space is blank in order that the possessor of the journal may record the messages being conveyed to him by his Higher Consciousness.

Two of the quotations from the spiritual journal follow:

"Life is an experience meant to train the individual for a higher, deeper, more expanded state of existence through the experience of the results of his action."

"To give up all the promptings of desire in the mind is the negative process; to install attachment to God is the positive process."

In order to get electricity flowing, both a positive and negative pole must be present. In order to get our ships sailing Godward, we also must have both the negative and positive processes.

Chapter Eleven

"No boy can enter college the moment he steps into school. Several stages have to be passed. So, too, we have on the spiritual path, the stages of work, worship, wisdom, and sacrifice. Sacrifice is when the ripe fruit falls from the tree, sacrificing its affection and attachment, weaning itself away from its support and sustenance. Work is for the physical level; worship, for the mental level; and wisdom, for the spiritual. Each of you will have to pass through these three stages."

—Baba
Words of Jesus and Sathya Sai Baba

"Whichever the book, whoever the master, whatever the institution, the goal is one and the same. The path is the ancient one, laid down by saintly pioneers. You can also picture it as the four-storied mansion, the ground floor being karma yoga, and the second, third, and fourth stories being devotion, wisdom, and detachment. Or it may be pictured as a fruit tree. As a seedling, it is called karma, that is, the activities all are capable of—the first step in spiritual discipline. As the tree matures and is rendered free from egoism and greed, it becomes worship, and it leads one to the flowering of devotion. When the fruit becomes ripe and sweet, that is to say, when the aspirant achieves complete surrender, then wisdom has been acquired. When the fruit drops from the tree, it marks full detachment, and the fourth floor of God's mansion has been reached. Pure love is the motive power in karma yoga, the yoga of action. Love is the very breath of the yoga of devotion. Love is universal and infinite in the highest form of wisdom, and, when total detachment has been achieved, Love is seen everywhere and in everything."

—Baba

12

"MAKE THE MIND FORGET ITSELF"

As we peel off the ego layers one by one, some of our everyday incidents are more fun than others. At least that's the way the ego judges them. This incident, which was no fun at all, will probably turn out to be one of the most valuable of all. It started innocently enough. The Sathya Sai Baba Center of Cherry Valley meets every Tuesday evening at 7:30 P.M. in our home, and the time was approximately 7:25 one Tuesday evening. A half-dozen or so members arrived at the same time, removed their shoes, and started to enter the front door. Raye opened the door and in walked the most pathetic specimen of a cat anyone has ever seen. It was completely emaciated, with almost all of its fur gone, and barely able to walk. It appeared to be quite determined, however, because it was able to avoid all efforts to block its entry.

Reactions were instant and varied among the members. Everybody had suggestions as to what to feed it. One member said that she would take it home after the meeting and nurse it back to health. Another asked me, "Do you have any cheese?" I responded, "No." Meanwhile, Raye had gone to the kitchen and poured a saucer of milk. While the cat followed the saucer of milk out to the patio, other suggestions were coming in. Raye came out of the kitchen, carrying slices of cheese and a slice of bread. These were added to the milk. The consensus of opinion was that a starving cat, once fed, would lie down and not leave the place where it had been given food. Therefore, the meeting began.

An hour later, however, the only sign of the cat was the empty plate. Everyone remarked on the strangeness of the experience. No one had seen the cat on the patio prior to the time it walked in the door, and no one saw it after the meeting. It has never been seen in the neighborhood again.

After everyone had left and I had time to think, I went into shock. I could not believe my own behavior in this confusing and unusual situation. I went over and over the fact that, when asked if I had any cheese, I said, "No." I tried to think up excuses. I really had never heard of a cat eating cheese, and I wasn't sure whether there was any cheese in the refrigerator or not, but I couldn't let myself off the hook. All of the alarm signals were going off inside, and I knew this was a big one. I wanted to rebury it quickly, but my desire to get rid of it for good was even greater.

The next morning I drove to West Covina to work on the Newsletter. I tried to put the incident out of mind, thinking, like Scarlett O'Hara, that I would worry about that tomorrow. However, on arrival at my work station, I began to open the mail. The first letter on the stack was from a devotee who had attended a recent Sai Baba retreat. She told a story about a cat, relating how someone had joked that it was Baba visiting us, but the relationship with the cat had not been a joke to her. She had experienced a healing of grief through the love expressed to her by the cat. The cat had not come into her experience by accident; neither had the cat come to the Center by accident. These had been obligatory scenes in our life dramas and the leading role in each had been played by a cat.

I managed to get through the day reasonably well, but as soon as I pulled out of the parking lot to drive home I began to

Chapter Twelve

sob. I cried uncontrollably all the way home. If anyone had asked me twenty-four hours earlier whether or not I was greedy, I would have said "Of course not!" But what else could it possibly be called? Anyone who would deny a piece of cheese to a starving cat is greedy.

The more I pondered the cat incident, the more convinced I became that immediate action was required. I was vaguely aware that the surfacing of this inner enemy was something for which I could be very grateful, but my uppermost thought was to become free from it just as soon as possible. As described in *Cutting the Ties That Bind*, the inner enemy can assume many forms, and a great deal of energy is usually tied up in it which can be released for use in daily activities. This monster assumed the form of a leech. I could feel it in my upper abdomen, filling the entire area under the rib cage, covering and surrounding the solar plexus. I called Phyllis Krystal and asked for an appointment to see her as soon as possible.

The night before our appointment, I had the following dream: I saw a young man I know well. He was working hard, as usual. His project was underground. As he worked, he was hidden from view except for his feet. They were protruding above the ground level. I was walking past him, and I laughed indulgently, saying, "All we ever see of you is your feet." Phyllis asked me about the characteristics of the person in the dream, saying that when we know the person, his outstanding characteristics usually reveal the aspect of ourselves being symbolized. When we aren't able to identify the person, then either masculine or feminine aspects of ourselves are being represented without further delineation.

I began describing this young man in glowing terms. He was a hard worker, usually holding down two jobs. He was ambitious. He had accumulated a lot of money very quickly. He made wise investments, and he was willing to do without minor comforts in order to take advantage of opportunities to advance himself financially. Phyllis asked me if I knew what I was describing, and I replied, "Ambition." "Which," she said, "is another word for greed."

The dream then became quite clear. Greed is only to be seen at the ground level, the action level. It is on the ground floor of the four-storied mansion described by Baba in the quotation preceding this chapter. Karma (action) yoga is the first step in spiritual discipline. When it is rendered free from greed and egoism, it leads one to the second floor, which is devotion. This was a lesson I would not soon forget. And, oh, how I want to be a full-time devotee, not obstructed by attachments, desires, and other inner enemies.

At this point we formed the triangle and asked the Hi C for guidance to free me from this black thought form which had been uncovered in its dark hiding place. Listening for the High Consciousness and utilizing our imaginations, we created pictures with which to get the message through to the subconscious that I was now ready and willing to be free from this thing which had been controlling my behavior for over fifty years. The subconscious has no sense of humor. It takes everything literally. It responds more quickly to emotion and to action than to words. The action may be vicarious, imaginative, or physical, but when it is performed with emotion, the subconscious receives the desired reprogramming most effectively. In this situation, the emotion generated by the cat incident was a powerful force to help release me from this inner enemy.

The rational mind will try to discount the effectiveness of such exercises, calling them just imagination, just psycho-drama. That is because the mind is ignorant of itself and does not comprehend the fact that it creates external experiences in the same way it creates internal experiences.

For most people, however, the freedom which follows the performance of a ritual such as the one just described is undeniable. In this particular instance there was an immediate and unexpected response. I not only felt lighter and freer, but I was aware of a dramatic contrast in my desire for food. I seemed to feel more in tune with the body and less dominated by habitual or hidden thought patterns.

Excess body weight has been a problem for me most of my life. I have occasionally managed to reduce, only to have the weight return. It had become clear to me a few years ago that any solution which was designed to remove the symptoms was self-defeating. When I asked Swami what to do, He had replied, "Forget it!" This seemed to indicate a need to remove the problem from the mind, rather than concentrating on feeding or not feeding the body.

Gradually a program unfolded which requires moment-by-moment attention. It seems to have been made possible through the increased freedom from domination by the mind, and also to be a response to Swami's instruction. It requires constant acknowledgment of God's presence and power in my life, especially remembering to dedicate every bite of food that I take to Him. The perfect diet had been revealed. It is: **Make the mind forget itself; fill it with thoughts of God!**

Along the way, we may be given little signs of encouragement as well as tests of our courage. Since this all began with the appearance of a very sickly, underfed cat, it seemed to me to be a sign of encouragement recently when a very healthy, loving cat came into my experience. At a retreat in the nearby mountains, a very well-fed, demonstrative cat presented himself at the door of the lodge where we were housed. He was just as determined as the cat had been at the Center meeting, but, otherwise, quite different. Although he was not at all averse to being fed, he was more demanding that he be loved. He gave and received love from everyone, but I felt that there was something special going on between him and me. As he curled up in my lap, licked my hand, and purred, I felt forgiven for my former lapse. Baba's familiar words came to bring this particular segment of the game to a close: "Whatever happens, has to happen."

******

"The person who is a slave to the mind will not find peace or happiness in life. The body is a mansion which has been built by the mind for its own joy and protection. The mind is the cause and the basis of every body—every human being. Some persons are wasting their lives by expending all their energy in looking after the body, basing their existence entirely on food. Others increase their attachment to the body through thoughtless repetition of spiritual practices, reducing them to mere physical exercise. The wise man controls the mind and purifies the heart by removing bad thoughts and replacing them with good thoughts. Do not underestimate the power of good thoughts. They are sacred and divine, having great impact on the individual entertaining them. On that day when we free ourselves from the evil thoughts which have solidified within us, we will be able to have a vision of God."

—Baba
Guru Pournima Address, 1986

Chapter Twelve

"Really, if only you have faith in the Name, you need not struggle to secure the chance to detail to Me your desires and wants. I will fulfill them even without your telling Me."

—Baba
Words of Jesus and Sathya Sai Baba

THE WAY

I did it my way—
until the pain exceeded the gain.

I did it His way—
until His way and mine were the same.

We did it Our way—
and peace, love, and joy were retained.

But when action gives way to Being,
the goal of all life is attained.

—Joy Thomas

13

"I AM THE DOER"

The next episode in my game of life began following a tie-cutting ceremony in which I asked for guidance as to what I was to work on next. The answer seemed quite clear: that I was to separate myself from any attachment to particular foods. I began visualizing various foods in the figure eight, but I had no strong feelings about any of them. I seemed to take little interest in the procedure—so little that I forgot to do it on several days. This being the case, I continued with the figure eight for several weeks, trying to identify problem areas, but seemingly without success. Finally, on the day of the week when I meet with my partner regularly to do whatever work has been revealed to us by the Hi C, we both felt guided to proceed with cutting whatever tie I might have to food.

We began by asking our Higher Consciousness to guide and direct the session, revealing to Betty whatever questions needed to be asked and providing whatever experiences I needed to have. As I attempted to visualize the figure eight with food in the circle in front of me, I felt the same lack of definition that I had felt all of the weeks I had been working with it. No particular food stood out to me, and I didn't see any ties at all. We have learned to be patient, however, and so Betty did not pressure me. Gradually, as I watched the inner scene, a vision of myself preparing food came quite clearly into view. I realized then, with considerable surprise, the superlative accuracy of the revelation. It was quite true that, rather than attachment to any certain foods or types of food, I was attached to food which I myself had prepared.

As I continued to watch, I saw a steel wire, such as many coat hangers consist of, coming from the vision of myself preparing the food to the self sitting in the other half of the circle. It appeared at the solar plexus of the one preparing the food and encircled the neck of the "me" sitting in the opposite circle. The wire was tightly wound around my neck, embedded in the flesh, and the end was twisted firmly around itself in the same way the wire of a coat hanger is twisted around itself. The straight end of the wire extended out to the side of my neck about fourteen to sixteen inches. I described what I was seeing to Betty, and it came naturally to designate the person I saw across from me as my ego-self. She realized that I would be unable to separate myself from the wire around my neck, and so readily agreed to do that for me. We were shown the appropriate instruments to use and proceeded to free both the ego-self and me from the tie.

When the wire, now cut in half and untwisted, lay on the floor in front of me, Betty directed me to ask Higher Consciousness for the best way to permanently dispose of it. As I did so, I saw a blacksmith working in a nearby location. I approached him, carrying the wires in my hand. His face was covered with a protective shield, but he reached for the wires and I gave them to him. He placed them in a heavy metal container with a long handle. He put the container into the fire, and I watched as the wires melted down into a liquid. When they were completely molten, he poured them out into a small round mold.

As the metal hardened again, he lifted the face mask, and I saw that the blacksmith was Swami. He smiled at me very lovingly as he removed the circular object from its mold. As he took it into his hand, I watched the color change from gray to gold. I realized that he had transmuted the tie which had bound me to my ego-self from a steel bond into a gold coin. I accepted the coin with great eagerness and joy. The vision of Swami and the forge faded then, but the coin remained. I carried it with me through the remainder of the ritual, and it comes readily into view whenever I think of it. The golden disk seems a perfect symbol of the gift Baba tells us so often that He came to give us—the return to unity from multiplicity—or liberation.

Betty and I both realized that something quite significant had occurred during this cutting, but that can be said of each cutting. There are never two experiences alike, and they are always a surprise. My parting from the "ego-self" had been somewhat similar to parting from a parent. I realized that the ego had been a necessary part of my development as a student in this University of Planet Earth, but that I was no longer in need of it and that it was now retarding my growth, obstructing my path. I was not prepared for the extent of the reaction which followed, however.

Beginning immediately on the day following the cutting, every project which I had underway began to fall apart. It seemed to me that nothing remained with which I might in any way be useful. The sudden drastic change in circumstances threw me into a depression such as I had not experienced since the time I had contemplated taking my own life. Even in the worst of this turbulence, I felt its purposefulness, but that did not mitigate the sense of despair which assailed me. Even the writing of this book seemed to be a dead end. Information came at me from several different sources that it could never be published, or, at least, that its publication would have to be postponed for a considerable time.

I had a dream the night before the cutting. It involved my traveling to some kind of yard sale and asking for a loudspeaker, such as those used in public arenas, and a signal light, such as are standard at intersections. When the man who was to obtain these for me tried to purchase them, he was told that the price had gone up. Instead of being only five dollars as I had been told earlier, they would now cost nine dollars. When he told me, I was unconcerned. I said, "Oh, that's all right. Just put four more dollars with the five I gave you and go ahead and get them."

During the three days following the cutting, even my old bugaboo, car trouble, showed up again. One car was overheating; the other needed extensive repairs on its braking system. This lack of transportation contributed to my sense of being cut off from all of my useful activities. Finally, on the morning of the fourth day, as Raye and I were meditating, I felt a sense of peace descending upon me like a divine benediction. With it came the knowledge which had been completely hidden from me up until this point. I saw that my attachment was to achievement, self-expression, or the fruits of the ego-self's actions—especially those of a creative nature—**my** cooking, **my** writing, **my** problem-solving, or **my** doings, whatever they might be.

Through study of Swami's teachings, I had become aware of the ego-involvement regarding the acceptance of payment, thanks, or compliments from others, and, though not completely free from the experience of pleasure which resulted from those, I had made considerable progress in lessening my desire for them. It came to me quite clearly that, although I had ceased to look for such acknowledgement of **my** good works from others, I was still experiencing quite a lot of inner satisfaction from such activities. My ego-self was still taking credit which rightfully belonged to the One Self, to the Eternal Absolute, to Swamiji.

I had wanted a green light to publish or broadcast, thinking that my five years of experience could be useful to some newcomers. My thinking had been that, because I was not a

Chapter Thirteen

longtime devotee of Baba or "advanced" (whatever that means) in my spiritual endeavors, these beginning steps might be encouraging to others who were just starting on their journey also. Sometimes it had seemed to me that the available books were all written by people who were so far beyond me that they were almost impossible to relate to my own situation. I had hoped to decrease that gap for other newcomers. Now, however, it seemed that my dream was telling me that five years was not enough. By adding another four years, making nine in all, I would be able to get the green light to publish.

The auto (self) needed brakes, and it was overheating. This seemed to be an indication of the need to slow down and to temper my over-enthusiastic urge to "do it now." Even more than that—it indicated the need to stop believing in my own ability to do anything. God is the only Actor—the sole Doer. Why do I have to keep learning that lesson over and over?

I hope that, each time I pull up this weed, I am getting closer and closer to the root—the ego-self itself. Moment-by-moment listening, moment-by-moment watching, moment-by-moment surrender of the ego-will to the divine Will—in every thought, no matter how fleeting, and in every activity, no matter how mundane—these became the ideals to which I aspired.

Raye works with me to help me remember, and we are both constantly blessed by the endeavor. For example, when we put seatcovers on the car, we declared over and over, "Baba, you are the Doer. Use our hands as you wish. The work is Yours; the outcome is Yours; the car is Yours. We are Your instruments." The task might have been a frustrating one, since nothing on the car seemed to relate in any way to what was described in the instructions for installing the seatcovers. Nevertheless, step by step, we listened for Baba's guidance and overcame each obstacle as it presented itself. When the job was complete, we gave thanks to Baba for His action and its resulting neatness and cleanliness.

Another incident illustrates the application of this principle of God being the only Actor in even our simplest, most routine duties. Early on a day which seemed packed with things to do, I took out some soybean granules to prepare for dinner. I usually began this particular dish by sauteing an onion. When I reached into the bin for the onion, I found that there were none. This might have been somewhat disconcerting, since it seemed as if taking time to go to the market would decrease the time which had been allotted for other activities. A quick survey of possible choices open at this point included: borrow an onion from a neighbor, go to the store, change the menu, or take no action at all, trusting Baba to make the way clear. I chose the latter, acknowledging God as the Planner, the Provider, the Creator, and the Actor, asking Him to use my hands and feet only for His purposes. I then went right on to my next activity, feeling quite confident that even a little thing such as this was not out of His realm.

Sitting down to the typewriter, I gave my full attention to some correspondence which needed to be handled in a timely manner. Suddenly a picture appeared on my mental screen of a packet of seasonings located on a shelf in the kitchen cupboard. I went to the cupboard, found the envelope of seasonings exactly as pictured, and prepared the food in much less time than it would have taken if an onion had been available.

By dinnertime all of the chores which had been scheduled for the day had been completed. As Raye and I sat down at the table, we thanked Baba for His moment-by-moment guidance during the day and for the food which He had provided and prepared. Our repetition of the grace which Baba has given to the students in His schools was especially meaningful that evening. We recited together:

Oh, Lord, Thou art the food;
Thou art the enjoyer of the food;

> Thou art the giver and preparer of the food;
> Therefore, we offer all that we consume
> > at Thy lotus feet.

At that instant, the fragrance of vibhuti surrounded the table and we both felt tangibly enfolded in His Love. We know that God is where our feet are—on the action level. He is the Doer—not only of our loftiest deeds but also of our humblest ones. Jesus' declaration that He, of Himself, could do nothing, has been assumed to mean that, without God, Jesus could not have performed the miracles of healing and regenerating those who came to him. But that is not what He said. He said that He could do **nothing**. He knew that God was the only Actor. It was God who washed the disciples' feet, who broke the bread and poured the wine at the last supper, who prepared breakfast for the fishermen on the Galilean shore. And it is God who prepares all of the meals in our homes, too.

Many have had the experience of Baba's loving hospitality as He serves food to His guests. I have been told that He is extremely solicitous of each one's needs and preferences, even to sometimes handfeeding one or more of the guests. My own experience of His (in-the-flesh) serving of food took place at the Sixtieth Birthday celebration at Prasanthi Nilayam when He gave each one present at darshan one evening both a spicy and a sweet rice dish, served up in dainty cups made of leaves sewn together. The joys and blessings of knowing Baba are many, but one of the greatest is to allow Him to do the same things, using our hands and feet, that we see Him doing with His hands and feet.

The consummation of this particular series of lessons brought with it the realization that, in a negative frame of mind, I had placed an earthly interpretation on the dream of the speaker and the signal light. The ego—though frustrated in its desire for instant gratification—was still planning to get its reward four years later. Realizing this, I set about to more accurately decode the symbolism of adding the four to the five, making a total of nine. Four is a number sacred to the Supreme Spirit. Almost all of the ancient people had a four-lettered name for God. Among the Gnostics, Four was the name of the Supreme Being. Five is the number of the human values and of human activity. [3] Therefore, my dream was not saying that I should postpone doing any righteous activity, but that I must be absolutely sure that God was recognized as the source and substance of the human virtues. By acknowledging God as the Doer of all activities, they would be brought into fruition or completion for His glory.

Nine represents synthesis of the corporeal, the intellectual, and the spiritual. [3] It is the symbol of truth, frequently referred to as Baba's number. By recognizing Baba as the Doer, we are completely freed from responsibility, fear, criticism, and frustration in our endeavors. *A Course in Miracles* teaches: "When peace comes at last to those who wrestle with temptation and fight against giving in to sin; when the light comes at last into the mind given to contemplation; or when the goal is finally reached by anyone, it always comes with just one happy realization: 'I need do nothing.'" The anxiety which is so often expressed in the words: "I just don't know what to do" or "I must do something" is only the ego's avaricious craving for that which rightfully belongs to God. The ego aspires to be the creator, the actor, and the doer, and to receive the rewards of its actions. Baba alerts us to this pitfall when He tells us: "Anyone who accepts compliments is dealing in stolen merchandise!"

******

"The students utter in chorus a deeply meaningful prayer before every meal, as directed by Baba. It instills into their consciousness the highest truth reachable by intelligence, insight, or grace.

"It teaches that we cannot formulate any thought, word, or phrase; we cannot conceive of any being or thing or incident, which will separate God from anything else that we know, including ourselves.

"It is a sloka from the Gita: 'Brahmarpanam...samadhinah.' It means: 'Everything is an offering to God; provisions used for food are essentially God; the fire which cooks the provisions as food is God; the process of cooking is also God; the person who consumes the food is God; the work that the consumed food enables us to perform is also God.' What a synoptic vision of the cosmic power of God!"

—N. Kasturi
Hridaya Brindavan

"When we are mostly unconscious (unaware of our soul nature) we are inclined to be egocentric, selfcentered, and involved in personality needs. We may be driven with a passion to experience, with the result being desires which cannot be fully satisfied, or we may avoid involvement out of fear of bondage or rejection. The better way is to learn to appreciate living but without attachment and without avoidance of necessary experiences. In this way we can participate in life's unfolding drama and be involved in the flow of events, but with understanding."

—Roy Eugene Davis

"The message of the fatherhood of God and the brotherhood of man, which Christ Jesus proclaimed two thousand years ago, should become a living faith for the achievement of real peace and the unity of mankind. The oneness of creation, affirmed by the ancient seers and sages, can only be expressed in a transcendental love which embraces all people, regardless of creed, community, or language."

—Baba

14

"NOT SISTERS"

On one of our visits to Prasanthi Nilayam, Raye and I had traveled with Karl and Barbara Trisler. Although Barbara and I were sitting some distance apart, when Baba stopped in front of me during darshan, He pointed to to her and asked, "Sisters?" "No, Swami, not sisters," I replied, "but good friends." He feigned great surprise. "Not sisters?" he questioned. "Oh, no, Swamiji, not sisters," I assured Him again.

Thus began my rumination on the idea of the sisterhood or brotherhood of man. One morning, in a Sai Baba study group, one of the members shared some experiences she had had with language prejudice while traveling. This recalled to memory my early years in the southern part of the United States. I had been completely unaware of having a language pattern any different from anyone else's. However, when I went to college, I was told that my speech was "nonstandard." Enrolling in speech and language classes, I ultimately earned a master's degree in language arts and found great satisfaction in teaching others how to speak properly. Pride of scholarship, criticism of others, and a feeling of superiority crept into my thinking, producing prejudices against anyone speaking what I classified as nonstandard English. I was quite comfortable in this prejudice for many years, without ever realizing its negative and destructive elements.

When I became aware that there were others who were just as prejudiced against my language as I was against theirs, it came as quite a shock. I found that American English was just as unacceptable to many British subjects as certain dialects had been to me. As I pondered these things, awareness came that I hardly ever thought about the language of my sister or my husband, both of whom had learned and practiced the same form of nonstandard speech. I realized that what irritated me and alienated me from others, I completely overlooked in my loved ones. The oft-told story of the young lad carrying another boy almost as large as himself returned to my memory. When asked how he could possibly carry such a heavy youngster, he had replied, "He's not heavy! He's my brother."

It was evident, then, that Swami wanted me to see everyone with that same lack of judgment. To judge anyone, at any time, for anything is to usurp the prerogative of God—a prerogative which God Himself never exercises! To prejudge another is to be caught up in two of the ego's webs. To judge is to be vainglorious or prideful, but to judge one person in the present, based upon an experience with another person in the past, is not even logical human reasoning. *A Course in Miracles* warns: "If you place your faith in the past, the future will be like it." I began to be extremely aware of criticism, judgment, and prejudice—first in others, but finally where the root of the problem really existed—in myself.

One day Betty and I were listening together for directions from the High Consciousness to guide a cutting of ties between me and a person who seemed to be the archetypal critical parent. As I waited for the inner vision to focus on the other person, I saw instead a mirror. I recognized it to be a magnifying glass and, as I watched, the image which appeared in it was the reflection of myself. The self in my circle was its usual size, but the reflection of that self in the magnifying mirror seemed to be ten times larger. It was not the other person—not the one I had

Chapter Fourteen

been visualizing in the figure eight for two weeks—who needed to be separated from me. I needed to separate again (and again and again!) from that ego-self who criticizes, judges, and condemns. The ego criticizes others for criticizing, judges others for judging, and condemns others for condemning. And if it gets caught doing that, it criticizes itself (naming itself you or me) for criticizing. Anyone looking for fault will find it; but he who relinquishes that right will find God.

The only solution in this battle with the ego is to refuse to see anything but God. Swami gives us the way when He tells us to constantly identify ourselves as God and not as the ego. We will ultimately become so tired of the ego's machinations that we will surrender joyously to God, become one with Him, and state with conviction: "I am God. I am God. I am not different from God. I am Being. I am Awareness. I am Bliss. I am the Totality—all of it!"

The ego cannot be eliminated from the outside in; it must be erased from the inside out. When we are identifying ourselves as a body, it makes no difference whether we call the body J.D., John Doe, or Dr. John Doe, we will still be equally as ego-ridden. When we genuinely identify ourselves as God, we realize—as Baba does—that all names are ours and that it makes no difference at all by which one we are called. We will have the calm assurance that Divinity, however labeled, is complete, perfect, and unchanging. To understand the coincidence of the human and the Divine is to allow our Divinity to enhance our humanity.

Both waking-state and dream-state experiences help bring consciousness to a place from which it can accept its Divinity. A dream was given me at this time which I have found to be a continuing blessing. I dreamed that I was in a restaurant, sitting on a sofa. Baba came in and sat down beside me. My right hand had been on the sofa beside me, and, as Baba sat down, I didn't get it out of the way fast enough. It was between His back and the sofa, not touching Him, but in such a small space that I knew I couldn't get it out without touching Him. I considered whether to try or not. Finally I decided to take it out. I did touch His back in the process, and He looked at me and frowned.

He then got up and got His breakfast on a tray and sat down across from me. Another gentleman had his breakfast on a tray also, and, as he stood beside Baba, he poured boysenberry syrup on his food. The syrup filled his plate, his tray, and began running over and streaming down in beautiful ribbons of clear reddish purple sweetness all over his feet and the floor.

Baba finished His breakfast, got up, and went into an adjoining room. He came out dressed in street clothes. His hair was flat to His head and He had on a beret. I recognized the beret as being one which a friend, Lucille Sheets, had been wearing the previous Sunday. I looked at him and thought, "Why, He looks a little like Lucille."

Then He stepped into a small alcove with a mirror. He removed the hat and reappeared. Neither His hair nor His clothes had any distinguishing features. He could have been any American businessman. He looked around the room briefly, then opened the side door. I could see the sidewalk filled with busy people, hurrying to and fro, shopping, doing errands, on their way to work, or perhaps just out for a morning walk. He looked back at all of us in the restaurant once more. It seemed He wanted to assure us that He was aware of each of us and He wanted us to be aware of Him. Then He stepped out onto the busy sidewalk and was lost in the crowd.

In researching, contemplating, and pondering the symbols in this dream, I found that the open hand signifies any task which is specifically human. The right hand indicates the conscious, rational, logical, and virile. The red color of the boysenberry is of the heart and the blue of the head. Syrup is sweetness and love. Overflowing is the symbol of abundance. The height of the tray would indicate the spiritual level, and the feet and the floor, the action level. A change in hairdo signifies a change of roles. To put on a hat is "to put all ideas under one hat," thus ending separation.

The message of the dream seemed to be: "Do not separate the manifestation of Myself at the action level from Me. I perform all human tasks. I am conscious, rational, logical, and virile, as well as spiritual, divine, eternal, and Absolute.

"Your bliss, your fulfillment, is my food. My sweetness, my love, runs over to bless and permeate your every action. I am always aware of you and your activities. I am not only the positive heavenly Father but also the negative earthly Mother. Do not separate these two. Keep them unified under one hat—One Supreme Force. I am God; I am your Brother; I am your Sister; I am Everyman. See me everywhere."

******

"The devotee regards both persons of high character and persons of low character as roles in the divine play. When he insults or injures or rejects anyone, he is, in fact, inflicting insult and injury on the God he adores. He cannot reap the harvest of grace or the bliss of the Atma if he sows spiritual ardor on a heart full of the weeds of greed and hate. The basic moral prescription for the devotee who aspires to be near and dear to the Avatar is: Worship God and offer love to Him in every living being."

—Baba
Discourse given at Prasanthi Nilayam
August 2, 1986

"Bhagavan Baba says that we must know what our real duty is in life. We have come on a sacred mission to achieve victory over the forces of darkness within us, those that keep us ignorant of our divine truth. That is the inner war which everyone must fight. To win we need the grace of the Lord. Therefore, overshadowing all other consideration in our lives, we must earn the love of God. The Mahabarata war symbolizes the inner war which has gone on unabated in the hearts of men in every age. It is a war in which long-established impulses are pitted against our higher Self. These impulses are the brood of cravings and emotional needs that are deeply embedded within us, having been honed in the jungle of survival over countless lives. They show up as selfishness, greed, lust, pride, arrogance, hatred, anger, jealousy, possesiveness—a host of dark forces which well up from the inner depths. Eventually they create dilemmas of great anguish for us as we face conflicting calls of duty to the world and God. Baba has said, if, at that time, we turn towards the Lord in self-surrender, He will sing to us a *Gita* (song) that is especially meant for us, showing us the way to victory over these powerful enemies that have become lodged within us."

—Al Drucker

15

"LIVING IS NOT NECESSARY, BUT NAVIGATION IS"

Some time before my first trip to India, I had an experience which seemed to be a flashback in memory. I recalled sitting at a table with friends, who were advising me in regard to my forthcoming incarnation. I replied to a suggestion they had made, "All right, I volunteer to do that." Just what I had volunteered to do was not revealed. From time to time the desire to know what it was became prominent in my thinking for a day or so, but knowing was not an immediate necessity. My daily duties were usually enough to keep me from dwelling too long on such esoteric puzzles. However, recently without warning, the flashback came again. This time I recalled that there were three things I had volunteered to do, one of which seemed even stranger than the other two. It was: "To overcome the desire for a healthy body and to help others do the same." That seemed a little weird—even to me. I decided rather than lose my credibility entirely, I would keep that one to myself.

The next stage of development of this idea came in a dream. I was in a hotel room getting ready to leave on a journey. A friend and I were discussing travel arrangements. We knew that there was a very fine oceanliner at a nearby dock, leaving soon for our destination. It seemed possible to get to the ship before it left, but we could not take time to either pack or arrange for land transportation. We each just took two changes of clothing, and I said that I would drive my car. The closest route was through a flooded tunnel. We didn't know how deep the water would be because we didn't know anyone who had ever tried to go through it before. I commented that, since my car was a Mercedes, it might be able to make it. If it didn't, it wouldn't matter. If we missed the ship, we could take a plane tomorrow.

So we started out. I was driving. At first the water was only up to the hubcaps and we were moving right along. We enjoyed seeing the inside of the tunnel. It was natural, rather than man-made, and had beautiful stalactites and stalagmites. Suddenly, though, we found ourselves in deep water, and I started to turn back. The hood was completely underwater, but I could hear the engine still chugging away. We made the instant decision to continue. We came out of the tunnel safely, and a representative of the company was there ready to help us with our tickets. We had arrived in plenty of time and would have comfortable accommodations.

I asked if the car could be given necessary care until our return. The reply was: "Yes, but you will have to pay." I was already halfway up the ramp, looking forward to a joyous journey, and I called back over my shoulder, "Whatever is reasonable."

I felt no urgency to interpret this dream, but an interpretation gradually emerged with which I feel quite comfortable. Both the fact that I was traveling with a friend and that we took two changes of clothing seem to symbolize dualism. Edgar Cayce said that a tunnel represents the subconscious through which we approach the superconscious. [4] And Cirlot points out that a ship always indicates the desire to transcend existence. [3] Deep water symbolizes emotional involvement, and the stalactites and stalagmites in the tunnel have a special relevance to me, creating a perfect picture of the ups and downs in my life to

Chapter Fifteen

which I reacted with great emotion. This characteristic was remarked upon by Swami during one interview when he said to Raye that I was quite emotional.

The vehicle (body) which is carrying me through this earthly existence is sturdily built (like a Mercedes), and it has been able to keep going even when inundated by a flood of emotion. At one point during this incarnation I might have turned back (taken my own life), but decided instead to proceed. Having come out of the tunnel, and obtained passage on a fine oceanliner, I appear to be prepared to pay "whatever is reasonable" to repair the damage done to the vehicle which carried me through the dark tunnel and the deep waters of material experience.

In researching these symbols, I came across a reference which seemed to relate directly to the strange purpose of "overcoming the desire for a healthy body." Cirlot, writing on the symbol of the ship, said that "the most profound significance of navigation is that implied by Pompey the Great in his remark: 'Living is not necessary, but navigation is.' By this he meant that living is split up into two fundamental structures: living, which he understood as living for or in oneself, and sailing or navigating, which he understood as living in order to transcend...". [3] A healthy body is not necessary, even though highly desirable, but finding our way back to God is. Abraham Lincoln, who considered himself to be exceptionally ugly, said: "It teaches you—to be an ugly child." I can vouch for the fact that it teaches you also—to be a fat lady. It is effective for learning many things, including humility, which is one of my high-priority courses.

There have been many people who have achieved worthwhile goals, even though burdened with a body which was less than perfect. Helen Keller is one outstanding example, as is Ken Keyes, Jr., author of *The Handbook to Higher Consciousness.* The superb musician, who—born without arms—played a stringed instrument with his toes for the Pope and inspired the hundreds of thousands who heard and saw the performance, is another. David Viscott, M.D., speaking on a television show, mentioned a paraplegic Irish writer who wrote a highly acclaimed book by holding a pencil in his teeth to enable him to press the keys of the typewriter. He went on to say: "Any human being can, by totally accepting his lot and the world of which he is the center, transmit portions of that world to the greater world at large and humanize it." Perhaps even divinize it.

An incident from my first trip to see Swami now takes on added significance. It occurred in darshan several days after my arrival. Baba stopped in front of me, shook His head, and said, "Very, very fat!" I replied, "Please help me, Swami." He walked on, gave attention to several others, then suddenly turned and, from about twelve feet away, tossed me a large sphere of candy. It landed right in my open palm. It was about two and a half inches in diameter, crystalline, moist, with the flavor of honeysuckle nectar. He said, "Eat it!"

It struck me at the time that there was something rather odd about His giving candy to a person who had just asked for help with a weight problem, but I dismissed the thought. He knew what He was doing even if I didn't. Now, putting all the pieces of the puzzle together, I realize that He was clearly showing me by His action that my problem did not stem from what I was eating, but from what I was thinking. It was necessary for me to clear out all of the conflicting information in regard to right and wrong, fattening and non-fattening, every theory and opinion relating to diet which had been stored in my mind through the years. It was essential to erase all of the old parental tape recordings and dislodge the dark thought forms which were controlling my behavior beneath the level of awareness. With these out of the way, I would be free to listen to the messages from the body and to respond to its needs for simple care and fuel. My desire to be His instrument entails trusting Him to know what kind of

Chapter Fifteen

instrument He needs, thus leaving the outcome of the action strictly to Him.

Giving up the desire for a healthy body does not mean to either abuse it or indulge it. It is wonderful to forget the body when we are totally absorbed in our service to others. It is blissful to forget the body when our mind is filled with thoughts of God. But as long as we are in the body, it is dharmic to give it the best possible care. This was brought out vividly to Al Drucker when Swami told him to treat his body as if it belonged to Swami Himself—as if it were Baba's very own body. If the body we are in right now were Swami's very own body, we would certainly care for it as if the world depended on it! We would not indulge the desires of the senses at the expense of Swami's body. We would not turn the care of Swami's body over to the mind or intellect, either our own or anyone else's. We would not ignore any message that Swami's body was sending us. We would strictly limit desires. We would remove all of the old programming from the mind and fill it with thoughts of God. We would listen for guidance from the Highest Source. Then we would act in accordance with that guidance, trusting the results to Infinite Wisdom.

Learning to accept ourselves where we are right now—without guilt, without pride, without self-pity, without self-justification—is an extremely valuable exercise, and the body is a useful tool for performing this exercise. Acceptance of what is, discipline, and right action add up to commitment to giving the body the best possible care, without being attached to the results. If we have done the very best we know how, then we can surrender the outcome entirely to Him. Swami has said: "Life is a water bubble. It comes and it goes. Don't worry. I will take care."

Each of us has the body which is exactly right for us at this stage in our development. It is delivering the messages we need to hear. It is forcing us to be where we need to be, to do what we need to do. It is a very important part of the game plan, but we must not be deluded into identifying ourselves with it. It is the token that moves around the board, but it is not the object of the game. The goal is God and God alone.

A vivid illustration of this principle was given on the television show, **There is a Way,** recently. Dr. William Hornaday, minister of Founders' Church of Religious Science in Los Angeles for forty years, found himself incapacitated by a knee problem. His faithful mental treatments did not seem to help at all. He was in considerable pain as well as being quite embarrassed by his inability to heal himself with the methods which he had been teaching the members of his congregation.

Finally he determined to seek medical assistance. He located the surgeon who was reputed to be the finest in the world and made arrangements for the knee to be operated on. Following the operation, the surgeon assured him that the operation had been successful and that he would have no further difficulty with the knee. However, he found that such was not the case. To his great dismay, he was not only still unable to walk but the pain was, if anything, even worse.

The surgeon was at a loss to determine what had gone wrong, but, knowing the success rate of his technique, he could only assume that he had made an error. The operation was repeated with great care and precision, but the results were no better. Dr. Hornaday, lying in his hospital bed in pain and unable to walk, realized that there was nothing more to be done. He had utilized the best mental treatment he knew and had employed the best surgical treatment available, but his knee had refused to respond to either. He asked that he might be left undisturbed for several hours. In total surrender, then, he prayed with great earnestness over and over again the same prayer: "Lord, let me feel Thy presence." No longer focused on the body, his purpose became solely to experience God. Giving that one goal his total attention, he desired nothing else.

After a number of hours spent in blissful contemplation of his Oneness with God, his attention was once more drawn to the body. He lowered the side of the bed, put his feet on the floor, and walked across the room to the bathroom without pain. At the time of this writing, he is still ministering to his congregation in vigorous health with no regard for his advancing years.

During this experience he relinquished his desire for a healthy body and realized his purpose to be God and God alone. At some point in the spiritual development of each of us, we will be given the opportunity to make that choice. When we establish our goal as God-realization and look at it with one-pointed concentration, we will reach it more speedily. No, even more than that. When we look at the goal with singleness of vision, we will find that we have been there all along.

******

"Most devotees seek health, wealth, power, and fame from God, which are all trivial assets, yielding momentary pleasure."

—Baba
Santhana Sarathi
August 1986

Referring to the fact that stalactites and stalagmites grow towards each other and ultimately join, Baba said: "Similarly the compassion seeping from the stalactite of God will keep dropping on the individual soul, and he by his austerity grows up as the stalagmite reaching up to the Supreme Soul. Ultimately some day they merge. Nonetheless, the effacement of karma and eradication of past tendencies is a very slow process—like the stalactite-stalagmite growth."

—Baba

"There are two kinds of teaching: direct and indirect. Scriptural teaching (deduction and induction, reasoning and inference) is indirect. When the understanding gained is experienced and realized, it becomes direct. The understanding of the Supreme Godhead, which is Truth, Knowledge, and Bliss, can be, at best, only indirect. From one point of view, the Absolute knows neither direct nor indirect. It is beyond both.

"The first step to direct knowledge of God is spiritual practice; the first step in spiritual practice is service to the guru performed in total faith and total submission. At the same time, the responsibility of the guru is to instruct the disciple on the nature of God, to instruct continuously and in simple ways. When the disciple grasps this instruction, it becomes indirect knowledge. This indirect knowledge can be transformed into direct knowledge by constant recapitulation, constantly turning it over in the mind. Indirect knowledge is as evanescent as letters drawn on water. Direct knowledge is as indelible as letters carved in rock."

—Baba
Prasanthi Vahini

16

"LOVE MY UNCERTAINTY"

To know God's will has been one of the deepest desires of sincere spiritual aspirants throughout recorded time. It is an end which most will agree provides comfort and security. And yet Baba says "Love my uncertainty." This has seemed to me to be a hard teaching, so Baba, in His infinite mercy, has given me an experience to help engrave His words in my heart and set my feet firmly on a foundation of faith and trust.

As summer neared its end in 1986, I began to long for Baba and Prasanthi Nilayam. I wrote to Him, asking if Raye and I might come, but did not get a clear feeling of His reply. Raye felt confident that he was to go for one month, but I was hoping to stay at least two months. Since Baba has said that ladies should not travel alone, I wasn't quite sure how that could work out. One morning, as I again asked for guidance on this issue, the telephone rang. When I answered it, the voice on the other end of the line said, "We want to go to India with you and carry your suitcases." The caller was Stanley Bertsch. He and his wife, Sharon, had visited Southern California, learned about the advent of Sathya Sai Baba, and attended some of the same study groups and seminars that we attended. However, they had left California on the way to the Eastern part of the United States, and the call, which was from New Mexico, came as a complete

LIFE IS A GAME, PLAY IT!

Chapter Sixteen

surprise. I felt it was the answer for which I had been waiting, and jumped to the conclusion that this was the clearance to proceed with the plan for me to stay two months.

Weeks passed, however, and nothing firmed up in the way of reservations, dates, tickets, or visas. We were met by obstacles on every hand. Finally, one day when it again seemed as if there were no way for the trip to become a reality, I wrote to Sharon and Stanley and asked if they had received any guidance as to whether they were to "carry my suitcases" or not. On receipt of my letter, they both took up my question in their meditation. I received Stanley's answer first. He wrote that he had awakened "with the picture of a sign on a billboard with two legs and black writing. The sign said, 'Don't look for an obscure date on the ground.'" He went on to say that when he had asked his Higher Consciousness for an answer to my question, he had received three symbols in rapid succession. They were: a mountain, which he recognized as San Gorgonio, a very pleasant valley, and a bunch of cherries. Since we live in Cherry Valley and have a view of Mount San Gorgonio, Stan said the symbolism didn't seem to leave much doubt that he was to return to Southern California. He also enclosed a photocopy of a page from his dictionary which contained the definition of "obscure." He had highlighted the words: "out-of-sight, hidden, the obscure beginnings of mighty things.'

A billboard is an accepted way to get important messages to consumers of various types of merchandise, so why not from the Higher Consciousness to the lower mind? The message seemed quite easy to interpret. They would be coming back to Cherry Valley, but no date was yet set for the departure to India. However, promise was given of "mighty things" to come. Before I had answered Stan's letter, one arrived from Sharon. In it, she included drawings of the symbols she had received from the Higher Consciousness upon asking for further guidance in regard to the trip to see Baba. The symbols were a knot, which she drew to show its intricacies, a small red-orange cross, two lines which ran parallel to each other for a distance but then curved in different directions, and a waterfall.

She said that the words "a camp divided" were connected with the two lines and that those two lines became the waterfall. Near the bottom of the fall there were beautiful clear sparkling crystal objects, which might have been drinking goblets. She concluded by asking that I ponder and research these symbols to see what came to me in the way of interpretation.

The next day, as I was driving to the Newsletter office, I seemed to see a sign at every corner and every freeway offramp which was exactly as Sharon had drawn the "camp divided" symbol. It is the standard California highway sign to indicate that the left lane will curve to the left and the right lane, to the right. A camp is a temporary residence. We are only camping on Planet Earth, and it is, by its placement in space and time, composed of opposites. There always seem to be two or more choices available to us and frequently it seems that one choice will take us one way and the other choice will take us in the opposite direction.

Looking up "knot" in several dictionaries of symbols, I found agreement that it meant "divine inscrutability." This reinforced the reminder I had been giving myself daily to "Love My uncertainty."

Water symbolizes 'the unconscious, dynamic, motivating, non-formal, female side of the personality—intuitive wisdom."[3] The Chinese philosopher Lao Tse noted that "Water is outstanding in doing good. If a dam is raised against it, it stops. If a way is made for it, it flows along that path. Hence it is said that it does not struggle."[3] The fall of water is always toward the center of gravity. The path of the spiritual aspirant is always toward His center—Divinity. The flow of water conveys the idea of inevitable progression along a given path. Crystal goblets symbolize the grace of God. And the red-orange cross seemed

Chapter Sixteen

to me to represent Sai-Jesus, a name which Baba has given Westerners permission to use for Him if they wish, since all names are His.

The message seemed to be that we should not look for the right date to leave or time to stay in accordance with desire or human reasoning (both ground level processes). There seemed to be assurance that, even if we should make a wrong choice or take the wrong direction in this everchanging world of illusion that we would inevitably be guided back to the unchanging flow toward our God center. Being in tune with Baba and Jesus, we will be the recipients of grace.

Upon awakening the following morning, I felt a clear direction to call the airline. We had been given the information that all space was taken until after the first of the year, but guidance came to ask for four reservations on the closest departure date to November 25. I did this. I was told that the closest date on which there was a through flight was November 29 but that there were no seats available. I requested that we be placed on the waiting list for that flight and also that return reservations be requested for one month later. This time there was no hesitation or feeling of tentativeness. I felt strongly that the **divine inscrutability** was, through **intuitive wisdom**, becoming as clear as **crystal**. This was through no virtue of our own, however, but by the grace of Sai-Jesus.

Validations came in several ways. Raye was delighted with the arrangements. Sharon and Stanley, who had been enroute to California at the time of the call to the airline, felt that it was exactly right. Within twenty-four hours the airline confirmed all of the reservations except one segment of the return, which they assured us could be cleared before our departure date. We did not expect anything further. However, several days later, as I was looking up a symbol unrelated to this experience, I "accidentally" glanced at the definition of "labyrinth." These lines leapt from the page: "Some labyrinths shaped like a cross, known in Italy as

Solomon's knot, and featured in Celtic, Romanesque, and Germanic decoration, are a synthesis of the cross and the labyrinth; they are known for this reason as the 'emblem of divine inscrutability.'"[3]

The labyrinthian knot, which Sharon had seen together with the cross, was the **emblem** of "divine inscrutability." The symbols sent by the High Consciousness were precise, exact, and left no room for uncertainty. Once more I felt a tremendous shift taking place within me as the knowledge grew that there was certainty within the uncertainty, as well as uncertainty within the certainty. The human mind demands certainty in order that it may feel secure. But the only certainty is to be found in complete surrender to the divine uncertainty.

Paul must have reached this conclusion also. He wrote to the Romans: "O the depth of the riches both of the wisdom and knowledge of God! How unsearchable are His judgments, and His ways past finding out!" The human mind which struggles and strives to find out is itself the barrier to the knowing. The coincidence of the human and the divine is the supreme mystery. It will never be possible to understand it, but it is inevitable to Be It.

When Dr. Bhagavantam, who had frequent opportunities to interact with Baba, told Him that he still could not understand Him, Baba replied: "You have lived with yourself for a longer time. Do you understand yourself? If not, try to do so. Do not worry about understanding me."

******

"You must have not only freedom from fear, but freedom from hope and expectation. Trust in my wisdom. I do not make mistakes. Love my uncertainty, for it is not a mistake. It is My

Chapter Sixteen

intent and will. Remember—nothing happens without My will. Be still. Do not ask to understand. Do not want to understand. Relinquish the imperative that demands understanding."

—Baba
Sanathana Sarathi
August 1984

"You are God! All humanity is God! Everything with life and everything without life is God. I am God, but I do not have to know I am God, for I have always been that. I am Avatar. I have always been Avatar.

"Of the countless lives which have been on this planet, few, relatively speaking, have known their God Self. Most have groped helplessly, unaware even of the existence of their true Divinity. To them the light was not elusive, for it had not been revealed to them.

"As My devotee you have taken a step that is incomparable in magnificence and magnitude—even greater than the giant step forward which was acclaimed by man when he first walked on the moon.

"I am here beside you. I am within you. I am in your Heart of Hearts. I am here to help you and guide you. Turn to God. I cannot do that for you. You must do that yourself.

"I can draw the God in you toward Me, but you must come to Me. You must become one with Me and try to see God everywhere. See His Love in all people. Feel His Love in you, for it is above all other Love.

"When I go about My work, I impart the Love of God. My Love is God's Love. Am I not giving you a hint as to the real glory of God's Love that reposes within you? Let Me awaken you from your slumber. Let Me help you open your eyes for you to see the

Love of God that awaits you. This is My work. This is My joy. I am tireless in My quest to let you be filled with the Love of God.

"As I look on you, I see the Lord within you. His divine sweetness bathes you. I want you to know that this Divine Heritage is yours. Know this and come to the Lord's Kingdom. You will live forevermore in a treasure house of blessed happiness.

"A rare chance to find God is in your grasp. Do not sacrifice even one breath without coming closer to your own God Self. Benefit from every means I give you to find God. Become ever aware of the Love of God. Impart God through your Love to all.

"Your dawn of knowledge is approaching. Each day is your chance to achieve the greatest of all earthly accomplishments: to become Yourself—God!"

—Baba

17

"I WILL COME, AND I WILL STAY AT YOUR HOUSE."

American devotees of Sri Sathya Sai Baba have long prayed that He would come to the United States. He has been asked many times, and many times has indicated that His visit would take place at some time in the future. When Raye asked Him the question, he replied, "I will come, and I will stay at your house." It seemed so unlikely that this would occur at the action level that we recognized almost immediately that it was, once again, a mystical reference which would require some interpretation. In conjunction with another of Baba's frequent sayings: "My home is in your heart," the interpretation did not seem to be terribly difficult. The message seemed to be that God is a resident within the heart of each one, or as Jesus put it, "The kingdom of heaven is within you." House symbolizes consciousness. Therefore, to be assured that God would come and remain (stay) in consciousness, by His choice, requiring no effort on our part, was wonderful enough. And yet I never felt the sense of resolution or knowingness about this saying that I had learned to recognize when I had followed other sayings of Baba's to their Source.

Recently, as I pondered the words again, I felt the shift occur. It isn't really possible to describe what the shift feels like, but one is in no doubt at all when it occurs. It was, in fact, one of the first things I became aware of after my first visit. On my return to the United States I was asked, "Well, what benefit do you think you got from going to visit Sathya Sai Baba?" And, without having thought about it previously, the words—which still seem to me to be the perfect answer—came spontaneously from my lips: "He took all of the cold knowledge which I had in my head, warmed it in the glow of His love, and installed it permanently in my heart."

With the shift came the realization that, as Baba identifies Himself, so we must ultimately identify ourselves. I saw that He seldom uses the designation "I," but when He does, He means God. When He refers to himself as a separate body, He usually calls Himself "Swami." The interpretation which my head had placed on His words had been accurate. He did not mean that "Swami" would come and stay at our house, but that God made His permanent residence in our house—our consciousness. And at the moment of the shift, He made His residence felt—realized. What had been only one part of a belief system now was installed as a permanent fixture of the heart.

To know Him as our very Being, to hear Him speak as the Inner Voice, and to see Him in all people is the unspeakable gift of His Omnipresence. He tells us repeatedly: "Call Me by any name all names are Mine." I was given a very beautiful vision in illustration of this profound truth. As I asked for His guidance in regard to the use of names of individuals in this book, there suddenly appeared to me a thousand-petaled lotus. It's center was Baba's face and on each petal was a name I recognized. Some were of people I knew well; others were names of people I have only heard or read about. The message was clear. Whatever names appear within these pages are all His. They may or may not be people who are known to the reader, but their names are recognizable as His. He plays every role in each of our life dramas, and, as we learn to see Him there, we will dwell with Him "forevermore in a treasure house of blessed happiness."

Chapter Seventeen

"To light a fire, strike one match to start;
To light your life, take one word to heart."

—Baba

"God has a million names...a million forms. Select any name of His that appeals to you. Choose any form of His. Every day when you awaken to the call of the brightening East, recite the name, meditate on the form. Keep the name and form as your companion, guide, and guardian throughout the waking hours. When you retire for the night, offer grateful homage to God in that form, with that name—for being with you, by you, beside you, before you, behind you, all day long. Know that within the many forms and many names, God is present in all of them. The inner being is, in reality, only One."

—Baba
Images of Sai Baba
Alexi Allens

"God is the source of supreme delight, of extreme ecstasy. The joy flashes as sport, as prank, and as purposeless play (leela).

"All the living and non-living entities God projects are led towards acquisition of the very ecstasy whose overflow they are. God is the paramount principle of bliss that is not affected by time or materiality, for He is the basis for the material world of time and matter. His bliss pervades all creation. That is the way His leela works.

"God has no gain to achieve, no need to project the cosmos. He has everything. He is everything. He plays motiveless and unattached, out of sheer elan."

—Baba
Sanathana Sarathi
June-July 1986

******

"Learn! Experience! Be happy! It does not matter a bit if you have no faith in Me or in God. Have faith in yourself. That is enough. For who are you really? Each of you is Divinity, whether you know it or not."

—Baba
Sathya Sai Speaks, Vol. III

18

"HAPPY, HAPPY, HAPPY!"

Most of us who have had Baba's darshan have at some time heard Him say, "Very happy, very happy!" He is always happy. He may occasionally frown to impress us with steps we need to take to make our own lives happier, but He never feels anything but pure joy. At the end of one interview we had with Him, He placed His hands on Raye's shoulders, then made several sweeping motions across his chest, saying, "Happy, happy, happy!" In whatever circumstances we find ourselves, we can still be happy. Even though Baba is totally dedicated to serving the thousands who come to Him, as well as to personally administering a growing network of educational institutions, overseeing construction of buildings, and carrying out esoteric duties of which we can only be faintly aware, if at all, He still finds time to have fun.

Aurelia Nauroth and I were waiting for Baba to appear one day at Brindavan. She and I were nextdoor neighbors at that time and we had traveled to India together. However, we were not sitting together, and there was nothing to indicate that we even knew each other. We were in different rows and about ten feet apart. I had lent her a pen because she hoped that Baba would sign one of His pictures for her. When He had made the rounds under the banyan tree that day, He stopped and spoke a few words to me. Then He moved on. When He was right in front of Aurelia, He stopped again. He held out His hand for the picture, signed it with the pen, then handed the picture back to her.

At that point He turned around, walked back to where I was, and put the pen in my hand. I was so intent on watching His face and maintaining eye contact, that I held out my hand for the pen quite automatically. Baba shook the pen in my hand to bring my attention to it. Then He said, "That's not your pen." Aurelia, who had been watching all this very intently, called out, "Oh, yes it is, Swami; it's her pen." He laughed in delight and continued on His way. This whole little play, which was enjoyed by a dozen or more onlookers, seemed to be just for the fun of it. The message, if any, was that we can all enjoy playing the game. We don't have to take it so seriously that we forget to be happy.

Recently, in a Sathya Sai Baba Center meeting, two members told of beautiful experiences of Baba's tender, constant care in their lives. After the meeting was over and I had retired for the evening, I found that my mind was dwelling on the two "miracles" which had been reported. I know that miracles fulfill the law of God by dispelling the illusion of chaos and revealing the natural order. Nevertheless, my thoughts refused to settle down.

After hearing the clock strike eleven o'clock, and twelve o'clock, I asked Baba for help to fall asleep. At one o'clock, as the clock began to strike, I was surprised to hear it continue. Wondering what was happening, I counted each stroke. The clock had my full attention. After striking one hundred and ninety-one times, it was finally silent, and I fell asleep.

The next day I told the story several times and everyone agreed that it was a typical Baba leela. He uses ordinary things in an extraordinary way to produce a desired result. Who but Baba would see the relationship between a runaway grandfather clock and the vision of sheep jumping over a fence?

The story was just too delightful to keep to myself. Two days later, I related it to a group. Someone asked, "Why 191?"

Chapter Eighteen 147

Admitting that I hadn't really given it any thought, I asked if anyone else could offer a suggestion. Lee Katchen spoke up. "Well, let's see," he said. "We have a nineteen and the nineteenth letter of the alphabet is 'S'; a one, which is 'A'; and a nine, which is ' I '." Before he could put together what he had spelled, the rest of the group gasped almost in unison: "Sai!" It was the perfect signature to a perfect leela.

All of Baba's creations are designed to bring pleasure to his devotees. They not only please and delight the recipient of the talisman, but everyone who witnesses the manifestation enjoys it. When Swami produced the ring I presently wear, He had an especially happy time doing it. With a wave of His hand, He created a golden image of Himself on a setting of panchaloha (an amalgam of five metals). He placed the ring in my palm and turned to talk to Raye. I began trying to put the ring on my fourth finger right hand, pushing as hard as I could. Just as I realized I had pushed it so hard that I could neither get it on or take it off, Swami turned back to face me and asked sweetly, "How does it fit?" Hedging, I replied, "Well, it's just a little tight, Swami." He took my hand in His then and tried to pull the ring off. He gave it several vigorous tugs before it came off. He held it up and looked at it quizzically. Then He said, "Oh!" as if He had just made a great discovery, "you had it on backwards!" With that He slid the ring on my finger easily, much to the amusement of all present.

Recently, at a meeting in Ojai, California, Al Drucker mentioned one of the instances in which Baba has described Himself. "Swami says, 'I'm like a serene, lonely little child in a room full of mirrors. Some of those mirrors face one way and others another. I take out my marking pen and put a moustache and beard on that one, and I put a sari on that one and long hair and something else on this one. Then I just turn my back to the whole room and walk out. It's just play—play—our play.' And so the first thing on a spiritual journey that is going to set the tone for us—for the whole trip, the whole journey—is: Be happy! It's not: Go and find happiness, run after happiness. It's BE Who We ARE; BE HAPPY. Swami says, 'Spiritual path is not pressure; it is pleasure.'"

I heard a wonderful story on television recently which illustrates this point very well. It was told of a young Buddhist monk. The aspirant had been wealthy, self-indulgent, pleasure-loving, and had experienced a sudden transformation. He left his home, all relations and possessions, and entered the monastery. When the other monks fasted for a day, he fasted three days. When the rest meditated for eight hours, he meditated for twelve hours. He seldom smiled. He seemed to be determined to win liberation with the intensity of his sadhana (spiritual practices). Finally his mentor took him aside and explained to him that, whereas his living had been too loose prior to entering the monastery, it was now much too intense. He was advised to be gentle with himself, to be happy, and to find God right where he was.

Raye and I have been through these stages in our development. We are only now beginning to find a peace, contentment, and lighthearted joy which stays with us most of the time. Our desire for liberation is greater than ever before, but we have learned to be gentle with ourselves. Baba has given us a most beautiful direction in asking us to place a ceiling on our desires. He does not say that we may be wantonly self-indulgent, but neither does He ask us to immediately give up every earthly pleasure. He tells us not to let our desires escalate. They can easily do that here in the United States where so many things are readily available. We can be very happy without having the latest models, up-to-the-minute styles, or new home decorations every year. Happiness which is dependent on externals is fleeting, but happiness which comes from within will be permanent.

Telling the difference between these two kinds of happiness—or even understanding that there are two different "happy's"—

has not been easy for me. In my first marriage, there was a basic disagreement between my husband and me as to whether or not happiness was a worthwhile goal. He said it was not; I said it was. We thought that we had a major philosophical conflict. Actually, we only had a problem in semantics. We were both right. Happiness, if it is considered to be a temporary pleasure which comes about from an external cause, is not a worthwhile goal. It is, as Baba frequently tells us, only an interval between two pains. We want something, and we feel dissatisfied until we get it. We get it, and we feel happy. Then we lose it, and we feel great disappointment or grief. However, happiness which comes from the desire for God, thinking about God, experiencing God, and finally knowing ourselves to be That, is a very worthwhile goal. This happiness is a steady, unchanging joy, which requires no particular incident or circumstance to bring it into being. It is bubbling up within us from an inexhaustible source. It has neither opposite nor opposition, but it is the basis and substance of Being.

The philosophy of the Tahitians is: "Happiness is all that matters." I pondered that statement earnestly when Raye and I were privileged to spend some time on the island of Moorea, but I concluded that it could only be laziness and lack of ambition which could be expressed in such a philosophy. I was, at that time, willing to work toward happiness as a goal, but I was unable to accept it as my birthright.

Since knowing Baba, the war for or against happiness no longer rages within me. Joy may not always be easy to achieve, but it is simple to understand. Attachment to, union or identification with God—with the Eternal Absolute—always brings about happiness. Attachment to anything of a fleeting, temporary nature always results in unhappiness.

James Sinclair, a successful international financier and businessman, went to see Sathya Sai Baba for the first time, expecting to receive mystical wisdom which was available only to very few. Baba told him: "I've given you a lot, but you've never been happy. Be happy." It would have been understandable if James had rejected the advice as too simplistic, but, in a state of humble receptivity, he saw in those two words the sum total of all knowledge. He recognized that God had created us for His pleasure and that it was our purpose and our destiny to be happy.

It is easy to be happy when everything in this world of dreams is shadowed out the way we like it. The test comes when all is not in accordance with our preferences. Such a test came to me when Shail Rastogi called to tell me that Baba's biographer, translator, and faithful devotee for over forty years—Sri N. Kasturi—had departed from the earth plane in the transition we call death. Having looked forward to seeing him again on our next visit to Prasanthi Nilayam, I became choked with emotion and was having difficulty continuing the conversation. At that moment, the grandfather clock began to chime. Shail commented on the beauty of it, as she could hear it quite clearly on her telephone. Then, as we both realized that it was striking more than twelve times, she said, "Oh, Joy, how wonderful. The church bells are always rung at the time of someone's passing." And, of course, they are. But, what Shail did not know was that this was the second time that the phenomenon of the clock's overstriking had come to my rescue. Since I had identified Baba's instruction on the first occasion as: "Be calmly and peacefully happy—neither elated and overjoyed nor sorrowful and depressed"—I recognized the message that I was receiving through the clock this time to be the same. Death is not an occasion for sorrow. It is, in fact, the glorious opportunity for which we incarnated. If we have cut all ties to binding relationships, given up the desire for control, and detached from all pleasure which is dependent on objects or achievements, the soul can soar free from the body and attain the ultimate joy of merging into the Light—into changeless Being-Awareness-Bliss.

19

"MY LIFE IS MY MESSAGE"

One of Baba's most well-known sayings is "My life is my message." It is now clear to me that this statement is true for each of us. Everything that we feel, think, say, or do is a message we give to everyone around us. The love we feel for others will bless them as well as ourselves, softening the more difficult messages they have to hear. Even though we are not rescuers, and cannot if we would or should not if we could, save others from the messages they need to receive for their own growth, we can become an exemplification of a good player of the game of Life. Our acts of kindness, deeds of mercy, and service to others provide better messages of how to play the game than any speech we could make or book we could write.

The difference between us and Baba at this stage of our growth is that we are still on the receiving end of Life's messages, and He is not. Our everyday experiences bring us messages which we can decode and learn from. Our dreams bring us messages which we can decode and learn from. Significant others in our lives are our messengers. Insignificant others in our lives are our messengers.

Isn't it interesting that those of us who have gone everywhere, read thousands of words, and tried hundreds of techniques for achieving liberation, still spend thousands of dollars obliterating the messages that are being given us in order to help us achieve liberation. We divorce a spouse because we don't like the message we are getting from him or her about ourselves. We change our place of residence because we are unwilling to decode and accept the messages the environment is giving us to help us know ourselves. We criticize and blame others because they don't treat us the way we think we deserve to be treated. And the body, which may be the most valuable messenger of all, is probably the one least listened to. We rush to have the offending part drugged, soothed, or cut away, rather than hear what it is trying to tell us. We are willing to take it for a walk or a run, feed it vitamin tablets and live food, but we aren't willing to listen to what it has to say.

One of the most useful rules of the game is: When the message has been received, the messenger is no longer needed. Do you want this to be your last incarnation? Then be sure you cut every tie and hear and heed every message. Do you want to be free of attachment to a body? As soon as you have heard its message, you will not require it anymore. Freedom is to have a choice. We only begin to have the right to choose when we no longer have appetites, cravings, and impulses hidden so deep in our subconscious mind that we are not aware of how they are controlling us or of how to get free from them. Once we have gained awareness, we will find Baba's statement to be the truth in our lives: "Hunger, thirst, joy, sorrow, grief, suffering, appetite, and anger, are only impulses helping us to attain the presence of God."

Baba's life, His incarnation in this name and form, is far beyond my ability to explain or describe. However, it has been necessary for me to ponder His life many, many times in order to gain a clearer view of my own. He is my Exemplar. He is Love, showing Itself as constant caring. He is Principle, manifesting Itself as scrupulous obedience to divine law. He is Truth, expressing Itself as honesty. He is Life, expressing Itself in

Chapter Nineteen

tireless righteous activity. He is Omniscience, expressing Itself in perfect knowing. He is the Eternal Absolute, expressing Itself as a living symbol. And He constantly reminds us that what He is, so are we.

I have found Baba's teachings to answer all of my questions and fulfill all of my needs. They are universal, complete, and multilevel. They are Truth, the same Truth that is expressed in the Vedas, the Bible, the Dhammapada, the Tao Te Ching, all of the scriptures, and all of the spiritual teachings of saints and sages of the New Age as well as in ages past. But the **way** He teaches these truths is unique. At least, it is without parallel in my experience. He poses a problem, stimulates an inner search, then whether we solve the problem or follow through with the resulting instruction is up to us. Once we unravel the puzzle, we are no longer believers—we become knowers. Baba's teaching techniques are Life's teaching techniques. Both begin and end the game with Love. Life may present some hard knocks; Baba may frown and scold; but both do it for only one purpose: to help us achieve our goal of perfect wholeness, union with the Eternal Absolute.

******

"From the form to the Formless, from the Formless to the form—both processes are possible and progressive. The personal God is an expression, a symbol, a representation of the impersonal God. The impersonal does become personal and assumes form and attributes. This is the very nature of the Divine."

—Baba
Prasanthi Nilayam, August 2, 1986

"When troubles come, look beyond the mountains to the blue skies. See that you are only witnessing My play. See that your life is as temporary as the dancing clouds. Your coming and your going is just part of the performance.

Take God alone seriously, and play the parts you are given by Me with love. I will grieve should you misunderstand your roles. You are the Spirit within you; you are your blessed Self. My Kingdom that is within you is your real home.

"Oh, how I love you. How I care for you. Come! Rejoice with Me. You are ever dear to Me."

—Sathya Sai Baba

"In the symbol, the particular
represents the general,
not as a dream, **not** as a shadow,
but as a living and momentary revelation
of the inscrutable."

—Goethe

20
"YOU ARE ONLY WITNESSING MY PLAY"

    Having been a student of theater arts and an avid theater goer most of my life, I relate very well to the reluctance which many have to become witnesses of, rather than participants in, the dramas of their lives. In order to gain the greatest enjoyment from the theater, we are told, there must be "a willing suspension of disbelief." And as long as one is still deluded by the promise of finding happiness in these temporary goings and comings that we call life, he will be willing—even determined—to suspend his disbelief. As I have sat in the theater sobbing with sorrow, shaking with fear, or burning with anger over some experience which is being portrayed by the actors and actresses, a companion has reminded me that it is only a play. I have responded, "Oh, I know that, but I don't enjoy it unless I let myself get completely caught up in it."

    In recent years I am no longer willing to suspend my disbelief. I do not respond emotionally to stage plays. To my surprise, however, I still enjoy them just as much. I am a disinterested witness, but the pleasure I derive now is in the skill with which the actors and actresses play out their roles, the creativity expressed in the scenery and costuming, the beauty of the music, and the correlation of all of these ideas into a meaningful and purposeful whole.

The same change is now occurring in relation to my own life drama. It has taken many reminders, given by many companions, that "it is only a play," but I am finally beginning to be unwilling to suspend my disbelief in the reality of this temporary show. It is, as Shakespeare wrote, "full of sound and fury, signifying nothing." And yet, as witnesses, we can be fully aware of the becoming and the Being, feeling only peace, equanimity, and contentment as we watch the show.

Giving up the attachments and promptings of desire in the mind has been referred to by Baba as "the negative process," and He places emphasis on the importance of both the negative and the positive processes for those of us who desire to achieve full Self-realization. The ego puts up only slight resistance to the positive process: i.e., our efforts to establish an attachment to God. But, when we begin the negative process, we frequently experience great turbulence. The reason for this becomes clear when we visualize our consciousness as a mansion with many rooms. As long as each room is filled with relatives, friends, enemies, possessions, co-workers, employers, employees, and casual acquaintances, we can invite God to come in everyday. We can sing to Him, plead with Him, pray to Him, and worship Him, but it will be useless. He cannot come and stay in our house (consciousness) because there is no room for Him. Before God can come in, the other tenants must be evicted.

Each time we are able to extricate ourselves from entanglement with a desire or attachment, we must fill the vacant room with God. If we do not, the danger is great that another—or several other—counterproductive relationships will move in to replace the one we have just separated from. This was my experience. After I had specifically performed the rites which separated me from parents, grandparents, a favorite aunt, and other relatives, I found myself still experiencing distress in a relationship. The reason for this situation was not at all clear to me at first.

Chapter Twenty

After several years, during which a friendship was fraught with ups and downs, and many prayers had been uttered, I finally began to see it all clearly. The ego maintains its association with the familiar as long as it possibly can. My familiarity with seeing critical people and being a critical person was still holding me in bondage. It continued to take up too much space in the mansion of my mind—space I would prefer to have filled with thoughts of Baba. The relationship with the other lady could be described like this: She was willing to be the nurturing parent if I would play the role of docile child. She was also willing to play the role of child when I played the role of nurturing parent. But she was on the alert constantly lest that nurturing parent should become critical and/or controlling. If she sensed or even imagined that any control was being exercised, she instantly switched roles with me. She became the critical/controlling parent, and I willingly became the hurt child. We were into a symbiotic relationship which was occasionally pleasant but more often quite painful. I gradually became aware of the roles we each were playing in this game. We had been drawn together like magnets because of our complementary attachments. Neither of us merited blame or shame. Love and gratitude were in order between us. She had showed me myself in a way I might have taken a great deal longer to discover without her help. Her role in my play had been assigned by Baba, as was my role in her drama. No one appears on our stage unless the Director has placed him or her there for our benefit. To believe otherwise is to willingly deceive ourselves.

Baba frequently addresses us as "Embodiments of the Divine Atma." And so we are. If we are relating to anyone as other than an Embodiment of the Divine Atma, we have relegated ourselves to a lesser role as well. The playwright is a master craftsman and does not deal in stereotypes or misfits. Therefore, when the conflict has been resolved, the curtain comes down, the houselights come up, and only contentment remains.

Having seen through the game and recognized it as interaction between two fictional characters, we are then faced with the question of where the real is to be found. Knowing Baba, our thoughts will turn naturally to Him. Though He cannot be described or explained, His devotees have feelings and experiences that they express among themselves in ways which are sometimes confusing to others. For example, Sathya Sai Baba in form—the personal—does not channel messages for one individual through another individual. He conducts necessary business person-to-person in much the same way as anyone else. However, His freedom from ego enables Him to show forth the Formless—the Impersonal—with such clarity that His person—His name and form—become the symbol of the Absolute for His devotees.

Each of us is also both in form and Formless. Our ability to demonstrate that truth is, however, short-circuited by our many earthly attachments. As we strive to maintain our disbelief in the reality of this earthly drama, we turn again and again to listen for the voice of our High Consciousness, frequently naming it "Baba" or "Swami." When we are at our state of greatest freedom from the ego, we are experiencing the highest degree of Oneness with the Absolute—our Self, who is symbolized to us as Baba. Baba has made it very clear that He never channels messages through anybody, and we can have great certainty on this point. But we have access to the same source of Wisdom which He has, and as we are obedient to His instructions we will let that limitless Wisdom express Itself through us to a greater and greater extent.

In view of this, a little, lighthearted prayer comes to me each time I sit down to my typewriter:

> Beloved Baba
> Let my fingers do the walking,
> And Your Wisdom do the talking.

Chapter Twenty

The words remind me of Absolute Reality, but allow me to function at the action level—hopefully, as the instrument of Divinity rather than of the ego. The ego is in control whenever we get caught up in any role other than that of "Embodiment of the Divine Atma." I have played a long series of roles in this incarnation, as have most of us. In most cases, I took those roles quite seriously, getting so completely caught up in them that I was elated when they went well and dejected when they faltered or failed. Many of those roles have now been relinquished. I no longer play the role of "Mother" to the children or "Daughter" to the mother, but even more important than that, I no longer play "critical/controlling parent" or "injured/demon child." (Well, not very often, anyway!) The goal is to witness the play from the audience as the Embodiment of the Divine Atma—not to experience the ups and downs of the actors on the stage.

I had a very happy, bright, technicolored dream which confirmed these conclusions. It was Mardi Gras time, and I was in New Orleans. Everyone was in costume, and the celebration was in full swing. I was walking toward a bus stop, thinking that I might catch the next bus. Before reaching the stop, however, I saw the bus. It was gaily decorated with balloons and streamers. The balloons were all different carnival faces. They had three dimensional noses and each face seemed to be one of a kind. I thought I would just let that bus go on by as there would be another along soon. My own clothing seemed to be new, and I glanced down admiringly at a very pretty silk blouse I was wearing.

The symbology here is as delightful as the dream itself. Balloon faces represent our roles. The spiraling streamers with their loose cut ends symbolize freedom from bondage. Mardi Gras is a time of rejoicing. The word "carnival" comes from folk etymology "carne vale," which means "Flesh, farewell!" And the new silk clothing indicates an upgraded or improved position. The bus is a form of public transportation. Walking relates to earthly activities and, in this dream, to upward movement.

Witnessing the bus go by would seem to indicate letting go of all of the roles that have been played in public life. All of the other symbols provide reinforcement for doing that. Giving up identifying with our roles, but watching them with pleasure and contentment as they pass by in front of us, seems to be the way to carry out our earthly activities while we move upward—Godward.

******

"All living beings are actors on this world stage. They exit when the curtain is rung down or their part is over. On that stage, one may play the part of a thief; another may be cast as a king; a third may be a clown; and another, a beggar. For all these characters in the play, there is One who gives the cue. He will not come out on the stage in full view of all. If He did that, the drama would lose interest. Therefore, standing behind a screen at the back of the stage, He prompts each actor, irrespective of his role. The Prompter provides dialogue, speech, or song, just when the help is most needed.

"In the same way, the Lord is behind the screen on the stage of the world, giving the cue to all of the actors for their various parts. Each actor must be conscious of His Presence behind the screen of illusion. He must be eager to catch the faintest suggestion the Director might give, keeping the corner of the eye always on Him and having the ear pitched to catch His voice. If the player forgets the plot and the story (that is to say, the work for which he has come and the duties that such work entails), neglecting to watch the Presence behind the screen, the audience will laugh and he will have spoiled the show. For these reasons, every actor who has to play the role of Man on the world stage must first learn his lines well. Then, remembering the Lord behind the screen, await His direction."

—Sathya Sai Baba

******

"You have played many roles through many incarnations, but they were all given to entertain you—not to frighten you. Your immortal soul cannot be touched. In the motion picture of life you may cry, you may laugh, you may play many parts, but inwardly you should ever say, 'I am Spirit.'"

—Paramahansa Yogananda
Truth Journal
May-June 1987

"If you live on the level of the body and the individual, you will be entangled in food, entertainment, and frivolity, in ease, envy, and pride. Forget it, ignore it, overcome it—you will have peace, joy, and calm. On the divine path, there is no chance of failure; it is a path on which every milestone is a monument for victory. It is the path of Love."

—Baba
Sathya Sai Speaks, Vol. VIII

21

"FORGET IT...JUST REPEAT THE NAME!"

Several years ago I found myself facing what seemed to be an impossible dilemma. Both of the choices were equally repugnant. Not only were they disastrous in their implications for my finances and relationships, but both were in direct opposition to Baba's teachings. There seemed to be no way at all to avoid acting on one of the choices, and yet both seemed so wrong that I found myself immobilized. For several days and nights my mind ruminated on the two alternatives and the various results of selecting either.

I became more and more agitated. Finally, in great distress and with considerable emotion, I prayed to Baba to tell me what to do. The desire to be free of the problem was so great that it didn't matter at all which choice was to be made, as long as I could feel that I had done the best that could be done under the circumstances.

One evening I beseeched Baba for an answer until falling asleep but awoke in the morning with the dilemma still before me. I spoke aloud, "Oh, please, Baba, please tell me what to do." The thought that came vividly at that moment was: "Just repeat the name." I sat down in disbelief and continued addressing Baba out loud, saying vehemently, "That's no answer!"

I waited expectantly, hoping for a solution that my mind would accept as being more practical. "After all," I reasoned, "I could repeat the name of God for twenty-four hours—or even twenty-four days—and I would still eventually have to make this decision." No amount of complaining or resistance, however, brought any further direction. Resigned that I was ultimately going to have to act without Baba's intervention, I thought: "Oh, well, if I do as I seem to have been told, at least I can postpone taking action a little longer." So I began to repeat the Name I love. "Sathya Sai, Sathya Sai..." All day long I kept it going. When my mind tried to bring the problem to the forefront, I would say the Name out loud for a while. When bed time arrived, I fell asleep easily and the beloved Name echoed peacefully in my dreams.

On awaking the following morning, I began repeating the Name again, but—on another level—I gave my mind permission to look for the answer to the predicament with which I was faced. My mind began to search for the two alternatives which it had been so desperately trying to decide between, and a strange feeling came over me. There had been no change at all in the external circumstances, but all sense of urgency was gone. From a firm conviction that I must decide and act almost immediately, I now felt that there was no need to do anything at all. As I repeated the Name throughout the day, the memory of the problem surfaced a few times, but, instead of seeming to be a fearsome future decision to be made, it all now seemed to be more like a dream which had occurred in the past.

In a very short time, even the memory of the dream had disappeared. No decision was made. No action was taken. No miraculous solution appeared. The problem had simply dissolved. I found that I could not even remember what it had been.

Petitioning Baba again for His help, I asked, "Where did the problem go?" Waiting quietly this time, my expectant heart received a gentle response: "When you removed the problem from the mind, you eliminated it from the only place where it even claimed to exist."

Contemplating these words, I recalled that when I had asked Baba for His help to heal the relationship with my son, He had replied: "Put all of your attention on your Center activities." Then when I had asked Him what to do about the condition of my health, He had replied, "Forget it!" Both of these answers involved removing the problem from the mind. In addition, when I had been concerned about all of the negativity surfacing from deep within the subconscious, I had been led to become conversant with Phyllis Krystal's work, which is specifically designed to remove old habitual thought patterns from the mind. Guidance to "Just repeat the Name" was not different in essence from the answers which Baba had given me in person or previous guidance I had received from the High Consciousness. I began to be aware of a pattern, which was not only consistent, but which also seemed to be one for which I had been preparing long before I had ever heard of Sathya Sai Baba or consciously desired to travel the path home to God.

And yet, this instruction, which seemed to be uniquely designed to remove my personal obstructions, also had a universality which I was shown almost immediately following the incident related at the beginning of this chapter. I happened to see a television interview with Herbert Benson, M.D., Associate Professor of Medicine at Boston's Beth Israel Hospital, Harvard Medical School, and Director of the hospital's Division of Behavioral Medicine and Hypertension Section. Dr. Benson has authored two successful books, *The Relaxation Response* and *Mind/Body Effect,* outlining the benefits of stress reduction through meditation. In this interview, however, he said that he had recently discovered a remarkable new technique which, when combined with meditation, measurably and dramatically improves health. "This technique," he said in the interview, "is the repetition of the Name of God—whatever Name you love." He went on to say that he had, under carefully controlled conditions, documented the strengthening of the healing effect when the "Faith Factor" (repetition of the Name) was added to the "Relaxation Response" (meditation), and that it mattered not at all which Name for God was used, as long as it was one in which the person had faith. Baba has told us this many times, saying: "Call Me by any Name; all Names are Mine."

Dr. Benson has now published a new book, *Beyond the Relaxation Response,* in which he tells how he came to recognize the benefits of the "Faith Factor" and also the results which have been witnessed when this new technique is added to standard meditation. He outlines the resultant sequence of events which he has observed in his practice as follows:

1. "There is less concern about the symptoms or illness; in other words, the anxiety cycle is broken.
2. The symptoms become less severe.
3. The symptoms are present less of the time and short periods of complete relief are noted.
4. The periods of relief become longer.
5. The symptoms are completely gone or remain in a fashion that no longer interferes with everyday activities. In fact, I have found that many patients have difficulty remembering their original symptoms.

"The time duration for a person to experience these full benefits is quite variable. For some, it can be as short as one to two weeks. For others, up to a year is required. Most people can expect improvement to occur in approximately four to six weeks."

Chapter Twenty-One

Thus Western science confirmed what Eastern mystics have known for centuries. Further validation of the power embodied in those simple words, "Forget it...just repeat the Name!" which had come into my experience from Sathya Sai Baba, seemed to rush in from everywhere. *A Course in Miracles* teaches: "Repeat God's Name and all the world responds by laying down illusions."

To forget the illusion while holding the thought steadily on God seemed such a practical and effective way to proceed that I even imagined myself having arrived at a state beyond imprisonment in a body. On that plane, I might think something like this: "You know, I used to live in some sort of form which took me from place to place. I needed it almost all the time. As a matter of fact, there was virtually nothing that I could do without it. It seemed paramount to my existence then, but now I can't remember what it was." In the New Thought churches such a statement is called an affirmation. It is common knowledge among students of Unity, Science of Mind, Divine Mind, and other metaphysical teachings that an affirmation exerts the greatest influence over the mind when it is stated as having already been achieved. Professor Kasturi referred to the affirmation quoted earlier in this paragraph as a "step toward what is truly a Vedantic victory—the knowledge that there is only One..."

As long as we're playing this game of life, should we not play to win? The victory has been won by our Being Self, and with the example and the grace of Baba, our becoming selves are rapidly moving into conformity with Being. The use of spiritual exercises such as meditation, the triangle, the figure eight, affirmations, prayers of petition, and repetition of the Name, along with decoding daily experiences and dream experiences and utilizing them for self-inquiry, will enable us to love and serve All. Service of man will expand awareness until God and man are seen as One, and we can affirm with Bliss:

The game is done;
The victory, won;
Our Baba's work is plain.
The longing to be One with Him
Has brought the Light again.

And Being now is what I am—
No more deception-bound—
I'm All-in-All, this Baba-Me;
I've played a perfect round.

Chapter Twenty-One

THE HAND OF GOD

How small it is, the pale brown hand
That holds the world!
How gentle is the mighty strength
That lifts humanity from self-destruction!
In future aeons of Time,
When my struggling soul
Climbs slowly SAIwards,
Embedded in my consciousness
To spur me on, will be the knowledge
That I looked into the Face, the Eyes of LOVE,
That once—nay twice!—I held and kissed
The small brown hand of God.

—Peggy Mason
The Embodiment of Love

22

"ASK FOR WHAT I CAME TO GIVE: LIBERATION"

After an 8:00 A.M. arrival in Bangalore from Madras on December 2, 1986, we had barely unloaded the taxi and set down the bags in the hotel lobby when we were given the news that Baba had arrived in Whitefield the night before. He would be giving darshan at Brindavan within the hour. Everyone assured us that our luggage would be cared for, our room would be ready for us on our return, and all that mattered was that we be in Whitefield by 9:00 A.M. So with great joy we got back into the taxi and careened through the streets of Bangalore at breakneck speed, horn blaring, passing huge buses, loaded trucks, bicycles, three-wheeled rickshaws, pedestrians, cows, oxen, goats, and dogs—all the while feeling as if we were on the wrong side of the road. It takes a day or so to readjust to traveling on the left instead of the right, and to regain confidence in the driver's ability to somehow miraculously avoid each obstacle as it looms ahead of us. Accidents, which seem continuously and momentarily imminent, are relatively rare occurrences.

So we saw Him on December 2. The next day He took the letters I had brought, asked me when I had come, and said, "How many in your party?" I replied, "Eight, Swami!" This was a rather clear example of His doing both the asking and the answering. On the way to Whitefield from Bangalore that morning I had instructed

Raye and Sharon and Stanley that in the event that Swami should ask, "How many in your party?" they should say, "Six!" We had met two beautiful devotees in the L.A. airport as we were checking in at the ticket counter. They were Katie Brown and Pat Aiken from Tucson, Arizona. We found that we had identical itineraries both going and returning and that we were quite compatible and so it seemed to us that Baba had brought us together for His purposes. We considered ourselves to be a party of six. Pat Bradley and Barbara Hill were to join us in a week, but they had not yet arrived, so I had very carefully instructed everybody to tell Swami, if He asked, that we were a party of six.

Immediately after the darshan in which I had told Him that there were eight in our party, a very personable young lady addressed me, said that she had come alone and that this was her first trip. Her name was Heidi Kugler and she was from Palo Alto, California. I felt right away that she must be one of the eight. Then Vidya Alekal spoke to me. She is an associate editor of the Newsletter, our next-door neighbor in R-1 (the American Round House) at Prasanthi Nilayam, and a lovely lady. So she became number eight and I relaxed. I have heard it said that Baba doesn't appreciate it at all when someone tells Him there are a certain number in their party and then when He calls them there is an entirely different number.

Two weeks passed. We went to darshan every morning, but we weren't called. Then we got the news early one morning that Baba had left Whitefield and gone back to Puttaparthi the night before. We packed in a flash and were on the road to Puttaparthi before noon. By this time, Pat and Barbara had arrived; Vidya was too close to her leaving date to feel it was practical to return to Puttaparthi; Heidi (though leaving on the same plane that Vidya was) went to Puttaparthi to get every possible moment with Baba. She would spend a week in Germany with her mother before returning to Palo Alto. So now we were nine. Since Heidi was leaving December 18, I hoped somehow it would all work out. On the afternoon of

Chapter Twenty-Two

December 17, Pat Bradley decided that she wanted to have some time to be alone and so did not attend darshan. That was when Baba came straight from the veranda to me and said, "Pakora, you go!" And we were eight!

Baba began teasing me as soon as He came back to the veranda. He said, "Pakora, where do you come from?" I replied, "California, Swami." He said, "They sure grow 'em big in California!" "Is your husband so big?" he asked. I replied, "Well, he's not getting any smaller, Swami." (He weighs in at over 200 pounds.) After He opened the door to the interview room and some started in, He looked me over again. He said, "We've got a problem. There are no strong chairs inside." I said, "Never mind, Swami, I'll sit on the floor." But, when we got inside, He and one of the college boys brought in a nice chair for me and I sat in the back, right in front of the door. He manifested a black lingam for a lady whose husband was diabetic, telling her to put water on the lingam each day and have him drink it. He manifested a medallion for a little boy about ten years old. He made a ring with nine gemstones for a gentleman. Then He began taking one or two of the group in for personal interviews.

While Baba was in the inner room with a couple, Stanley wanted to write down the words which were on His chair. It had been Stanley's joy to learn to write the Hindi characters or Sanskrit words on this trip and Swami had blessed these efforts on a previous occasion. Therefore, Stanley asked the student sitting next to him if he might borrow a pen. The student gave Stanley his pen and Stanley carefully copied the words "Sathya, dharma, shanti, prema" into his journal. When Swami returned to the larger room, He glanced at Stanley and the student, circled His hand in the characteristic motion of creation, and produced a gold pen which He gave to the student. Then He signalled to another couple to come inside with Him. This time, after His return, He again looked at Stanley and the student. He said to the student, as if He had forgotten, "Oh, you'll need some ink, won't you?" With a quick wave of His hand, He brought forth a cellophane packet with two ink cartridges. He opened the packet, took the pen back, and showed the young man how to install the cartridges. Then He said, "It will not start writing until tomorrow." Raye and Stanley were sitting beside the boy and saw him try to write with the pen, but it was not yet ready to perform.

Suddenly, the lights went off and the fan slowed until it became still. We were all wondering what effect this electrical failure would have on our interview. Will we never learn? With a quick wave of His hand above His head, Swami said, "Light!" The lights came on instantly and the fan began to turn again, giving us all just one more view of His Omnipotence.

One lady asked about a clicking sound she heard in her head almost constantly, and Swami demonstrated the alternate closing of the nostrils in order to balance the prana. Upon my arrival at home, Vidya gave me a beautiful calendar which has a quotation from Baba on the front (Jan./Feb.) page. It is: "Thoughts can be managed through regular silent sitting (meditation), devotional singing, and rhythmic breath." On the same day that I received the calendar, I received the January Lesson in Truth from Roy Eugene Davis. In it Roy gives a detailed explanation of the importance of rhythmic breathing. I have learned from past experience that Baba will emphasize his message in several ways if I fail to pay attention to it the first time. Since this message came three times in rapid succession, it seemed to be a message for me as well as an answer to the questioner.

The highlight of the interview for Raye and me came when He took our group into the inner room. He took Raye's hand as if He were going to shake hands. They both had to stretch as Raye was sitting a distance away—though there was no one between him and Swami. Then as they joined right hands, Swami also put His left hand on Raye's and Raye put his left hand up as well. With their four hands together, Swami seemed to lift and pull and Raye floated and/or scooted across the floor until he was at Swami's feet. Swami looked into his eyes deeply for a few moments. Then He said, "This

Chapter Twenty-Two

is a good man." He turned to me and repeated, "This is a very good man." I said, "I know that, Swami, and I thank You for him."

He then pointed to the ring that Raye was wearing. It was a large portrait of Baba. He said, "You don't need such a large picture of me. I am always in your heart." Raye agreed, and he pointed out that he had recently knocked a chip out of it. Swami asked, "Would you like me to change it?" Raye replied in the affirmative. During this interchange Raye's eyes were as big as saucers and his smile was literally from ear to ear. In the outer interview room, Baba had made the ring with nine stones, which I mentioned earlier. He asked Raye if he would like one like that. Raye said, "Yes." Baba asked Raye three times if he really wanted nine diamonds, and Raye assured Him each time that he did. Baba said, "Ask Me when we get back into the other room."

Upon returning to the larger room, Swami had some delightful interaction with the young boy, took the medallion back, and added a chain with a circular motion of His hand. He commiserated with a man whose wife was quarrelsome. He called Katie up to Him, placed His hand on her head, and showered her with love. He told her that she might choose to marry or not—either choice would be fine.

Baba distributed vibhuti from a red bag to all of those present, giving each a generous supply. I was taken aback just for a minute to see that it was in tiny Ziploc-type bags, printed with the sarvadharma emblem. I realized I had become attached to having the vibhuti in folded papers, frequently with the children's handwritten mantra or a few of a devotee's thousand and eight names of God appearing on them. So I adjusted my thinking to accept the new idea and expressed gratitude for the ease with which the vibhuti could be shared or preserved in the new little bags.

Then Baba turned to Raye and asked him, "What do you want?" Raye seemed unable to grasp the fact that Baba was really asking him. So Baba asked again, "What do you want?" Then I realized that Raye was so blissed out that he probably didn't even hear the question. I couldn't stand the idea of having the moment pass with no action, so, with the intention of just reminding Raye of what he was supposed to say, I said "Nine diamonds." I had meant it to be a stage whisper, but it came out in a full-bodied voice that could have been heard in the Poornachandra. Raye says that it's a good thing that I did because it was the sound of my voice that brought him back down to earth. Anyway, he then responded by asking for nine diamonds. Swami asked him three times and he replied "nine diamonds" three times.

Then Baba took the big ring, passed it around for all to see, took it back, and blew on it three times. It was instantly diminished in size, the silver was changed to gold, and the portrait of Baba became the nine gemstones. It was exactly like the ring he had manifested for the other gentleman. Baba then showed them that they had rings alike and said, "No jealousy, no jealousy."

Pat Aiken said that she could see three lines of vapor with staccato-like dots in the lines on each side of the ring. She said that they appeared to be little sparks of energy coming from His mouth as He blew on the big ring. She was close enough to catch sight of the big ring as it diminished into the smaller one. I was too far away to see, but was ecstatic that Baba was giving Raye so much attention. I had felt before we left home—and said several times—that this would be Raye's trip. It was, but it was mine, too. Each one always gets just what he needs but not always exactly what he wants. This time we got everything we wanted and more.

Stanley had been asked by Elsie Cowan to deliver a message to Baba for her. She had kissed Stan on the cheek and told Him to give it to Baba with her love. When Stanley told Baba, He said, "Yes, yes! Already received!" Then He stroked Stanley's cheek and said, "You're a good boy."

When it was time to go, Baba walked to the back door. As I mentioned earlier, my chair had been placed right in front of the

Chapter Twenty-Two

door. No one could leave until I moved. I just sat there. Baba waited a few moments, then he said, "Well, get up!" I replied, "I want to stay, Swami." But I got up. As I did, He placed His hand on my cheek and stroked it a few times, saying, "You're a good girl—a very good girl." I wanted so much to kiss His feet, but I knew that it wasn't practical there in the doorway, so I asked, "Swami, may I kiss your hand?" He said, "Yes, yes," and held up His adorable little soft hand to my lips. I kissed it three times and reluctantly went out the door. The little preview of paradise was over.

That night, just before I fell asleep, I asked that inner Wisdom reveal the significance of the ring to me. As I awoke the following morning, it seemed clear to me that Raye would no longer be subject to the influence of the orbiting planets but that he had now placed himself within Baba's orbit, acknowledging that he was being cared for, watched over, guided, and protected by Him. Raye had made an appointment to discuss the ring with Professor Kasturi, knowing that he would be able to explain the significance of the stones. We also had a hazy memory that Baba might have created a similar ring for His close friend and biographer, Sri Kasturi.

We were welcomed into the Kasturi home with an outpouring of love and hospitality. It was a fact that Swami had manifested a ring exactly like the one He had made for Raye. This was done in 1950 and the dear professor had worn it until only two years previously. At that time Baba had glanced at the thirty-five-year-old ring and said, "Kasturi, are you still wearing that old thing?" Taking it back, He changed it into the one which was on Kasturi's graceful, long, slim finger in December, 1986. The new ring has the same stones but the setting is round instead of square. The central stone, a ruby, is larger than the others.

In his autobiography, *Loving God*, Professor Kasturi described the one that Baba gave him in 1950 as follows: "It was a gold ring set with nine precious gems, extolled in legends as capable of winning for the wearer the boons the nine planets can grant. [The stones are] pearl, ruby, topaz, diamond, emerald, lapis lazuli, coral, sapphire, and zircon." Baba told Kasturi that he would eventually discover that His grace (anugraha) was sufficient to remove any bad effects which might accrue to him from the nine planets or his birth horoscope, but that in the meantime the ring would provide protection and be a reminder. Our talk with Kasturi confirmed the unfoldment which had come to me the night of the interview: that Raye is no longer subject to the influence of the orbiting planets but that he is now within Baba's orbit, cared for and watched over, guided and protected by Him.

All of us were asking the same question: Why did He tell Raye to ask for nine diamonds when His intention was clearly to give him the nine precious stones? The night after we arrived in Cherry Valley, I awoke with the answer to that question quite distinctly in thought, without having exercised any reasoning or analysis at all. It was that Baba has always referred to the diamond as a reminder to its wearer that the mind must die. Thought must become completely still in order for the God-Self to be realized. Diamond = die mind. The number nine is frequently referred to as Baba's number—the number of completion, the end of the cycle, or liberation. Baba always says: "They come to me asking for trinkets and trash, but few come asking for what I came to give: liberation."

When He told Raye three times to ask Him for nine diamonds, and then had Raye ask three times for nine diamonds before He made the ring, He was telling him to ask for liberation—to ask for that which Swami came to give. The ring with the nine precious stones is only a symbol to remind Raye that he has been granted liberation—it is already his by virtue of his having accepted Swami's teachings and asked Him for liberation (nine diamonds). Professor Kasturi explained that when Baba placed the ring on Raye's finger it indicated that Raye was now wedded to Him. They are no longer two individuals, but One. Duality has ceased. The merger is complete.

More and more I realize that we must be constantly alert to symbols. Everything on this plane is symbolic of the reality but it is not the reality itself. Just as the $ symbolizes money. It is a useful symbol. We use it. We understand it. But we can't spend it! We must decode the symbols and see the reality beyond them if we want to have anything of genuine and lasting value.

The ring is a beautiful piece of jewelry. But it symbolizes so much more. Baba came to bring us to the awareness of our freedom from all earthly and planetary influences—our Oneness with Him and, hence, our present perfection. Liberation is not a goal to be struggled toward. It is the Truth to be real-ized.

******

"Superstitious awe of astrology makes one an automaton, slavishly dependent on mechanical guidance. The wise man defeats his planets—which is to say, his past—by transferring his allegiance from the creation to the Creator. The more he realizes his unity with Spirit, the less he can be dominated by matter. The soul is ever free; it is deathless because it is birthless. It cannot be regimented by stars.

"Man is a soul, and **has** a body. When he properly places his sense of identity, he leaves behind all compulsive patterns. So long as he remains confused in his ordinary state of spiritual amnesia, he will know the fetters of environmental law.

"God is harmony; the devotee who attunes himself will never perform any action amiss. His activities will be correctly and naturally timed to accord with astrological law. After deep prayer and meditation, he is in touch with his divine consciousness. There is no greater power than that inward protection."

—Sri Yukteswar

Do good
See good
and Be good
this the way to
GOD love
Willi
Babu
1.1.87

23

"FOR YOU, OR FOR ME?"

Right from the beginning, the "mighty things" which had been foreshadowed by Stanley's intuition regarding the trip began to occur. The desire uppermost in my thought was to receive reassurance from Baba that the publication of this book had His approval and was under His guidance. Therefore, after we had been blessed with His recognition and delivered the letters to Him which had been entrusted to us by other devotees, our next project was to see whether or not He would accept the manuscript of the first twenty-one chapters.

With the help of many others, I had prepared it to be as close in form and appearance as possible to the way I visualized the published version. The front cover was a beautiful full-length picture of Him and the title appeared in gold letters against a dark portion of the picture. Four days after our arrival, I carried it with me to Brindavan. It was in my lap as He approached me in darshan. He looked at it and asked, "What is it?" I replied, "A manuscript, Swami." He took it, then, and holding it with both hands, read aloud: "Life Is a Game, Play It!" Turning back to me, He asked, "For you, or for Me?" I replied, "For You, Swami."

I watched Him continue around the banyan tree, collecting letters and handing them off to one of the Seva Dals (volunteers), but carrying the manuscript. With His grace, I was given the bliss of watching Him carry it across the sand and into the university building (where He presumably spoke with the students), and fifteen minutes later come out again with it still in His hand as He disappeared into the inner compound.

Three days later, He came to me again in darshan, and, speaking in a manner which seemed to me to express acceptance, He said, "I have seen the book." Pondering this statement, I reviewed the sequence of events. When He asked me what I had handed Him, I replied that it was a manuscript. Yet He did not say, "I have seen the manuscript." He said, "I have seen the book." It sounded to me as if He were saying that He saw the project complete now—a finished creation—not just a possibility somewhere along a space-time continuum. However, when I mentioned this interpretation to another devotee, whose opinion I highly respected, I was told not to try to read anything into the words. I allowed the reaction of the other person to shake my faith in the Inner Voice and accepted the suggestion that I was only hearing what I wanted to hear.

The desire which remained seemed to be almost too much to hope for. I wanted Him to write something for the book in His own handwriting. His handwriting, like His face and His form, is so symbolic of Divinity to me that my heart leaps with joy each time I see it. I wanted the readers of the book to have that sublime experience, if they were indeed ready to appreciate it. But how to win that boon from Baba, I didn't know. The time passed so quickly.

After two weeks, Swami returned to Prasanthi Nilayam and we, of course, followed. We were granted a long, wonderful, sacred interview, but the opportunity to ask Him to write something for the book just was not there. He was completely in control, and I was completely immersed in the joy of His proximity.

There was only one time during the interview when I felt He made an oblique reference to the book. It was when He spoke to

Chapter Twenty-Three

the gentleman in regard to his quarrelsome wife, and said, "Marriage is five minutes pleasure and twenty-three hours fifty-five minutes grief!" He glanced at me very briefly before turning to Raye, saying, "You know what I mean." He was not joking. His voice and His response were completely serious. He was not referring to Raye's marriage to me. He had somehow conveyed that assurance to me wordlessly before He made the statement to Raye. It seemed quite clear to me that He was, as always, relaying several messages in a very few simple words.

First, He was speaking only to the one gentleman. His remark was for that person only and should in no way be taken as a blanket condemnation of the institution of marriage. I have heard Him say, "Yes, and soon!" when asked by another whether that one should marry or not. With His natural ability to know the questioner's present earthly condition, the stage of his evolution, and his purpose for incarnating, He is able to give an answer which is precise to the individual. It is supreme folly for anyone to assume that words spoken in private to one devotee will necessarily be applicable to another. They must be deeply, earnestly, and sincerely pondered in the heart until the answer becomes a conviction within and the seeker knows with a certainty which only comes with divine revelation that the words are also guidance for him.

In this particular instance, His remarks on marriage had no application at all to Raye and me in our human condition, but His glance at me, followed by His remark to Raye, spoke volumes. It said to me: "You see, I do know what is in the book," and it said to Raye: "I know your past, and I know the suffering that you have experienced in marriage." Once when I happened to be sitting beside a longtime resident of the ashram and a similar interchange took place, she remarked: "It never ceases to amaze me how He can get so much action out of so few words."

But the interview came to an end without any words being spoken which referred directly to the book. As our leaving date approached, I decided to write Him a letter. I told Him that every minute of our stay had been perfect. I said that we had been given so much grace that it seemed impossible that I should want more, and yet my state was still so very human that it craved constant evidence of His love and approval. I asked for two things: (1) help in sorting out feelings and attitudes in relation to money, and (2) a few words in His own handwriting for the book.

On New Year's Day outside the Mandir of the Avatar, I sat awaiting His appearance. Our bags were packed, the cars and the drivers were waiting, and we would leave for Bangalore immediately after darshan. Baba appeared on the veranda, spoke briefly to some of those seated there, and then stepped out onto the sand. He appeared to be coming directly toward the area where I was sitting. I had a pad of unlined paper in my lap and a pen in my hand. I watched Him as He spoke to several others and accepted letters from them. Then He stopped directly in front of me. With His most beautiful, loving smile, He said, "Well, Pakora, you are leaving today." I replied, "Yes, Swami." He put His hand out for the pad and pen. He wrote: "Do good See good Be good This the way to God With Love Baba." Then, handing the precious gift back to me, He said, "Very happy, very happy."

Back in Cherry Valley, I pondered His words. They were not a casual selection, I knew. Nothing Baba ever does is casual or offhand. Each word He speaks or writes is deeply meaningful. How does one know how to do good, see good, and be good, I wondered. On the surface it would seem to be axiomatic. No one would expect to find God by doing, seeing, and being evil. And yet, we are all struggling to find a way to God. What has Baba told me that I must pass on to the readers of the book? This teaching—unlike the one given about marriage—is not directed

Chapter Twenty-Three

to any one person. It is for everyone, everywhere, and for all time. Gradually I began to see that He had given me the answer in our first conversation about the book. When He asked "For you, or for Me?" He had supplied the yardstick by which every action, every thought, every state of being can be measured.

Superficially, it might be assumed that He was asking simply whether or not I had brought the copy of the manuscript for Him to keep or if I was only asking for His acknowledgment, blessing, or perhaps His autograph. It had been clear to me right away that His question had a much deeper meaning than that. I felt that He was asking whether the book had been written to glorify God or to enhance my own ego. I had pondered the question many times in relation to the book, to my purpose in writing it, and to the answer I had given Him. Now I had to go further.

Most of us are faced with decisions every day. Some of them seem trivial—insignificant—hardly worth giving thought to. Many, however, require deep soul-searching and have long-lasting effects on our earthly experience. How can we know whether or not we are doing that which is good? We can ask ourselves the question Baba asked me: "For you (the separate, individual ego), or for Me (the One Self or Universal Absolute)?" Will this action which I am contemplating only satisfy the senses and enhance the ego, or will it help me achieve my ultimate purpose of union with God? I find this question to be applicable to every behavior, to every act—whether trivial or otherwise. I have given it to others who have been wrestling with decisions and have been told that they also found it clarified the entire situation for them. What freedom there is in the joyous conviction that everything we do is for the purpose of union with Him!

On arrival in the United States, I felt a firm conviction that the events of the 1986-87 trip should be written up before the manuscript was submitted to a publisher. When the final six chapters seemed complete, I airmailed them to Baba, requesting that He signify His approval or disapproval in a manner which would be clear to me. Nine days later, on a morning when I had an early appointment, I felt drawn to a particular book. It was Roy Eugene Davis's spiritual autobiography: *God Has Given Us Every Good Thing.* I had not found time to read it in the fourteen months since its publication, and with only forty minutes in which to bathe, dress, have breakfast, and do a few necessary household chores, this seemed a highly unlikely time to begin. However, the urge to open the book was so persistent that I finally gave in. Opening it to page 109, I read: "In God's mind, it [the book] is already published."

Instant realization flashed. Nine days is the time it usually takes for airmail to reach India. Baba had not only sent a definitive answer to my most recent question; but, by the words chosen, also chided me for allowing anyone else's opinion to shake the faith which is to be accorded to one's own Inner Voice. His frequent references to the need to develop self-confidence became clearer to me than ever before. We cannot if we would— and should not if we could—push our inner convictions on anyone else, but neither should we allow anyone else to weaken or destroy them. God speaks to each of us in a way we can understand at our present stage of development, and the messages may be highly personal. In this case, the specific message received will probably have little or no meaning to the average reader. But the lesson it entailed—trust your inner guidance; have confidence in your High Consciousness—has universal application. Whatever we are doing for Him is also guided and directed by Him.

******

"Whatever we do in order to gain name or fame is a waste of time and is not of lasting value."

Bhagavad Gita 17:18

Chapter Twenty-Three

"The fault lies in the belief that things happen as a result of human effort and planning, human intelligence and care. No one can succeed in any venture without divine Grace. It is God's plan that is being worked out through man, but man prides himself that it is he who is working for it. Man will realize his mission on earth when he knows himself as Divine.

"Man must worship God in man. God appears before him as a blind beggar, an idiot, a leper, a child, a decrepit old man, a criminal, or a mad man. You must see the divine Sai behind all physical veils and worship Him through service. All names are His and all forms are His, including yours. You appear as separate individual bodies because the eye that sees them seeks only the outer bodies. When you clarify your vision and look at them through the Atmic eye (that is, the eye which penetrates behind the physical with its attributes and appurtenances), you will see others as waves on the ocean of the Absolute...

"See Him, serve Him, and revere Him in all. Pray: 'Let the whole world prosper and let all mankind be happy.' This is my special message."

—Sathya Sai Baba
Vision of the Divine
By E. B. Fanibunda

24

"I WILL CARRY THE BURDEN OF YOUR WELFARE"

When I had asked Baba to write something for the book, my mind had thought that perhaps He would write the title, or something similar to it. I could not stretch my imagination beyond half a dozen words. When I asked for help in sorting out attitudes and feelings about money, I thought that we might have the privilege of hearing Baba discuss the differences or similarities between His use of money as Sathya Sai Baba compared to the way He handled it as Shirdi Sai Baba (His previous incarnation). However, in both cases, He gave more than I asked and in a manner which was much wiser and more expansive than the limited concept I had formulated.

The first indication that my request for help in sorting out our feelings and attitudes about money was being answered, came about in a rather spectacular way. Shortly after our arrival in India, we had been approached after darshan by a lady who seemed to be well-educated, friendly, devoted to Baba, and who seemed to be interested only in doing what she could to help us. It was not long, however, before a long, sad, and very complicated story began to come out. Although we were never asked for money, the implication was clear that money would be very helpful. We knew that Baba had cautioned against such entanglements and our instincts were sensing that all was not as it appeared on the surface, but we found it difficult to avoid a daily conversation.

When we followed Baba to Puttaparthi, the friendly lady did also. For me, it was easier to avoid the contact at Prasanthi Nilayam, and I did. However, others in our party were still being drawn into various situations each day by what seemed to be only a desire on the part of the other lady to be helpful. Finally, the climax in this little drama came when two members of our party were called into the Accommodations Office because their names had been given as references by this woman. Evidently she had managed to work upon the sympathies of some foreigner visiting the ashram and had been given a large sum of money. Even though the members of our party had never given her money, the situation was brought to their attention. They were told that, due to the great differences in attitudes and feelings about money between some Indians and some tourists, the Indian government had passed a law to prohibit foreigners from giving money to Indian nationals. Only those organizations specifically licensed by the government to receive donations for charitable purposes could legally be given money. Any other gift-giving could result in the foreigner going to jail and would result in the Indian national going to jail.

As you can imagine, this incident began our sorting-out process. We asked ourselves whether we ever were caught up in bargain-hunting or in looking for a "good deal," or taking advantage of things advertised to be 'free.' Were we ever deluded into looking for something for nothing? Did we carefully discriminate between giving God's substance for God's glory and giving to enhance the ego? It is not an easy determination to make. These questions are not easily or quickly answered. But in our efforts to answer them, we became increasingly aware that giving and receiving are one continuous motion—that until we have our giving right, our receiving cannot fall into place either. We recognized that many times we give for very selfish purposes, hoping to receive friendship, love, gratitude, or respect in return—or just to free ourselves from the nagging insistence of one who has been carefully schooled in techniques of persistence.

Other lessons followed in rapid succession. On our return to Bangalore, we found that the travel agency which we had paid to reconfirm our reservations had done nothing and that we were now without reservations from Bangalore to Madras. It became necessary to go directly to the Indian Airlines to work out this problem. Even though the reservations were restored, we found ourselves faced with the question: "What had we paid the travel agency to do?" It seemed as if we had paid for a service and gotten nothing for the money. How did we feel about that? Again, it was not an easy question. The amount involved was negligible, but we recognized the importance of becoming clear in our own thought about it. Due to the timing, there was nothing that could be done other than examine our feelings and attitudes. I now see the incident as being part of the perfect plan. We realized that action can be used to avoid self-inquiry. In this case, we were determined to know ourselves better, and we acknowledged that the money was a valuable instrument to promote inquiry. Resolution came for me when I realized that all substance is God's, that no matter how it is rearranged it can never be lost, and that the travel agency was only playing its role in our drama. When we utilized the situation for self-inquiry, we got more than our money's worth!

On arrival in Madras, we checked in without incident, were promptly and easily cleared through immigration and security, but soon realized that three other members of our party had not followed. When they finally appeared, they told us that there had been some mix-up in regard to their reservations. Since the flight was full, the decision had been made to give them two seats in the first-class compartment. Then they held out the two first-class boarding passes and said that they wanted to give them to Raye and me for a special treat. Here was another lesson by example! We saw the love, caring, generosity, and beauty in giving with no thought of return at all. They freely gave because they put others first and themselves last. We felt our hearts expand to be the witnesses and recipients of this pure love.

The trip from Madras to Kuala Lumpur was part of the lesson, too. We were alert to notice those things which distinguish first-class from economy-class service: first, more space; second, more food; and third, more personal attention. However, our inquiry during this portion of the trip was somewhat lackadaisical as our comfort increased. Can it be that too much comfort, like too much action, slows us down in our discovery of that which has true and lasting value?

Fortunately, we were not to languish in that state for long! As we had left Los Angeles without confirmed reservations from Kuala Lumpur to Los Angeles, we found ourselves faced with the prospect of spending two weeks in Malaysia. Again, money was foremost in our feelings and reactions to this situation. Time was a factor, of course, but it did not seem to generate as much concern as the extra expenditure involved. As we sorted out and identified our feelings, trusting that the Universal Wisdom would put us in the right place at the right time to do whatever we needed to do and to learn whatever we needed to learn, we found attitudes around us changing. Though at first we had been told that the airline would do nothing at all for us, since our tickets clearly showed that the space had been requested but never confirmed, after several hours of patient exploration of the various options available, we were told to go back to the hotel and wait while attempts were made to find some routing which would enable us to continue on our journey. After about an hour and a half, the counter supervisor came to our hotel with our tickets. We had confirmed reservations to Tokyo for the next day. On arrival in Tokyo, we would be given hotel accommodations in order that we might rest comfortably between

Chapter Twenty-Four

flights, then continue on to Los Angeles on a different airline. The supervisor explained that the airline would pay our hotel bill for the additional night, but that we would not receive food vouchers. We should arrange to pay for our own meals.

Being extremely grateful that our situation had changed so dramatically, we were more than willing to pay for our meals. We changed some U.S. dollars into Malaysian dollars in order to pay each restaurant tab in local currency. As we were preparing to leave the hotel to board our flight to Tokyo, we noticed one member of our party having a rather animated discussion with the hotel desk clerk. Raye went over to see if he could help. To our surprise, the hotel records had been lost or in some way confused and the clerk thought that we owed them for three rooms plus meals. We explained the situation as thoroughly as possible, giving the name of the airline supervisor who had made the arrangement with the hotel. Unfortunately neither she nor the clerk with whom the arrangements had been made were on duty at this time. Finally it was necessary to leave to board the plane with the hotel personnel feeling that we had somehow managed to cheat them out of a fairly large sum of money. This was the other side of the picture which we had seen in Bangalore.

Whether it was because I was not a principal player in this drama, or whether it was because my guilt feelings had been handled by the vibhuti leela reported earlier in the book, I'm not sure—at any rate, this particular incident caused me little difficulty. I recognized, however, that earlier in life the same situation would have caused me great distress. I had been a compulsive bill-payer. If, through some computer error, postal delay, or oversight on my part, I had received a second notice to pay some obligation, I had felt greatly distressed. I must have thought the Southern California Edison Company, Sears, or Texaco wouldn't love me anymore. Now, in pondering these feelings and attitudes, the quotation which is used for the title of this chapter came into thought. In *Gita Vahini* Baba translated Chapter Nine, verse twenty-three of the *Bhagavad Gita* as "I will carry the burden of your welfare." Eknath Easwaren, in his book *The Bhagavad Gita for Daily Living, Volume II,* has freely restated the same verse as "I will even pay your bills." That is a comforting thought to me. I still pay my bills promptly, but if through some mistake I get a second notice—or, as in this case, I am suspected of trying to get away without paying what I owe— no feelings of guilt or fear are generated. I know I can trust God to bring everything back into complete equilibrium, granting each one the experience which will be most valuable to him.

Upon arrival at the check-in counter, we found that again our seat assignments were a subject of concern to the airline personnel. They had assigned seats to us which were, in fact, occupied by passengers already on board. Either five members of a traveling hockey team or five members of our party would have to be placed in first class. It seemed to be settled that we would be the ones to go into first class, when it was discovered that we had ordered vegetarian meals. With the plane filled, there would be no extra meals and no economy-class passengers to eat the meals we had ordered, and so it was decided that the hockey players would go to first class and we would be in economy class wherever the vacant seats were located.

When we arrived at the airplane, everyone was admitted and seated except Raye and me. We were kept waiting on the ramp outside the door. We could see the flight personnel going back and forth throughout the plane, talking with each other over their radio-phones, and we were not sure what the result would be. In this process the plane was delayed twenty or thirty minutes beyond departure time. Finally the stewardess came to the door and beckoned to us to enter. We were ushered in and seated in the first-class compartment. Arrangements had been made with two of the hockey players to sit in economy class and have first-

Chapter Twenty-Four 195

class food service, while we sat in first class and would be given economy-class food. Such a leela!

Sitting in first class, but being treated like economy class, engendered a totally new set of attitudes and feelings. We realized vividly how much of our judgment is based on comparison. We had been given luxury accommodations. The added space was clearly a blessing. And yet we had a tendency to feel like second-class citizens when mealtimes came around. Even though we had exactly what we wanted—what we had ordered—it was made to seem like poverty rations compared to the feast being served to those around us.

We began to see true wealth in the many and varied opportunities for learning which were being granted to us, through His grace, at our request. We felt, like Paul wrote to the Phillipians, that we had learned "both how to be abased and...how to abound," and we hope the day is near when we can say that we have learned "in whatever state [we are] therewith to be content."

On the last leg of the journey, everything seemed to go smoothly. Our hotel reservations were in order; two taxis were sent for us; we had a very pleasant ride through a part of the countryside we had not seen before; our time at the hotel was especially pleasant and restful; and our arrival at the airport was timely and our check-in without incident. We boarded the plane on time and were shown to our various seats. Raye and I were not sitting together but, as the flight was an all-night one, we both planned to sleep anyway and attached no importance to being together.

The seat next to the one I had been assigned had some sort of mechanical problem. Two members of the ground crew were working on it and finally gave up, placing a sign on it that said it was inoperable. I felt that this was a blessing to me as it meant the arm rest could stay up and there would be plenty of room. I had just said, "Thank you, Baba," when a family boarded with three small children. The inoperable seat belonged to one of them. As the stewardess evaluated the situation, she approached me and asked if I would give up my seat so that the family could be together. I agreed promptly and waited while she made sure that they were comfortably situated.

Then she was gone for a few minutes, evidently checking to see where she could find another seat. She returned and asked me to follow her. Once again, I was led into the first-class compartment and seated in the first row. I had unlimited leg room and two seats for this, the longest part of our journey. I slept all night—not even waking up for breakfast. When I awoke, the plane was making its approach to the Los Angeles airport. It had been a beautiful trip from beginning to end. In thinking back, it seemed as if I had been given first-class seats on the first leg of the journey through the love and generosity of our friends; on the second leg, due to overcrowded conditions on the plane; and on the third leg, due to a mechanical problem—but I remembered what Paul said to the Corinthians: "God is able to make all grace abound toward you; that ye, always having all sufficiency in all things, may abound to every good work."

The three words **GRACE, SUFFICIENCY,** and **WORK** stood out in my thought as if they were in flashing neon lights. Of course! Our human reasoning has put the process backwards. WE think that through our labor—the sweat of our brow—we may earn barely enough to get by, perhaps, or even great wealth; and if we are good enough, we may also earn God's grace. Not so; not so. The **GRACE** comes first. It is ours because we are His. Not having enough or having too much is also just part of the human illusion—false perception. The fact is **SUFFICIENCY**. I saw quite clearly (even though I have absolutely no knowledge of economics) that we have based all of our human laws of economics on scarcity instead of sufficiency and that this error is the basis of all of the poverty on the planet. Grace and sufficiency are His gifts to us; work is our worship—our gratitude to Him.

Chapter Twenty-Four

I recognized that if I thought that I could help others, I denied them their heritage: the grace of God and sufficiency. Baba has said: "If you think that you can either help or harm others, you are mistaken." I had never truly understood this before. Now it was clear. We work in order to express our gratitude to God for the grace and abundance of all good which He has given us, and we serve others for the same reason. In serving, we celebrate the God in ourselves and in those we serve. We worship Him in all. If we think we are helping, we deny the God in the other person and increase the ego in ourselves. If we work to get money, possessions, or fame, we deny God and invest in our own ego. God gives us richly all things to enjoy. We worship Him in others, as others. What a privilege to worship Him through our service and righteous activity! And what comfort and security there is in the knowledge that no one's abundance is dependent on anyone or anything except Him.

I was given an opportunity to prove these truths in an incident which occurred as I was working on a service project. It was necessary to make one hundred copies of an eight-page article and the decision had been made to print on both sides of the paper. At first, the copier performed well while using the automatic paper-feed on both sides of the paper. As I began running the second side of the third sheet, however, the paper frequently jammed inside the machine. I finally decided it would be quicker and easier to hand-feed the eighty remaining pages than it would be to have to open the machine to remove jammed paper every two or three copies.

As hand-feeding is a somewhat slow and tedious process, and it seemed that I had other things which needed attention also, I found it helpful to remind myself of what I was doing and for Whom I was doing it. Each time I placed a sheet of paper in the machine I said, "Swami, this work is my worship of You."

Using that statement repetitively, I completed the sixth page of print and quickly ran the one hundred copies of the seventh page automatically. When I began attempting to run page eight on the back of page seven, however, the jamming problem recurred. This time I found myself unable to remove the paper from the machine. A small part had torn off and was not visible. I read the Owner's Manual carefully, but there was no instruction that applied to the problem with which I was faced. It was late Friday afternoon, and we live thirty miles from the nearest authorized repair service.

During the eighty times that I had repeated the words, "Swami, this work is my worship of You," I had truly surrendered to Him. I now felt that if He wanted to use my hands for this project or for another I accepted His will either way. I spoke out loud, "Baba, this is Your work. You are the Doer. Just make it clear to me whatever way you wish to use my hands today because they are here only for You." As I waited quietly for His direction, a vision of the inside of the copier appeared to me. I saw where the paper was and what I would need to do to remove it. Even the name of the part which had to be opened came to me. I went back to the machine, then, pressed a small spring which was not located on any of the diagrams in the Manual, and easily removed the paper. Within a short time the copying was completed and the pages assembled for distribution that Sunday at the guest meeting of the Sathya Sai Book Center of America. Once again, He had given all sufficiency in all things.

******

"The wealth you earn is not true wealth! True wealth is the grace of God."

—Baba
Discourse, October 21, 1986

Chapter Twenty-Four

"The Lord does not weigh the status or caste of an individual before bestowing His grace. He is all-merciful and His grace falls like rain or moonlight on all the people."

—Baba
Vision of the Divine
By E. B. Fanibunda

"You are my forms all. When I love you I love Myself; when you love yourselves, you love Me. I have separated Myself from Myself so that I may love Myself."

—Baba
The Embodiment of Love
By Peggy Mason and Ron Laing

25

"YOU ARE MINE"

On a number of the days when we went to darshan at Brindavan, Raye bought a rose and gave it to me to give to Baba. Occasionally Sharon and I were able to sit side by side. One day when both of these occurrences coincided, I felt guided to offer the rose to Sharon. She declined the gift, saying that it didn't seem right to her to take it when Raye had sent it to me to give to Baba. Several days later, Raye again sent me a rose. Sharon was sitting beside me, and once more I felt an overwhelming urge to give the flower to her. This time she accepted it somewhat tentatively, and I felt a sense of relief that I had followed my inner guidance.

When Swami passed in front of us, Sharon held out the rose to Him. He did not seem to notice it. He continued on His way with no acknowledgment of the proffered gift at all. I was somewhat surprised at His lack of recognition because I had felt so sure that the rose was to play an important part in the relationship between Him and Sharon. After darshan, Sharon made only a brief reference to the incident, but I could see that she was deeply hurt. She told me that it had been terribly difficult for her to offer the rose—that she felt in giving it she would be giving herself and that it was not an easy thing for her to do. She felt strongly that Baba's refusal of the rose symbolized His rejection of her. It seemed to her that she had made a mistake in thinking that Baba had called her to Him. "But, He says that no one can come to Him unless He calls them," she said to me. "What am I doing here?"

I must have tried to make some comforting sounds, though I don't now recall what they were. It was difficult for me not to slip back into the old guilt pattern and berate myself for not being able to know the difference between inner guidance and head stuff. Gradually, for both of us, the rose incident receded into the background as our daily views of Baba became more and more fulfilling. On the day of the interview, when Sharon was sitting in front of me in the outer room, His eyes went to Sharon and He said, "Ni mama." He repeated the same words again, looking in Sharon's direction. No one was quite sure whether He was speaking to Sharon again or to Barbara, but my own feeling at the time was that the comment was directed to both of them.

We all heard it, and we all made an effort to find out what it meant, but there seemed to be no such expression in common usage. Several people told us that "mama" in Sanskrit means a relative. One said it meant an uncle, another told us it referred especially to a grandmother. But none of these translations gave us any insight. We returned to the United States still wondering what "ni mama" could mean.

One day, while working on the Newsletter, it occurred to me to ask Vidya Alekal if she had any ideas about the translation of these two words. I had not mentioned the incident to her before, so when she promptly replied that it could mean "You are mine," I felt instantly that the message was correct. Almost as soon as she had said the words, she began to doubt her own interpretation. She said, "'Ni' is from the language of Kannada and 'mama' from the Sanskrit. I don't know why Baba would have put those two together or why He would have used either to English-speaking devotees."

Chapter Twenty-Five

Whether or not those words are factually, intellectually, or academically correct—they were spoken at exactly the right time for me. My inquiry had once more blossomed into the fruit of knowing. My heart expanded to let it in, and my joy flowed out across the telephone wires to share the inspiration with Barbara Hill and Sharon. How can we give ourselves to Him? We are His forms, His creation. Can the painting give itself to the artist? His message to us is: You are Mine; you have always been Mine; you always will be Mine. Anything else you may believe is only a passing dream. I do not need your gifts. Come to Me with empty hands. Let Me fill them with the boundless Love and Wisdom which is your birthright.

When I received the edited manuscript for this chapter from Sonia Nordenson, I found a short note which she had attached. It read: "Joy: What is it in the Bible about "rose of Sharon"? I reached for the Bible and located "rose of Sharon" in the concordance. Opening to the second chapter of the Song of Solomon, I found the following words: "I am the rose of Sharon... My beloved is Mine and I am [hers]."

The overwhelming sense of awe I feel at such a moment can best be described as bliss. His presence, His love, is manifested in our lives daily as synchronicity and finds expression through willing instruments such as Sonia. What a blessed privilege to be here and to be His. There are no boundaries and no limits to His love.

Twenty-four hours prior to receiving the message from Sonia, I had received word that my mother was seriously ill. She was in the hospital receiving intensive care, and the doctors held out no hope for her. The prognosis was that she would not live through the night. I immediately sent a telegram to Baba, asking that He be with her. When I read the words: "My beloved is Mine and I am [hers]," I knew that I had received His reply. The illusion of separation had come to me in the thought that my mother was not a devotee of Sathya Sai Baba. But He is never so deluded. My mother has been an aspirant—a devotee of God—throughout her life. Now, Baba's message was not only to reassure me that He was with her but also to gently chide me for doubting. He spoke to my heart, saying,: "Don't you know that I am always with her? She is Mine and I am hers." And, though I had not presumed to ask for her recovery, He granted that also. She was given another year to enjoy.

Sharon Robinson, who was with me at the time I received the note from Sonia, experienced the message as being from her beloved Baba to her, as well as to me and to Sharon Bertsch. She had felt some lack of attunement with the name "Sharon," and those uncomfortable feelings, which had been with her all her life, were instantly dispelled by the beautiful message.

He gently, tenderly answers each call, constantly reassuring us that there is nothing to fear because He is always with us. His home is in each heart. No one is ever ignored, overlooked, or denied.

******

"Whoever you are, you are Mine. I will not give you up. Wherever you are, you are near Me; you cannot go beyond My reach."

—Baba
Living Divinity
By Shakuntala Balu

Chapter Twenty-Five

"See God in everyone you meet. See God in everything you handle. His majesty is immanent in all that is material and nonmaterial. This whole creation is an expression of His majesty. God has His hands in all handiwork, His feet at all heights, His eyes beyond all horizons, His face before every form."

—Baba
Images of Sai Baba
Alexi Allens

"God saw everything that He had made and, behold, it was exceedingly beautiful."

Genesis 1:31
As translated from the original Aramaic
by Rocco Errico

26

HE CALLED ME BEAUTIFUL

The most precious stories are never told because they are too deeply personal to share. It is necessary to feel very safe in order to open one's heart completely. I feel safer now than I ever have. It is one of the gifts of this trip that I returned feeling very loved. I never knew there was so much love in the world.

"Ugly" is, I guess, only an outer symbol of lack of self-acceptance. I have always felt ugly and unloved, and—even though the feeling has become less and less prominent—it was still there when I left on this journey. Swami still called me "Pakora." He still teased me about my size—about having no strong chairs. But He made it so clear that He loves me—no more than He loves everyone else—but He loves me.

Then, wonder of wonders, a lady came up to me a day or two after the interview and said, "Do you know what Swami said about you after you went up to the veranda?" I said, "No, but I imagine it had to do with my size. He seems to find that terribly amusing." She said, "He said: 'That's a beautiful pakora—such a beautiful pakora.'"

Obviously He doesn't judge by appearances. As God said to Samuel: "The Lord seeth not as man seeth; for man looketh on the outward appearance, but the Lord looketh on the heart." (I Sam. 16:7) He doesn't even judge us by our shortcomings and mistakes. He looks on that spark of Divinity which He has assured us is there in each of us. I could hardly believe my ears. He called me beautiful! Those words have been singing in my ears ever since. He called me beautiful!

Baba's teaching methods are awe-inspiring. No ordinary teacher could ever begin to imagine the variety of motivational experiences, learning exercises, and culminating activities that just come about spontaneously when He is recognized as the Master Teacher. Not only did He know the value of having these words come to me through a second party, but He later gave me a clear example of what I was to learn and how it was to come about.

The incident occurred in Raye's experience. One morning after darshan Raye asked several of us if we had noticed the red spot in Swami's eye that morning. We all said that we hadn't noticed it. Raye found that quite surprising. He said it stood out to him, and he couldn't fail to have seen it. He mentioned it several times. The next day he and the rest of us were quite surprised. Raye had a bright red spot in his eye. It was different from anything I had ever seen before, and it was so unusual that it was—as he had said about the one he had seen in Baba's eye—impossible not to see it. After we had all duly noted it, and expressed varying opinions about its cause or significance, it faded and disappeared. My own interpretation was that, as we see God, so will we see ourselves. Whatever we think God is, that is what we will seem to ourselves to be.

The next lesson in this unit on "Love" came about through Stanley. Due to his interest in the Indian culture and languages, he had been invited by Professor Kasturi's grandson to come for a visit and discussion. As Stanley was leaving, Sri Kasturi said, "Say hello to that mountain of Joy!" When Stanley relayed the message to me, complete with gestures and smile, I felt only pure love. Whereas, previously, I might have felt hurt or offended, now my reaction was one of joy and reciprocation.

Chapter Twenty-Six

Kasturi loved me. He did not refer to my size because he was critical or judgmental. He—like Baba—referred to it freely because it didn't matter at all. How strange. I had always thought people who were polite and well-mannered did not mention anything relating to your personal affairs or bodily characteristics. Now I realized that the saintly Kasturi and my beloved Baba saw me as some thing so very different from a body that they could freely refer to it. I had seen everyone as critical of me only because I was critical of myself. Thus it also works the other way. We see God as we see ourselves. The validation of this theme came to me a month after I had been back in the States. Pat Aiken wrote to me, and, in summing up her experiences on this trip, stated: "I realized that Baba had been a perfect reflection of myself in the way he addressed me and what he had said to me."

All of the ancient petrified thoughts of ugliness began to crumble with the impact of these experiences. I realized that my love for Baba and His love for me were one and the same. There are no differences—no separation. There is only One Embodiment of Love and We are It. I knew this now beyond question. Baba loves me! Kasturi loves me! Many beautiful people love me, and I love each and all of them. We do not love each other as bodies, minds, personalities, or for the roles we play. We recognize each other as the expansion of deity which we really are. No one can love Baba without loving me, too. I cannot love Baba without loving everyone else. LOVE IS ALL THERE IS. This is His message. His mission is to install it in every heart. Our mission is to see it in every heart—to hear it, live it, and Be It.

******

"Seen through the eyes of Love, all beings are beautiful, all deeds are dedicated, all thoughts are beneficial, and the world is one vast family."

—Sathya Sai Baba
Sathya Sai Baba's Divine Teachings
Grace McMartin

"My affection and love for you is
that of a thousand mothers."

—Sathya Sai Baba
The Embodiment of Love
Peggy Mason and Ron Laing

"Man's distance from Divinity is the same
as his distance from himself."

—Sathya Sai Baba
Discourse, August 8, 1986

Chapter Twenty-Six

"Many spiritual aspirants are under a misconception today. If you ask them why they are doing various forms of sadhana (spiritual practices), they will reply that they are doing them in order to merge with God.

"Do not think that you are human and that you have to reach the state of the Divine. Think rather that you are God, and, from that state, you have become a human being. If you think this way, all the attributes of God will be manifest in you. If you feel that you are ascending from humanness to Godliness, you will be taking all that is undesirable with you.

"Know that you have descended from God, as a human being, and that eventually you will go back to your source. Do not regard God as something separate and distinct from you. God is very much within you."

—Baba
Images of Sai Baba
Alexi Allens

"It is part of human nature that man desires to reach the presence of the Almighty to see Him and be ever with Him, for deep within the human heart is the urge to reach the place from which he has come, to attain the joy he has lost, the glory which he has missed. Man is himself divine and so it is a matter of the deep calling unto the deep, of the part calling for the whole..."

—Baba
The Embodiment of Love
Peggy Mason and Ron Laing

27
"BEING IS LOST IN BECOMING"

An incident which occurred on the second day we were in Kuala Lumpur stimulated further self-inquiry and learning. Since this extra day was unexpected and since none of us had ever been in Malaysia before, it seemed appropriate to see something of the country. Sharon and Stanley made arrangements at the tour desk for us to take the "Country Tour." I looked forward to the five of us driving through the peaceful country side, sharing our observations and hearing about the various unfamiliar things we would be seeing.

I was, therefore, somewhat surprised when we found that we would be going in two separate cars. Sharon, Stanley, and Barbara got into the front car (a Mercedes) and Raye and I into the second car (a new Nissan). It quickly became evident that our driver spoke little English and did not intend to say anything by way of explanation as we sped through the crowded outskirts of a big city with a population of one and one-half million. Finally, I asked him where we were going, and he replied that he didn't know. He said that his only instruction had been to follow the car in front, which he valiantly tried to do under heavy traffic conditions.

At times it seemed as if we were hopelessly lost. The Mercedes had disappeared, and our driver admitted that he didn't even know how to get back to the hotel. But, miraculously, with split-second timing, the Mercedes would appear just as we would have gone off in the wrong direction.

The front car stopped at a rubber plantation, and we stopped also. Raye got out, and the driver of the Mercedes showed Stanley, Sharon, Barbara, and Raye how the trees were scored and the sap gathered from which the rubber was made. Then we stopped at a batik factory, where silk was being hand-painted in open sheds. The next stop was a museum where butterflies, scorpions, and various creepy-crawly things native to Malaysia were on display. At this point I mentioned to Stanley that our driver not only hadn't said a word the entire trip, but that he didn't even know what our destination was. They then insisted that we change cars, saying that their driver was a very good guide and that we could have the benefit of some of his knowledge of the city. After some resistance on our part, we finally allowed ourselves to be convinced and the switch was made.

It was certainly a different type of experience! Whereas we had been sitting in silence as our driver tried to keep up with the other car, now our driver was chatting with us in excellent English, describing many things along the way which we wouldn't have noticed if he hadn't pointed them out. And without missing a syllable, he would turn around and go back to an intersection and intercept the Nissan, just as it would have gone on to who-knows-where. It turned out that the destination, the high point of the tour, was a temple, which was accessible only by foot—up 242 stone steps! Sharon and Stanley climbed them while the rest of us watched.

Finally arriving back at the hotel, we realized that the tour desk had probably made special arrangements for two cars instead of a minibus, thinking it would be easier for me to get in and out of a car. But, as I have learned over and over again, nothing is by accident. Everything is meaningful. And so I kept

Chapter Twenty-Seven

asking myself the meaning of this little tour experience, which seemed incidental and insignificant. It was not until after we were back in L.A. that I awoke in the small hours of the morning with a sense of sudden clarity in regard to the symbolism involved.

The driver of the lead car was a very handsome Indian gentleman, of Muslim persuasion, whose name was Atma. He was extremely well-educated, and spoke beautiful English with a cultured British accent. He was well-informed, competent, caring, and considerate. The other driver was doing the best he could. It was his second day on the job. He didn't know the city, the tour sites, or English. His intentions were good and he seemed to be a nice man, as far as we could tell, but he was ignorant of a great many important things.

It had been our intention to take the tour as a group, a unified whole. Instead we had been split into two parts. Instead of one auto, we had two. The one driven by Atma was able to move right along, but the one driven by the uninformed chauffeur was lost, or trying desperately to get around obstructions and catch up, most of the time. Each time it seemed that the second car was hopelessly lost, Atma would appear to rescue it and get it back on the right road. At the end of the tour, both arrived at the destination—the same place they started from. The group which had been separated became reunited, and the tour was over.

The tour symbolized our earthly experience; the two autos, two selves (dualism). The ego-self doesn't know where it has been or where it's going. The Atma or Higher Self rescues us, however, each time we think we're really lost.

In pondering this little vignette, I recalled some of the times that I had briefly caught a glimpse of the Atma. The first that I recall came about when I was in my teens. I had been studying the story of Moses, and I was particularly interested in God's revelation to him that His name was "I Am That I Am." The statement seemed enigmatic to me, and I longed to find the key which would unlock the puzzle. In contemplating the story and searching for further enlightenment, I reviewed it many times. Finally, one day as I let my memory range over Moses' various conversations with God, my thoughts put the events in an order which was different from any which had occurred to me before. The objection which Moses gave to accepting responsibility for leading the children of Israel out of Egypt was: "I am slow of speech." And God's answer to Moses' question: "When they ask me who is this God who commanded you to lead the children of Israel out of bondage—what is His name—what shall I tell them?" God replied: "I Am That I Am."

As I recalled the story to my memory for perhaps the hundredth time, I heard it this way: Moses said: "I am slow of speech," and God said: "I Am That I Am." The insight was instant. Moses was not the limited "I" or self that he thought he was, but he was the unlimited "I" that God knew he was. However, being quite caught up in my earthly tour, I lost the revelation before it became embodied or real-ized.

Ten years or so later, I was again striving to understand what God was and who I was. This time I was contemplating the definitions given by Mary Baker Eddy of "man," "Christ," and "God," in the glossary of *Science and Health with Key to the Scriptures.* In my efforts to understand the distinctions among these three, I wrote down each word with its definition, and placed all of the information side by side, determined to distinguish each from the other. To my surprise, this exercise revealed that there was no difference. They were all One. Again, I had a brief glimpse of the Monistic Absolute, but it did not stay with me.

Another puzzle I had attempted to unravel is located on the wall of the men's dining room at Prasanthi Nilayam. It reads: "Being is lost in becoming." Over a period of several years, I made every effort to get real meaning from that saying of Sai

Baba. Little by little, I began to recognize my own efforts to become that which I already am. It became clear that the struggle to become God causes us to lose sight of the fact that We are That already. It is, as has been so aptly stated by Robert Skutch in his book by the same name, *A Journey Without Distance.*

Baba has told us: "Life is a bridge. Cross over it, but do not build a house on it!" His clear instructions, together with the experiences which come in the wake of requests to Him for enlightenment, bring us into a more lasting awareness of reality. My life now seems to be a tour of the countryside and, for the most part, quite enjoyable. Temporary inconveniences are only that. Being is the firm foundation on which everything is based. It is unchangeable, secure, and permanent. The beauty of Being is reflected in the beauty of becoming, and ultimately the inseparability will make itself so apparent that we will no longer consider them to be two. We can play the game with joy, be All-in-All with bliss, and reside in the Abode of Eternal Peace forevermore, keeping the whole group together. No one is separate. None are left out. Our becoming selves love each other; our Being selves are each other in Love, as Love, ALL ONE.

******

"If you develop love, you do not need
to develop anything else."

—Baba
The Embodiment of Love
Peggy Mason and Ron Laing

"All are cells in the one divine Organism, in the divine Body. Awareness of this is your faith, your fortune, your fort, your fullness....You are agitated, I know, since the world today is tossed on waves of unrest and insecurity. But do not blame the world. The unrest is only the image of your own unrest. You have projected it onto the world....Correct your vision, and the world will be corrected....You create the world of your choice....Subsume the many in the One...and you will reach the stage of Unity in thought, word, and deed....Love is expansion, inclusion, and mutualization."

—Baba
Sathya Sai Speaks, Vol. IX

28

"AFTER ECSTASY, LAUNDRY"

As more and more of us become aware of our divine nature, we may feel in our enthusiasm that, by ruthlessly cutting ourselves off from our human nature, we can achieve the goal more rapidly. This tendency to seesaw between two extremes is typical of the ego. Baba's human emphasis on values is indicative of the need to enhance and improve the human moral nature—not to reject it.

Having won the right to a human birth, we can recognize ourselves as being divinely human and humanly divine, and rejoice in this. It is a perfectly balanced state of life, involving creation and dissolution, the perfect flow of Shiva and Shakti—positive and negative energy.

Concentration on and desire for enlightenment or Self-realization will naturally bring about unitive or God experiences. There are no special virtues required for the aspirant to succeed, except perhaps sincerity of purpose and perseverance. Since all wisdom is present in each human being, none are any more spiritual than others—none are any more capable than others—none are any more advanced than others. We simply make different choices. Many may say that they want enlightenment, but they devote the majority of their time and attention to other pursuits.

I recall an incident which took place when I was a newlywed. A young couple were happily showing my husband and me their new boat. Admiring it, I felt a twinge of envy and said, "I wish we were wealthy enough to buy a boat!" One of our friends responded by saying, "We have no more money than you. We just chose to spend ours on a boat, and you have made other choices." I was startled by the truth of the words. Now I recognize that the same principle applies to the desire for cosmic consciousness or enlightenment. It is a matter of choice. Just giving lip service to it will not achieve it, but establishing it as the top priority in our lives will enable us to reach our goal.

My first experience of expanded consciousness came about through a deep desire and constant attention. As an ego, I was so aware of my shortcomings, failures, and inadequacies that I found it difficult to accept that I had genuinely experienced what I thought I had experienced. While in India, I wrote a brief description of the experience and asked Professor Kasturi if he would read it and tell me what he thought of it. When I returned for his verdict several days later, he told me very matter-of-factly that he had approved it for publication and sent it to the office of the **Sanathana Sarathi**. That indicated to me that what had seemed so extraordinary was perhaps not too uncommon after all. The article duly appeared in the October 1982 issue of the magazine under the title of "The Still Small Voice."

At that time I was not acquainted with others who had had similar experiences and I was afraid to reveal the entire message spoken by "the still small voice." It might have been considered sacrilegious or even blasphemous by some. I have since met people who have had very similar experiences, even those who heard exactly the same words spoken to them that I heard spoken to me.

For those readers who may not have seen the article or who may have forgotten the details, what happened was this: While sitting in meditation, I felt a deeper and deeper silence, a higher, holier peace, and an acute objectless awareness. I became an unencumbered, boundless totality which cannot be described adequately by any word, but which has been referred to variously as bliss, ecstasy, samadhi, nirvana, or cosmic consciousness.

How long this state continued, I do not know. Perhaps it was only seconds. But within its occurrence was the timelessness of eternity. As boundaries began to reappear, I became aware of the fact that my body was not breathing—and yet was blissfully alive. My ears were not hearing, but in the profundity of the silence, a very small quiet voice spoke. It had an unusual quality, but it spoke in familiar Biblical language, saying: "Thou art my beloved son in whom I am well pleased. Ask what thou will, and I will give it thee."

I then heard, rather than spoke, the response which nevertheless seemed to come from me. It entailed no thought or reasoning, and it was: "That Raye may be fulfilled." Gradually my attention returned to the time and space of my earthly surroundings, and, in less than half an hour, a telephone call came offering Raye his first opportunity to serve in a capacity for which he had prepared himself. I have had the joy of watching him become more self-confident, more successful, and more self-realized over the succeeding years, up to and including the peak experience of receiving the beautiful nine-gem ring from the Avatar.

My own development has not gone in the same direction as Raye's, humanly. While he has become more active in the business world, I have withdrawn from almost all of the business, social, and recreational activities that previously filled most of my time. However, there are still a great many tasks that I perform each day which are quite earthly. At first they seemed to me to be interruptions or even deterrents to my spiritual activities. However, I now recognize them to be correlates. My humanness is neither separate from nor in opposition to my Divinity.

Another experience which illustrates this conclusion with great clarity came during a profoundly silent meditation. I became the observer of my body, and, as I watched, I saw it expand into multitudes of atoms. They seemed to be about the size of grapefruit, glowing with a soft light, and moving in a rhythmic flow around each other. There were atoms of different colors—all beautiful and in perfect harmony with each other.

As I watched this scene with interest and delight, I saw that the walls of the room in which I was sitting were composed of similar atoms. Gradually the atoms of my body and the atoms of the walls flowed together, and I became aware of the area surrounding the house. My attention was drawn to a large boulder and it, too, was composed of dancing atoms. I watched the atoms of my body and the atoms of the boulder blend together until one was no longer distinguishable from the other. Joyfully my awareness expanded to include trees, mountains, continents, the planet, our galaxy, and a multitude of galaxies, all merging in an ocean of light. At first each of the billions of atoms which were now a part of my body seemed to be dancing in ecstasy, but gradually the last sense of separateness vanished and nothing remained except awareness. Later, when my mind searched for words in which to express the awareness, they were: I am the ecstasy; I am the bliss; I am all of it.

The effects of the experience seemed, at first, to be permanent. I functioned in my daily routines as usual, and I was able to give the necessary attention to them without losing the cosmic awareness. After about six days, however, the effects began to fade, and I found myself caught up again in the illusion of separateness. Usually I was able to extricate myself more quickly than before, but at times it seemed as if my condition was not improved at all. The cleansing process which had been going on prior to the experience not only seemed to be continuing but even accelerated.

Chapter Twenty-Eight

The words of the beautiful nun Sister Carita, which I have used for the title of this chapter, have two meanings for me. Not only did I return to my daily chores after the ecstatic experience, but I also was returned to the cleansing process, which I like to think of as Baba's laundry. Baba has referred to Himself as "the great Dhobi" (laundryman). Howard Levin reported the following conversation in his book *Good Chances:*

> Tony asked Baba, "Swami, why do we get so many bad thoughts here in Prasanthi Nilayam?"
> "You see," Sai Baba answered, "the heart is like a garden. Grace is like rain. When rain comes, both flowers and weeds sprout. Only when weeds sprout can you recognize them and pull them out by their roots. God is like a great Dhobi (laundryman). You're like cloth. If stains are deep, the dhobi has to pound the cloth on the rock. If they are only surface stains, some light scrubbing will do. But God is best Dhobi. He never leaves any stain—always pure white." He made gestures with His hands as if He were washing clothes. "I'm cleaning. I'm doing my work."

In my case, it is quite clear that Baba is having to do much pounding. He is far from finished with me. A recent experience brought this to my attention quite vividly. Our Sai Baba Center had volunteered to make badges for the regional retreat, the theme of which was "Fill the World with Love." The Center members were enjoying the activity, knowing that their service to man was their worship of God. Because the name of each registrant was printed on his or her badge, it was necessarily a service which had to be postponed until the last possible moment. Otherwise, those who registered late would not have badges.

In order to prevent any last-minute surprises, I had made an appointment with our local printer to laminate the badges. I had explained the time factor involved and watched as the information was written on the calendar. However, when the time came for the work to be done, unexpected problems had arisen and there was a full day's delay before the laminating could be done. We had tested a few badges early in our process and found that we needed heavier laminating material than had been used on them. This had also been reported to the printer and duly noted.

With all of the cutting, punching, stringing, and alphabetizing left to be done, the badges were finally delivered only hours before having to be put to use at the retreat. I looked at them and realized in horror that not only was the laminating paper not heavier, it was lighter than the original. It seemed to me to be a tragedy. I visualized the badges falling apart after being worn only one day, and it would appear that we had performed a disservice for the retreat participants rather than a service.

I touched Baba's robe and asked Him to please help me do what could be done in the remaining time, to inspire and bless the others who would be working to finish the badges, and to help me understand and learn the lesson which I knew the experience entailed. During the night I awoke with the consciousness of His Presence and heard His voice speak to me gently and patiently, as a mother would to her child, "What? Did you want all your little world to sigh and whisper 'Wonderful'?"

It was a painful lesson. He had pinpointed the greatest cause of the distress and made me realize that I was very attached to the results of the action and even looking forward to the ego-satisfaction which is to be gained from doing a good and useful service. It was not public acclaim, compliments, or any external reward which was expected, but only to look around and see all of the retreat participants wearing the sturdy badges and feel a warm glow of satisfaction that they were so successful.

James Sinclair, a member of the World Council of the Sathya Sai Baba Organization, spoke at the retreat, saying, "The

Chapter Twenty-Eight

last bastion of the ego is in spirituality." Somehow, I had thought that there was protection inherent in performing a good and useful service—especially for other Sai devotees. This was a very foolish assumption. The opposite is probably true. We are most open to being taught of the Lord when we are performing service. The lesson is the reward. Being caught in the very heart of your faults is the greatest gift you can be given. Our Lord points out our faults, forgives them, and showers us with Love all the while.

As Baba works, each of us can watch Him and follow His example. We can do whatever is given us to do with enthusiasm. We can give up doing whatever is no longer ours to do, without regret. We can place our trust in the perfect process of Becoming because it is based on the perfect state of Being. And, however humble or however world-shaking our function may have been, we can assign all of the results to Him. "For Thine is the Kingdom, and the Power, and the Glory forever."

******

"The real and the unreal are not two distinct things; one is the absence of the other, that is all....There is only One appearing as two....The pure mind reflects the Reality clearly—God that is the basis of Self as well as the objective world. God is immanent in every particle in the universe. The clear vision can experience Him everywhere at all times, and that vision confers immeasurable, inexpressible bliss."

—Baba
Sathya Sai Speaks, Vol. IX

THE BLENDER

When the full-grown poet came,
Out spake pleased Nature
(the round, impassive globe,
with all its shows of day and night),
saying, 'He is mine';
But out spake, too, the soul of men,
proud, jealous, and unreconciled,
'Nay, he is mine alone';
—Then the full-grown poet stood between the two,
and took each by the hand;
And today and ever so stands
as blender, uniter, tightly holding hands,
Which he will never release until he reconciles the two,
And wholly and joyously blends them.

—Walt Whitman
Leaves of Grass

29
THROUGH THE SAI-LENS

In the Summer 1987 issue of the *Sathya Sai Newsletter*, a discourse which Baba gave on November 20, 1985, was featured. He was, as always, patiently helping each of us to come into the awareness of ourselves as the Atma, Divinity Itself, and to live our daily lives in such a way that God-realization might be achieved in this lifetime, obviating the need for additional incarnations. During the prepublication processes of typing, proofreading, checking the accuracy of the English translation, and making every effort to maintain the purity of the words of the Avatar, I read and reread the discourse many times. With each reading, my awareness of the power of the words increased, but it was not until the final proofreading—just before sending the copy to the printer—that the wisdom underlying the words seemed to open up to me.

From that moment in the Newsletter office, everything I saw, everything I heard, and everything I read confirmed and reinforced the inspiration which had come through His divine words and His grace. For nine days I ruminated on those words. Each time I turned them over in my mind the expression of them may have differed slightly, but the essence of them was that it is not what we see with our eyes or hear with our ears which is unreal, but it is our opinions, judgments, and decisions about those things that create illusion. Throughout the discourse, Baba develops this theme in beautiful poetic imagery such as: "The earth is a magnificence which enshrines significance.... Meru, the great mountain, proclaims to you the majesty of God. The ocean tells you of the might and dignity of God. The green plant life which you look upon—offering you fragrant blossoms and fruit with thirst-quenching nectar—proclaims God's compassion, mercy, and love. The sun and the moon intimate the omnipotence of God....It is impossible to locate anything on earth which does not at every moment bring home to you the truth that the Divine Reality (Paratattva) permeates everything."

The joy I felt in the continual contemplation of the Divine Reality was calm and sustaining. Above me, I saw Mt. San Gorgonio as the majesty of God. Around me, the cherry, apricot, and plum trees were literally pouring forth God's love as their abundant fruit fell to the ground, giving itself to us for nourishment and sweetness. The apple, pear, and fig trees were showing forth the certainty that more of God's provision for man was ready and waiting to come forth in its divinely appointed time. If I had ever felt myself to have been deserted, abandoned, or left without anything I needed, it was because I had become attached to receiving nourishment and sweetness from only one source. I recalled words from the Christian Science textbook, **Science and Health with Key to the Scriptures** by Mary Baker Eddy: "God has infinite resources with which to bless mankind." If I became attached to any particular source of sweetness, mourning its loss when its season was passed, it was that judgment, that decision, which blinded me to the next blessing which was just waiting to come forth. What a glorious, beautiful, compassionate way for God to assure us of His tender, constant care.

On the evening of the ninth day following the opening of my thought to the glories of God which were so readily available to all of His children, I was blessed by interaction with others from whom I gained many beautiful thoughts. Baba frequently expresses the importance of our spending time with others of like mind, and in the discourse which I had been contemplating day and night, he had again stressed the importance of leading "the kind of life which will satisfy the Atma." He said that, in order to free ourselves from vices such as hate and attachment, the first step is "satsang, companionship with other good people. When we are in the company of the good and noble, we have a chance of picking up noble qualities and thoughts." Raye and I had been blessed that evening with the presence in our home of eight friends whose "delight was in the law of the Lord," and we had spoken of those laws constantly for over two hours. We shared our holy experiences with them, and they shared theirs with us—all of us gaining strength and reinforcement from the leelasmarana (recalling, telling, and retelling the leelas of the Lord).

As I retired for the evening, filled with gratitude for Baba's presence on the planet and for His gift to us of so many wonderful friends who were also spiritual aspirants, I continued to recall words from the discourse which was the source of my current inspiration. This time the ones which stood out were: "To get beyond the body and the distractions which it offers, one has to transcend it by going deep within, seeking the Atma residing inside." As I contemplated these words, I felt myself going deeper and deeper into a profound stillness. My mind came to rest in a state of deep sleep, and yet knowledge began appearing as awareness which was independent of the mind, requiring no words or thoughts. Baba said in the discourse: "The principle of the changeless Reality (Brahmatattva) is to give rise to this creation, to sustain it, and finally to let it merge back into Itself." It was awareness of this changeless Reality which filled my heart, the room, and my being for the entire evening, during which I slept peacefully and dreamlessly.

On awakening the following morning, I began to attempt to formulate words to describe the knowledge which had penetrated my consciousness. The first ones, which seemed to come in Baba's dear voice, were: "You have been seeing through the Sai-lens." Oh, how lovable and loving He is! His lighthearted puns keep us from becoming too intense, even as they state the most profound truths. Though the experience had entailed no vision or sound, it can only be expressed as if it had. I seemed to see creation emerge from the ocean of Reality in the form of a huge clock face. The disk appeared not only as the beginning of time, but also as the outbreath and inbreath of the Creator, detailing both ontogeny and phylogeny—the development of the individual and the evolution of mankind. Baba had said that we "should go to the very basis of things and come to grips with that realization....the primary basis of existence and the final goal of our endeavors as the two wings which will help us proceed." I saw both the basis of existence and the final goal of our endeavors at six o'clock on the disk of time.

In terms of the individual, he emerged from the womb into a world of sense impressions, gradually developing the ability to focus his eyes on objects, to discriminate between sounds, and to react to various other stimuli. At this point, his development began to move slowly upward from six o'clock toward twelve o'clock. As the child accumulated sense impressions, they became more and more complex, but they were still basically recepts—things received. When the child's mind reached the highest possible point of receptual intelligence, it developed into the next stage and began to label or name those recepts. Previously, experiences of warmth, softness, pleasant sounds, nourishment, fragrance, sights of face, arms, and hands had been separate, but they gradually combined into one object. After these sense impressions had been received numerous times in the same or similar combinations, the child spoke his first word. He labeled the complex recept "Mama," and thus moved into the realm of conceptualization.

A concept, though it is nothing more than a named recept, nevertheless involves a giant step in the child's development. He now has a language. His mind can store all of the numerous recepts, which it formerly was required to laboriously combine, under one word: "Mama." At this point also, awareness of opposites begins to emerge. The child thinks: "Mama is either here or not here; I want what she is offering me or I don't want it"; and self-consciousness or ego has developed. From this point on, the developmental process is largely concerned with accumulation of concepts. Baba says that "The knowledge involved in mastering the scriptures and the lawbooks and the knowledge involved in professional disciplines such as sciences, visual arts, music, dance, etc.—all of this is worldly knowledge." It exists so that we can make a living. The individual spends most of his early years in gaining this type of knowledge. The body grows and changes in accordance with instructions received from the mind. As it develops into adulthood, the various choices it makes—the thoughts it chooses to think or the way it labels the stimuli which it receives—determine its experiences. It wrestles with attachments, rejections, losses, gains, success, failure, love, and hate, and deals with each in accordance with its own pattern of chosen responses.

Finally, having reached the zenith of earthly experience, having accumulated possessions, knowledge, friends, relatives, and achievements, the individual—sometimes only after having to suffer immense pain due to his attempts to cling to them—becomes willing to let some of these go. At this point, he has begun the journey from twelve o'clock back to six o'clock. He has begun the releasing, the undoing, which will bring his pilgrimage to an end and take him back to his beginning—home to his Father.

The leaving and returning home has been described by Avatars, seers, and poets in various parables and imagery. The parable of Adam and Eve illustrates vividly that judgment (eating of the tree of the knowledge of good and evil) brought about body consciousness (nakedness); and, with body consciousness, came the decision that work was difficult and onerous, and that competition with one's brother was necessary in order to survive. These judgments followed swiftly upon the formation of concepts and the development of language. Prior to that time, sense stimuli had simply been received. They were not labeled good or bad; they just were. It is this state of surrender, trust, and acceptance which exists at the point of emergence from or mergence with the Divine. Jesus said simply: "Unless you become as a little child, you shall in no wise enter the kingdom of heaven." Baba says: "If you wish to converse with the Atma, then the Pranava (universal sound, Om) is the language you have to use."ABus, both Jesus and Baba are telling us that we must return to the state of receptivity which characterizes a little child, which was ours prior to the development of language...prior to thoughts...prior to judgment.

I recently heard a lovely little story told on a television program. It seems that the mother of a four-year-old child gave birth to another child. The four-year-old asked her if he might have some time alone with the baby. The mother, fearing sibling rivalry, refused the request several times. However, when the four-year-old persisted, she finally gave in but stayed within earshot. The four-year-old leaned over the baby's crib and said with urgency in his voice, "Please, tell me what God is. I've almost forgotten."

In that wonderful night of seeing through the Sai lens, I saw that it was only in the same silence from which we emerged that we could merge again. The mind must become still, thoughts must cease, and judgment must become a receding memory. We become whole again, One with the Creator, the imperishable,

Chapter Twenty-Nine 233

transcendent Wisdom which requires no words nor thoughts with which to express Itself. Baba holds us in the palm of His hand—in the infinity of His love—and we again experience our inherent nature: Bliss. Time is no factor; judgment and comparison play no part. Outcomes belong to Him. When sense impressions return, we may find ourselves less inclined to judge them than before, or we may not. We may be less attached to them, or we may not. But it is almost certain that we will be more willing and eager to proceed with our journey home to our Father.

A sizable percentage of the human race is fast approaching a willingness to complete its journey around the face of time, and Baba has come to bring all of the pilgrims on earth back to the realization of their divine Origin. As children are developing the conceptual mind, Baba is providing the way for them to also develop their moral nature. For those children born to parents who will allow it, He offers Bal Vikas—instruction focused on the spiritual nature and stimulating devotion to God. For all who would let go of the I-sense, He encourages selfless service (seva). The Ceiling on Desires Program enables us to stop accumulating attachments and begin cutting the ropes that bind us to illusion. Spiritual practices (sadhana) such as repeating the Name, singing devotional songs, contemplating spiritual teachings, talking about God's leelas, and meditating in the silence are all means of "making the mind lose itself." And, finally, He tells us to be happy and to enjoy satsang, to share our spiritual experiences with others of like mind, and to acknowledge the Atma in everyone. His grace provides Godspeed on our journey back to six o'clock. Let's all join together on this wonderful tour. After all, getting there is half the fun!

30

"BE CAREFUL FOR NOTHING"

Our little apartment at Prasanthi Nilayam seems quite small for four people. There is hardly a place to step when there are four mattresses on the floor, or two beds and two mattresses, as was the case in 1987. And so, when one warm night I felt especially thirsty at bedtime and had decided to have a glass of tea before going to sleep, we turned out the lights and I sipped the tea while sitting on the side of the bed in the dark. When the tea was finished, I set the glass on the table and lay down quietly so as not to disturb the others. Suddenly the thought came that I had better be more careful. I had put the glass very close to the edge of the table. If I happened to move about in the night, I could easily knock it off and send it crashing to the cement floor. So I sat up, carefully placed the glass in the center of the table, and retired peacefully, feeling sure that the glass would now be safe.

About 2:00 A.M. I was awakened to the sound of breaking glass. One of the other sleepers, in attempting to get out of bed, had bumped the table. The glass had been jarred up against the alarm clock, which also occupied a space near the center of the small table, and the result was the same as if the glass had been sitting on the edge. These circumstances seemed to have some special message for me, but it was not immediately clear what that message might be. One obvious conclusion might have been that the thing which I had greatly feared had come upon me. I rejected that interpretation, however, on the basis that I had not "greatly feared" that the glass would be broken. I felt that my concern for it was quite a normal reaction—one to which most housewives could relate.

As I continued to ponder this incident, asking Baba in my heart to show me clearly the lesson in it, the words came suddenly and vividly to mind: "Be careful for nothing." Such a strange message! Isn't being careful an important human value? It must be one of the most important. Everytime I left home when growing up, I was told, "Be careful!" Now that I'm a senior citizen, almost everyone says, "Take care now!" instead of "Good-bye" on parting.

Yet, I've known from a very early age that I did not want to be a Martha during this incarnation. When I entered school at the age of five, I protested when called "Martha" or "Martha Jo," which was the name under which I was registered, and asked my teachers and fellow students to call me "Jo." I had no understanding of the reason behind this request. At that time, it was only a strong feeling. Later on, as I became a student of the Bible, I learned that Jesus had told Martha, sister of Mary and Lazarus, "Martha, Martha, thou art careful and troubled about many things." He went on to commend Mary for sitting at His feet to hear His teachings while Martha was "cumbered about much serving."

Putting these thoughts together, it seemed that it must be one of my major life tasks during this incarnation to rid myself of "Martha-ness." I had made great progress in my efforts to stop being full of care. I was not nearly as troubled about things as I used to be. The iced tea glass incident was an eye opener because it showed me that even though I was manifesting much more equanimity during major crises, the thought pattern which demanded that I take care was still there. The neural pathway

Chapter Thirty

through which it flowed had been reduced from a gorge to a mountain stream, but before liberation from the attachment could be achieved, it must be eliminated altogether. It was just one more subtle outcropping of the ego, calling itself "I," and awarding itself the role of caretaker.

I was beginning to see that when one behavior or aspect of the personality was being overused, there was another being underused. Was the opposite of taking care, **not** taking care? That didn't feel right to me. Baba had never said anything to indicate that we should be care**less** He teaches us to take proper care of food, money, time, and energy. None of these are to be wasted. How can I avoid wasting food and money if I don't take care of them? It seemed to be a riddle for which there was no ready answer, and so it became a koan. I pondered it day and night, just as the Buddhists contemplate and meditate upon the koans given them by their masters. The only answer that came, however, was still in the same words: "Be careful for nothing."

Those words were from somewhere in the Bible, but I didn't know where and I had no concordance with which to look them up. As a matter of fact, I didn't even have a Bible with me. It occurred to me that some of the residents of the ashram might have a Bible, and when the first person I asked said, "Yes, of course," and brought his Bible to my room promptly, I felt I was on the right track. The words were Paul's to the Philippians:

> Rejoice in the Lord alway: and again I say, Rejoice.
> Let your moderation be known unto all men.
> The Lord is at hand.
> Be careful for nothing;
> But in everything by prayer and supplication with thanksgiving
> Let your requests be made known unto God.

There was little doubt now. This was Baba's answer. It was clear, simple, and very much to the point. This is exactly the way He communicates with me face to face. In few words, He points out things that have been hidden from me. Paul told the Corinthians that the Lord would do this. He said: "Therefore judge nothing before the time, until the Lord come, who both will bring to light the hidden things of darkness, and will make manifest the counsels of the hearts: and then shall every man have praise of God."

The opposite of care-full was not care-less, it was rejoicing, moderation, prayer (letting requests be made known to God), supplication with thanksgiving, and praise. These words filled me with awe and gratitude for my beloved Swami. Although these learnings are available to us wherever we are, they seem to come so much faster and clearer when we are at Prasanthi Nilayam. "The Lord is at hand" here. Of course, Paul meant that we should not attempt to judge "before the time" that God spoke in our hearts. He will bring to light those things which He knows in His wisdom we are ready to handle. To attempt to unearth "the hidden things of darkness" before their time is to make the mistake which Baba cautions against: "Do not walk ahead of Me; I may not follow."

So this was the time for me to learn moderation, to be more grateful, to let my requests be made known to God through praise and thanksgiving, to surrender actions to Him, and to stop trying to be the Doer. Thank you, Baba, for the loss of the iced tea glass. What a small, insignificant sacrifice You require for the priceless truths You reveal. Thank you for Your teachings wherever they appear and however You choose to make them known to us. I rejoice in Your majesty, Your nearness, and Your Love. I praise You for Your tender, constant care. My supplication is that I grow more and more like You. My thanksgiving is that I am already that for which I pray.

31

"THE PROCESS *IS* THE HEALING."

Our 1987 trip to Baba was "the best of times and the worst of times." At least, that's the way it seemed to us as we experienced it. Of course, looking back now, we recognize that it was a perfect time—as every trip is. Our human tendency is to judge everything based on what we want, particularly ease, pleasure, and comfort. Our divine wisdom to see the perfect plan, based on our evolution toward union with God, seems to have to wait until the mind releases some of its excitement or resistance and God's plan can begin to appear through the fog of ignorance.

Dave and Betty Davidson had traveled with us, and we had arrived at the ashram before Baba's birthday. There were large crowds, and we had resigned ourselves to having little or no interaction with Him until after the crowds began to disperse. However, He greeted me on Thanksgiving Day and took the letters which I had brought from devotees in the United States. This gave me hope, even though I was sitting in the ladies' chair section. It has become known as the icy Siberia of the ashram, since Baba rarely goes there and seldom even looks in that direction.

Our days went along smoothly and somewhat uneventfully until Dave became ill. His problem seemed to be a recurrence of the dysentery from which he had suffered when he had been stationed in Calcutta during World War II. He had mentioned the experience prior to our leaving the States and expressed some fear of having it again. It was only his deep desire to see Baba which had given him the courage to return to India. Now it seemed as if that which he had feared had come upon him, and we all felt some concern for his welfare. And so it was that on that day in early December, when Baba called us for interview, Dave was not in darshan.

Raye and I had brought several copies of this book. There were only twelve copies in print at that time, and we hoped that Baba might grant a picture of Himself with the author prior to its publication. Raye had faithfully carried a copy with him to darshan every day in order that we might be prepared in the event the much-longed-for interview became a reality. When it did, our feelings of joy were dampened by regret that Dave was not with us.

Raye—always much more capable of keeping his wits about him in Swami's presence than I—asked Baba if He would sign the book and if we might have a picture of Him and me together as He did it. He responded, "Yes, yes!" and then asked, "Where is your camera?" Raye replied, "Back in the room, Swami." Baba seemed greatly surprised at that oversight. He may have been thinking, "Oh, ye of little faith," but He went to the curtain which separated the outer room from the inner and asked if anyone had a camera. A doctor's wife did, and Baba asked her to come in. He told her that we wanted a picture while He signed the book, and she agreed to take it. After that had been accomplished, Raye suddenly realized that He had left himself out. So he said, "And may we take one of You and me, Swami?" Again, the reply was, "Yes, yes." In his great joy and love for his Lord, Raye stood beside Baba and put his arm around His shoulder. The doctor's wife snapped the shot, but as she did the batteries flew out of the camera, going several feet into the air before clattering to the floor.

Chapter Thirty-One

Raye had become so fascinated with the intimacy and the captivating human qualities which Baba exhibits in the interview room, he had momentarily forgotten His Divinity. This is not an uncommon occurrence. As we seek to unify our own human aspect with the Divine, it is easy to forget that the Unity is on earth right now in the Poorna Avatar, Sathya Sai Baba. We have no other Being in which we can witness the complete expression of all human attributes merged with the attributeless. Since our training for interaction with such a Being has been limited to darshan and the interview room, we can, therefore, be forgiven, if our social skills are sometimes unequal to the occasion.

As for Baba Himself, however, His Grace is unlimited; and his skills, consummate. When the film was developed and our suspicions confirmed that there was no picture of Raye with his beloved Sai, Baba granted us a second interview. This time Raye had not left the camera in the room. Baba sat down beside Raye, placed Raye's right hand on top of His left, then placed His right hand on top of Raye's right. I took the picture, and we have a visual record of Swami's Grace—forgiveness without accusation, absolution without guilt, love without conditions.

Our supreme joy in Swami's gracious bestowal of His love was tempered by our concern for Dave. At the time of the first interview, Dave had only been sick a few days. He was being cared for by an American doctor friend. We were sure that he would be back on the darshan lines before Christmas. This was not to be, however. Instead of improving, he continued to grow worse.

My concern for Dave was undoubtedly due to attachment and ego. Pure love knows no fear nor grief. I prayed day and night for his healing. Over and over again, I asked Baba in my heart to please heal Dave. No improvement in the physical condition was in evidence, and I asked Baba to show me my own impurities in order that I might pray more effectively. Finally, the answer came in words which were clearly from the Kingdom of

Heaven within, for my mind would have been incapable of bringing them forth. They were: "The process *is* the healing."

This was a deeper understanding than I had ever experienced before. I had quoted Baba's words many times: "Whatever happens has to happen." I have affirmed "All is in divine order." I have known that this is Baba's play, and that He is the director, and all of the actors. But when the words "The process *is* the healing" came in response to days of petitioning for Dave's healing, my knowing reached another level of Awareness. I know now that whatever process anyone is going through is not a tragedy, not a catastrophe, not an illness or a problem—it is a process of healing. It is healing our ignorance and our sense of separation. We are never separate from Peace, Love, Unity, and Divinity. We are only confused. We become deluded by the senses into believing ourselves to be personalities who can own things—call them ours. We say, "My pain, my problem, my illness, my operation, my family, my friends, my property, and my mistake or my triumph." It is difficult not to use these words in our daily conversation, but step by step we become more aware of the marriage, the perfect unity of our humanity and our Divinity. Whatever process we are going through, it is the provision of the Eternal Absolute for healing, that is, for dispelling the mist—the mystification—that His creation has become engulfed in.

Just as we must maintain our Awareness of Baba's Divinity while we bask in the sheer joy of His humanity, we must also maintain Awareness of the Divinity of every human being. The processes of joy and sorrow, failure and success, ease and disease, and birth and death are solely for the purpose of healing the only illness from which we truly suffer: the schism between Self and self, between Being and becoming, between God and man. My prayer that Dave be healed was not answered in the way that I had outlined. He did not jump up from his mattress and immediately return to the darshan lines. But the process he was

Chapter Thirty-One

going through was bringing about a more genuine healing than I could have imagined at that time.

The body needs no healing, but the mind that thinks it is a body is sick indeed.

"If one thinks that God is separate from him, it may be so for him, but if anyone totally gives up his thoughts, he then becomes God Himself. All thoughts are illusions, so, if you give them up, you yourself become God. Therefore, you—all of you—give up all thoughts. Come forward and enjoy the Divinity that you are!"

—Baba
Discourse, October 2, 1986

32

"I WILL TAKE CARE"

"Who takes care of the body at any time?... The genuine saints and yogis in the Himalayas... have no way to take care of their bodies. It is God who takes care." —Baba (*Conversations with Baba,* by John Hislop, p. 110)

Dave was becoming weaker, and his illness was recognized to be of a serious nature. As a matter of fact, when he was placed on a litter and carried to the hospital, he seemed to have already let go of his tenuous hold on life. Raye and Betty were with him, while I waited in the apartment. They told me later that it was decided that he should be taken to the hospital in Bangalore because of his medical history. He had had triple bypass surgery for a heart condition. The hospital at Prasanthi Nilayam was not equipped with oxygen or other equipment which might be necessary in the event of an emergency, and so Dave was taken to St. Martha's. Betty accompanied him.

On Christmas Eve Betty returned to the ashram just long enough to gather up the balance of their belongings. She said that Dave was in the Intensive Care Unit (referred to in India as the Intensive Treatment Unit) and that it seemed certain he would not be ready to leave India at the time we were scheduled to depart. She also indicated that she was not feeling at all well, either, and feared she might be coming down with dysentery also. However, with bravery and determination, she loaded everything into a taxi very early on Christmas morning to return to Bangalore and keep her vigil at Dave's side.

Raye and I found ourselves in a quandary. This was Dave and Betty's first trip to India. They had come with us. How could we go off and leave them in such a situation? And yet how could we stay? Our tickets were of the "non-exchangeable, non-refundable" type and reservations were very difficult to obtain. We knew that with the doctor's statement, the airlines would honor their tickets and make every effort to open up space for them when they were able to travel. But whether they would provide for us also was quite doubtful. We felt an urgent need for Baba's guidance, and He responded to that need by calling us in for interview.

As soon as Baba had taken us into His private room, we began to tell Him of Dave and Betty. He listened patiently, knowing that we had a need to tell—even though He had no need to be told. When we said that one of our friends was in intensive care in Bangalore and that his wife was also very ill, He replied, "No, not so very ill." We were pleased to hear that Betty was not so very ill because we had heard from one of the taxi drivers that she had been admitted to the hospital also. Later, we learned that her illness had been a blessing—that it only persisted long enough to bring about her admittance to the hospital, which made it possible for her to be near Dave and to care for him as she wanted and needed to do. However, we continued our story and ended with the question: "Baba, what should we do?" He replied, "You must go. I will take care."

There I was, doing it again. Will I never learn that He is the Doer and that He will take care? I want to be His instrument, to go where He sends me, and to do whatever He directs, without trying to take things into my own hands and do them separate from Him. And so it was that we—not without some lingering

Chapter Thirty-Two

feeling of regret that it was necessary—left India without our traveling companions.

When all four of us were together again in the United States, Betty told us the rest of the story. After getting Dave admitted to St. Martha's Hospital, she had checked in at the Rama Hotel. Although feeling quite ill herself, she felt that she must remain ambulatory as long as she possibly could in order to take care of Dave's needs. The procedure in Indian hospitals is that whatever the patient needs, other than professional medical attention, is provided by the family. Betty found herself in the unenviable position of having to get herself around in a strange country, surmount the language barrier, purchase items for a sick-room, have numerous prescriptions filled (including the bottles of IV solution), and spend most of her time at the hospital without even a place to sit. There was no waiting room, and the only thing available to sit on in the care facility was a metal stool which was too high to allow her feet to touch the floor. There were several patients in the Intensive Care Unit with serious illnesses, and it was a beehive of activity with doctors, nurses, orderlies, and family members coming and going.

As Betty's condition grew worse, she realized she was in desperate need of rest and that she was physically unable to keep up the pace which was being required of her. Due to the difficulty of communicating over the telephone with persons speaking British English with an Indian accent, she asked that the desk clerk at the hotel call the hospital and tell them that she simply could not be there at the appointed time because she was too ill. She went to her room and collapsed into bed. However, in a few minutes people began to arrive at the door of her room. One brought flowers, the head housekeeper came to see what she could do, one of the gentlemen from the front desk came to tell her that he had made an appointment for her to see a doctor and that he would take her to the doctor's office.

The cab dispatcher, who spoke excellent English, came up to see what he could do, and he asked her why she had continued trying to do all those things when she was so sick. She said, "There was no one to do them but me." He replied, "Good heavens, woman, didn't you know that the Rama would help?" This kind and very efficient gentleman, whom we have all come to depend on as a friend as well as a source of transportation, is named Suleman. The name is another form of Solomon, which means "the wise one." I felt overcome by reverence and awe as I decoded the symbolism and realized what Betty was being told and was also experiencing. Rama was an Avatar, one of the ten Avatars of Vishnu. He was a symbol of the ideal human, the hero of the **Ramayana.** So, when Betty expressed the delusion that there was no one except her to do the necessary things, the wise one had asked her if she didn't know that the Avatar, the Ideal Man, would help.

Betty had come to India for one purpose. She had written it down before she left home. It was to have the actual experience of the love of God. Day after day in darshan when Baba did not come to the ladies' chair section, did not look in our direction, or even acknowledge our presence, Betty would think, "I didn't feel it. I don't feel the love of God at all." The day that Baba had first greeted me and taken the letters I had brought from Stateside devotees, Betty had been feeling a little queasy and had stayed in the room. By the time we were called in for interview, she had felt such great concern for Dave that her thought was not very open to experience the love she had come for. At that point she had an urgent question to ask.

Dave, being aware that his fear of getting sick in India had undoubtedly been a factor contributing to his present illness, told Betty that as soon as he felt well enough to travel he was going back to Singapore. He would await us there. Betty did not see how she could possibly let Dave go to Singapore by himself, but she wasn't ready to go. She wanted more time to have the

Chapter Thirty-Two

experience she had come for. So when she, Raye, and I went in for the interview, her first question to Baba was, "Shall I return to Singapore with Dave, Swami?" Baba assured her that He knew her husband. He said that they were both a little confused, but that Dave would not be going back to Singapore. We all felt great relief at that answer. We jumped to the conclusion that it meant that Dave would be getting well and staying at the ashram. Of course, it hadn't meant that at all. It had meant only that he would not be leaving India prior to the scheduled time and that Betty would not have to make the choice of whether to go to Singapore with Dave or to stay in Prasanthi Nilayam with Baba.

Dave did not leave India prematurely to go to Singapore, and Betty experienced the love of God that she had come hoping for. She was vividly aware of the care she was receiving. She experienced it when one of the nurses had brought her a second little metal stool to put her feet up on as she sat by Dave's bedside. She experienced it when one of the hotel managers had taken time off from his job to drive her to the doctor. She experienced it when one of the nurses, seeing that she did not really enjoy the strong tea with milk which is commonly served in India, took it upon herself to bring in a flask of boiling water several times a day so that Betty could make tea more to her own liking.

The most outstanding part of the whole lesson which this process entailed was that, in many instances, Betty had no need to do anything in order to experience the Love of God, the care of the Avatar. She felt herself surrounded by His tenderness and benevolence when two nurses came from the hospital in a van and told her that they had come to get her and all of her things. They were admitting her to the hospital so that they could care for both her and Dave. They took her to a large bedroom in the family section of the hospital. It had two beds and a private bathroom. She stayed there alone until Dave was released from

ICU. Then he was brought there. He was assigned an orderly to bathe him, shave him, feed him if necessary, pick up anything which needed to be purchased from outside the hospital, and to go with Betty as her guide and interpreter when she went to the airlines office to try to change their reservations. Even though Dave was getting better, he was not well enough to travel when it was time for them to leave.

The airlines were extremely accommodating. They required a statement from the doctor that Dave was now well enough to travel, but that was a normal precaution for all concerned. In the hospital, the nurses brought flowers and special goodies from their own Christmas gifts. On one occasion, when a special treatment was needed for Dave, one of the Sisters rented the necessary equipment out of her own monies and brought it to the hospital herself. No more love could have been shown, than was shown to two strangers in a foreign land.

At the ashram, no money was charged or donations solicited for medication, litter service, room accommodations, electricity, or water; neighbors in the Round Building brought in foods especially cooked to try to tempt Dave's waning appetite; everyone was expressing, through action, the Love that is God. The Seva Dals who served at the ladies' gate and particularly those who assisted the ladies who sat in chairs, were Love personified.

At the hospital, the loving service, freely offered, included both on-duty and off-duty time. After five days in intensive care for one, and nine days in a private room for two, many special services, especially prepared food and beverages, the total bill came to only two hundred dollars. The motivation was clearly not dollar signs. Love for God was being expressed through loving service to man. God's love for man is experienced through man's humanity to man. There is no difference, no separation. Love is One and is in All, through All, as All.

Chapter Thirty-Two

The love of Baba, which may not be recognized until understanding of the All is reached, came flooding back into the memory of both of His loved ones after the process of purification became less intense. Betty remembers now the incredible tenderness with which He leaned over her in the interview room, looked directly into her eyes, and told her that she and Dave were confused, and concluded by saying: "Happiness is Awareness." When I told her that He had said to Raye and me: "I will take care," she felt the same awe that all of His devotees feel, realizing that He is with each of us, caring for us, every minute of every day. He had certainly given her what she had come for: the awareness of His love as expressed everywhere through every body—Divinity as Humanity.

Dave remembers that he received an unusual amount of attention in darshan before he became ill. He had been in the front row many more times than the law of averages would dictate. He had been granted padnamaskar and had felt Baba's love daily while at Prasanthi Nilayam.

After arriving home, he wrote: "I am convinced that Sai Baba is the Avatar, complete with all the powers attributed thereto. There is no question in my mind that when you are in the presence of Sai at darshan, you are in the very presence of God, the Creator, the Only. At afternoon darshan on December 5, I was in the front row. I had a clear sight of Baba's approach for more than one hundred feet. Somewhere in that space our eyes met in prayerful contact, and I knew 'You and I are One' to be the absolute truth—specifically for me at that moment and then instantly for everyone and everything in creation.

"That night I had a vision. I can best describe it as though a window into heaven opened before my eyes. Inside was a view of a new world—a world without form—with only brilliant light. The activity was thought forms and only thoughts of absolute purity could exist—all others dissolved before completion. Afterward, I knew this to be 'heaven.' I knew that this was where we all belong and are moving toward in accordance with our choices and the strength of our desire. The route is commitment to the truth teachings of the ages, and my commitment seemed to be to the five human values: Truth, Love, Peace, Right Action, and Nonviolence."

******

Chapter Thirty-Two

Then said Almitra [to the prophet], Speak to us of Love.
And He raised His head and looked upon the people, and there fell a stillness upon them.
And with a great voice He said:
When Love beckons to you, follow Him,
Though His ways are hard and steep.
And when His wings enfold you yield to Him,
Though the sword hidden among His pinions may wound you.
And when He speaks to you believe in Him,
Though His voice may shatter your dreams as the north wind lays waste the garden.
For even as Love crowns you, so shall He crucify you.
Even as He is for your growth, so is He for your pruning.
Even as He ascends to your height and caresses your tenderest branches that quiver in the sun,
So shall He descend to your roots and shake them in their clinging to the earth.
Like sheaves of corn, He gathers you unto Himself.
He threshes you to make you naked.
He sifts you to free you from your husks.
He grinds you to whiteness. He kneads you until you are pliant;
And then He assigns you to His sacred fire, that you may become sacred bread for His sacred feast.
All these things shall Love do unto you that you may know the secrets of your heart, and in that knowledge become a fragment of Life's heart.

—Kahlil Gibran

33

"BOTH GOOD MEN"

"Let us not to the marriage of true minds admit impediments."
—Shakespeare

    Raye and I were somewhat surprised when, during one of our precious interviews with Swami in 1987, He began to speak about two of His devotees. He smiled like an indulgent, loving, forgiving parent as He said: "They can't agree on anything, but they're both good men—very good men." I couldn't imagine why He would be telling us this. We were in no position to do anything about it. It was really of no concern to us at all. As a matter of fact, the comment was so unexpected and meaningless to me that I couldn't stop trying to figure it out.
    When, during the summer of '88, I found myself in a disagreement with another devotee, I again tried to apply the statement to myself. In the throes of the problem, however, my self-search seemed fruitless. I already knew that I needed to be more humble and more accepting—more submissive to authority. Progress had been made along those lines, and I really thought that the character fault had been corrected. But here it was again, and it almost seemed to be worse than ever. I prayed to Baba for help to be free from anger and rebellion.

Little by little, step by step, the resistance to what was happening dissolved and disappeared. I became aware of Baba as the only authority and declared over and over again that He was the director of this little drama and that all I had to do was play the part He had assigned to me. It was also extremely important to recognize that all the other person was doing was playing the role which had been assigned to him. As the ego's resistance melted away, so did the problem. The end result was a sense of friendship, loyalty, love, and genuine admiration for the protagonist in the play.

Did he change? I don't know. Perhaps, being my mirror, he was always just as caring and generous as he seems to me to be now. At any rate, my perception changed and my thinking changed and my behavior changed. I feel that I am softer, sweeter, and more feminine than I have ever been before, and the dear person who played opposite me seems softer and sweeter also.

The connection between this happy outcome and Baba's statement to me about the two other gentlemen both being "good men" did not at first come clear. Then one day, as I was pondering it for perhaps the hundredth time, the light dawned. Of course they were both good **men.** Their male characteristics were highly developed. They were both scholarly, decisive, firm, efficient, and skilled in the use of language. I had heard others excusing them when they disagreed by saying, "They're too much alike." They had developed their male qualities to the detriment of their female qualities. And so had I. Can two people, both of whom are out of balance in the same way, ever be reconciled?

The Shakespearean quotation which introduced this chapter came to mind, and I began to question what a "true" mind is. Once more, consulting the dictionary, I found the definition of "true" was extremely enlightening. I found that it meant "in accordance with the parental type, having all the basic

Chapter Thirty-Three

characteristics, and conforming to the ideal." Our True Mother-Father, Sathya Sai Baba, is the Ideal Man and the Ideal Woman, possessing all of the basic characteristics of each in perfect balance. Those who have had the privilege of seeing Him in His present form have witnessed His graceful, soft, sweet, compassionate, loving femininity. Many have also witnessed and experienced His strict discipline, His administrative decisiveness, His strength, and His mastery of all languages.

Sathya Sai Baba is our Exemplar. As He is, so must we be also. I am resolved to balance my male and female characteristics in order that I may have a true mind—not just an educated, overactive brain, but that I may also exercise compassion, humility, and love. Balance is the key. When out of balance, we form symbiotic relationships with those whose excesses match our deficiencies, and experience conflict with those whose imbalances are the same as our own. Let us bring ourselves into true with the Ideal, thus bringing about happy relationships and peace on earth.

******

"As science develops and technology advances, humility and love should also develop to the same extent."

—Sathya Sai Baba
Sanathana Sarathi
June, 1987

Dear Baba,
    Each dawn my heart advances apologies to Thee
    For each night my soul knows where I failed,
    Although You were watching me.

—Hanna Hamilton
Sathya Sai Newsletter
Spring 1987

34

"WHEN THE TONGUE IS CONQUERED, VICTORY IS YOURS"

"The tongue of the wise is health.... A wholesome tongue is a tree of life.... Whoso keepeth his mouth and his tongue keepeth his soul from troubles." —Proverbs

Through a rapid and unusual set of circumstances, during the summer of 1988, I found myself spending three weeks at a health spa. This was my first such experience, and it was nothing I would ever have considered to be among my top priorities. It was only the fact that it seemed clearly to have been God-directed that made it acceptable to me at all. However, as the program unfolded, it became clear that there was nothing required of me which was not in complete accordance with Sai's teachings.

For example, we were fed only fresh, live, uncooked food. Baba says: "In creation there are 8,400,000 different life forms. Of these, only man cooks and changes his food. A seed, when planted, will sprout into life; but, when it is cooked, the life is destroyed. Eating food in its natural state promotes longevity; cooking partially destroys the life force.... Human diseases are increasing. The reason is that man does not like to partake of food as God created it. He is the victim of his own tongue. Since the tongue demands satisfaction in the form of taste, man's own likes and dislikes cause him to change natural foods to better suit his taste."

Meals were served on a regular schedule and there were no in-between-meal snacks. Baba says: "Eat at regular intervals, according to a well-established time table. Develop a biting hunger before sitting down to a meal." ***Summer Showers 1978***

We fasted one day in each week. Baba says: "Fasting for one day during the week is good for the body as well as for the country." ***Vision of the Divine***, p. 61

Meals were prepared so that there was one plate per person. Second servings were not available and first servings were small. Baba says: "Moderation in food; moderation in talk, desires, and pursuits; contentment with what one gets through honest labor; eagerness to serve others and to impart joy to all—these are the most powerful of all the health tonics and preservers known to the Sanathana Ayurveda, the eternal science of health." ***Sathya Sai Speaks,*** Vol. 1, p. 168

Our diet consisted mainly of sprouted seeds, nuts, and legumes. Baba says: "Food which is not cooked contains the largest amount of protein. For instance, the amount of protein in mung, dahl, and soybeans is great. The way to eat peas, beans, or lentils is to soak them in water and let them sprout. In this way, you consume them in all their richness. But because we are victims of our tongue, tastes, whims, and fancies, we boil them and add oil and various other ingredients. In this process, we deprive them of their basic contents and deprive ourselves of the nutrition they might have given us."

For more than a year prior to this time, feeling that my wisdom was not sufficient to discriminate among the hundreds upon hundreds of health plans, diets, and recommendations which were being made by various doctors, health institutions, and entrepreneurs, and following Baba's personal advice to me to "forget it," I had been practicing dedicating all food to Him.

Chapter Thirty-Four

This had purified my mind, cleared out all of the conflicting instructions, and prepared me for the next step. Baba says: "Without having purity of mind, we cannot achieve even a small thing.... [Therefore,] food must always be offered to God. Man has not created either matter or food. Brahma has created matter. God is in your body. Since God is in your body, it is as if He had said, 'this food is taken by Me and I will digest it.' While offering it in this way, the food becomes consecrated, blessed by God." The practice of dedicating the food to God was also followed at the health institute before each meal.

No salt, spices, or flavor enhancers of any kind were used on the food served to the guests of the spa. Baba says: "Food should not be too salty, too hot, too bitter, too sweet, too sour, or too steaming. These things heighten hunger and thirst." *Summer Showers 1978*

After three weeks of eating such food, prepared in beautiful, peaceful surroundings, by persons seeking spiritual enlightenment through healthy bodies rather than healthy bodies as a means of obtaining more ease and pleasure, I found that a totally unexpected result had occurred. I had no cravings. The live food which I was eating without flavor enhancers of any kind was totally satisfying. I was completely free from slavery to the tongue. It was a strange feeling, to say the least. After sixty years of selecting food which would satisfy the sense of taste, I was able to select food based on its health-giving, nourishing qualities only.

Back in the workaday world, I gradually slipped back into the habit of taking whatever food was available. The long airline journey, days of having to eat in restaurants, plus the time required to grow my own food, has caused me to lose the complete freedom from addiction to taste which was experienced for several weeks. However, the awareness remains, and I happily choose to eat fresh live food whenever I can. Some foods which I had never even questioned before have disappeared from my diet completely. I am learning to do better without feeling guilty and berating myself for each bite of food I take.

Another major aspect of controlling the tongue involves not trying to convert everyone else to this way of eating. It is important to be a gracious guest, eating at least a bite or two of whatever is served. Many of my friends are striving to follow Baba's teachings along these lines also, and so it becomes easier to accept invitations. Whenever it is noticed that I pass up butter, cheese, meat, eggs, rich casseroles, and desserts, someone almost inevitably says: "Oh, I see you're on a diet. Have you lost any weight?" I have to answer, "I don't know. If that is one of the results of my making better food choices, it will be a blessing." My purpose, however, in doing this is the same as in everything else I do: to follow Baba's teachings to the best of my ability and ultimately to experience mergence with Him—the marriage of self to Self—an achievement which freedom from domination by the senses can accelerate.

"It is nature that induces the belief that you are the body.... This identification has led to an inordinate degree of attention to the body and consequently to worry and misery.... The weighing machine on which you stand and read your weight with pride laughs at you for the silly exaltation you give it. It sneers at your conceit over physical victories.... Concentrate on the Maker, not the made."

—Sathya Sai Baba
Voice of the Avatar

35

"LIFE IS AWARENESS"

After Baba had given the first thirty chapters of this book His blessing, He read the quotation on the title page out loud—including the source from which the quotation had been taken. Then He looked at Raye and me intently and said: "Life is Awareness." At first I thought He might have been questioning the title. Later, however, I realized that He was making a statement of the theme of the book, which He had assured me that He had read.

To be aware implies vigilance in observing or alertness in drawing inferences from what one experiences. This is what is being reported in this book: the author's efforts to observe and draw inferences from what she has experienced. The fact or condition of being aware is knowledge, and such knowledge may be acquired by study, investigation, or observation, as well as by experience. As many others have written excellent books based on research, observation, and investigation into the life and teachings of Bhagavan Sri Sathya Sai Baba, it has been my purpose to emphasize the acquisition of knowledge which began in direct interaction with Sai, but which was strengthened and expanded through intuition, study, and the synchronicity of daily experiences.

Awareness does not dismiss anything as unimportant or without significance. It does not accept chance, accident, or coincidence as legitimate causes for the happenings in our lives. It engages in observation of natural phenomena as well as in meditation and introspection. It expects to experience boundless Being here and now and to have that experience become of practical benefit to self, to others, and to society. It is continually watching for and participating in the marriage of all opposites. Its purpose is to bring heaven to Earth today. It does not deny, reject, denigrate or eliminate; it assimilates, includes, appreciates, and glorifies. Awareness is Bliss and Being. Being is Awareness and Bliss. Bliss is Being and Awareness. The Trinity, **Sat-Chit-Ananda** or Being-Awareness-Bliss, is not a mysterious, esoteric appellation, which we may someday hope to attain. It is simply the happiness which is readily available to everyone who is willing to exercise vigilance in observing and drawing inferences from his everyday life experiences.

******

"Happiness is Awareness."

—Sathya Sai Baba
to Betty Davidson
December 15, 1987

36

"WHAT IS RELIGION?"

When Baba asked me "What Is Religion?" I answered from the standpoint of a sophisticated intellect. I said, "It is a systematized series of beliefs." He responded softly and patiently, "Oh, no. It is a path to God." This is one of Baba's basic teachings, and I have no excuse for answering the question the way I did. Ever since my first trip to see Baba, I have been learning to truly understand and appreciate my own religion, which for thirty-five years was Christian Science. Now He is expanding my awareness and my appreciation of other religions.

Catholicism has been difficult for me to understand in this incarnation. At times in the past, I felt prejudiced against the religion and all of its adherents. Recently, however, another devotee of Sai Baba sent me some information about events which are currently occurring in Yugoslavia. Feeling a sense of responsibility to reply, I read the material and found myself responding to it in a way I would have thought I could never do. A brief summary of the information which was sent to me follows:

Since June, 1981, Mary, the mother of Jesus, has been appearing daily to a group of young people in a remote mountain village of Yugoslavia. Medjugorje, Yugoslavia is by all ordinary standards one of the least likely places for such a phenomenon to occur. It is almost inaccessible even by automobile, devoid of tourist amenities, and located in a country which does not recognize any religion and denies the existence of God. Despite government attempts to discredit the appearances and make visits to the site difficult, millions of pilgrims have visited the village to see for themselves what is happening there.

The first appearance of Mary occurred on June 24, 1981. She appeared to six young people, two boys and four girls, who ranged in age from ten to seventeen. These were quite normal youngsters, of average intelligence, and without any more than ordinary interest in religion. The area is heavily Catholic and the government very grudgingly had allowed them to attend services in their church, but—prior to Mary's appearance—the attendance of these six young persons had been no more nor less than that of their peers.

Marija Pavlovic is the oldest. She is of average height, thin, serene, and the most spiritual of the group.

Vicka Ivankovic, the second oldest, has strong features and a particularly expressive face. She is obviously quite genuine, and also charming. She and Marija now see thousands of pilgrims each week, answering their questions and praying with them. Both girls plan to enter a convent when the appearances cease.

Mirjana Dragicivic, third oldest, is in her fourth year of college at the University of Sarajevo, where her family now lives. She returns to Medjugorje once a month.

Ivanka Ivankovic, the youngest of the four girls, is quite pretty. In 1981, she was a typical teenager, but also firmly religious. She married in December, 1986, and had a baby girl in November, 1987.

Ivan Dragicivic, the older of the two boys, is the most timid and retiring of the group. Although he has not succeeded in either of the two seminaries he has attended, he still hopes to become a priest someday. He finished a year of military service in June, 1987, and is presently helping his family in the fields.

The youngest and most lively member of the group is Jakov Colo, who was only ten when the first vision occurred. His presence seems to be of special value in convincing doubters of the authenticity of the miracles and messages from Mary. When people compare him to their own ten-year-olds, they feel that it would be highly improbable that a fidgety young boy would be spending two to three hours every day at church in prayer just to convince others that he had seen and was continuing to see holy apparitions. Now seventeen, he is still attending classes with local lads his same age.

According to the children, the message of the Blessed Virgin is simple and direct: She is appearing to the seers to tell the world of the urgency to return to the ways of God, to convert their lives to peace with God and with their fellow man. She has said that She would give each of the young people ten messages, or "secrets," of events which will be occurring in the near future. Ultimately, a visible sign will be given to convince all of mankind that the visions at Medjugorje are real and that the conversion to God must be started now.

Vicka, Marija, Ivan, and Jakov continue to see the Madonna each evening. Mirjana and Ivanka have received all ten secrets and no longer have daily apparitions. However, Mary visits them at least once each year. The Lady promised Ivanka that She would visit her on the anniversaries of Her first appearance. She told Mirjana that she would come to her on her birthdays and in difficult moments as long as she lives. When asked why Mary offered to help in her difficult moments but does not do so for the rest of us, Mirjana said, "I am not speaking of the ordinary problems of my life. My difficult moments stem from the secrets concerning the future of the world, which Our Lady revealed to me."

Of the ten messages, only four relate to the entire planet. Mary has already told Mirjana that the seventh secret, which was to have been a threat to the world, has already been eliminated by the prayer and fasting of spiritual and conscientious people. The ninth and tenth secrets, however, are also chastisements for the sins of the world. Mary has told Mirjana that these could only be eliminated by conversion of every person on the earth. However, the punishments due to befall the world can be mitigated. "You have forgotten that with prayer and fasting you can ward off wars and suspend natural laws," Mary said.

Both Mirjana and Ivanka received from The Blessed Virgin a piece of material which looks like paper, but it is not paper. It looks like cloth, but it is not cloth. On this substance all ten secrets are written, including the dates and times when certain incidents are to occur. Each of the seers can only read her own secrets. Mirjana's mother tried to read the paper given by Mary to Mirjana, but she could not. Mirjana told her that it could only be read by Mirjana herself and one priest whom Mirjana would choose to announce the secrets when the time comes for them to be revealed.

The material on which the secrets are written cannot be destroyed—not even by fire. The seers have been instructed to select a priest to whom they will give the secrets ten days before they are to happen. The Madonna will then give him the ability to read the messages. He will announce each one three days before it will happen, giving the full nature of the secret, including the exact time and place of its happening. After the first announcement, the others will follow within a brief period, still allowing a short time for those who wish to turn their lives around. However, after the visible sign appears, those who are still alive, according to Mirjana's report of the Blessed Virgin's statements, will have very little time for conversion. The time for each of us to take heed and begin praying in earnest is now.

Chapter Thirty-Six

Mirjana has revealed the name of the priest she selected. She said that Our Lady was pleased with her choice. "When I chose the priest who would announce the secrets," Mirjana said, "I revealed his name to Fr. Tomislav Vlasic, (who at that time was the spiritual director of the seers). Fr. Vlasic's response was: "He is far away from Medjugorje. You should choose someone closer." My answer to him was: "Our Lady will take care of it." A short time after that (August, 1984) Bishop Zanic had Fr. Vlasic removed from Medjugorje and replaced him with the priest whom Mirjana had selected to reveal the secrets. This action on the part of Bishop Zanic is particularly interesting in that he is not a believer in the apparitions and has done everything he possibly could to discourage them. Ivanka has not yet chosen the priest who will reveal her secrets.

Vicka has received only eight secrets thus far. She has taken dictation from The Blessed Virgin, however, which chronicles Mary's life on earth. Vicka has, for the last four years, been suffering from severe pains in the head caused by a water bubble situated between the small and the large brain. The doctors avoid surgery because of the delicate position. Her suffering is great, often resulting in a comatose condition. She always comes out of the coma, however, in time for the daily apparition, which occurs in her small, simple room.

Vicka's friends have offered to pay all of her travel, medical, and hospital expenses if she would be willing to go to the United States, England, or Switzerland for surgery. Her simple answer is always, "No." She explains: "Our Lady has told me that God sent me this illness for a special purpose, and I accepted it." When asked whether Mary has promised to heal her, Vicka replied, "No, she has not offered, and I have not asked her to do so." This is seen by many as clear evidence of the authenticity of the apparitions. When a young girl in the prime of life turns away from physical comforts and financial benefits in order to further spiritual purposes, who will dare accuse her of deception? Her face is radiant with the love of God even when she is experiencing pain.

Marija, who has received nine of the ten secrets which are to be revealed to her, is also being given messages which are specifically for the parishioners of Medjugorje. All six seers are well aware of the fact that they are misunderstood, criticized, and even condemned by many who should be supporting and protecting them. However, they are convinced that The Blessed Virgin Mary is using them as instruments for delivering Her heavenly messages to the world and that this task for which they have been chosen far outweighs earthly praise and the approval of other personalities.

Ironically, a government that was initially hostile and constantly harassing the locals and visionaries alike is now working at a furious pace to add new hotels, cottages, restaurants, and other tourist necessities to accommodate the ever-growing crowds. Medjugorje is now the number one tourist attraction in Yugoslavia. The economic benefits to the country far outweigh the Marxist, atheistic aversion to religion. [5]

On a visit to see Sathya Sai Baba in December 1987, Polly Kirby, a devotee from the San Francisco area, asked Baba if He was in any way connected with the events in Medjugorje. He replied: "Wherever Love is, there is My connection."

As I began to read the messages from Mary as reported by the children, I found that there were striking correspondences between the messages from Medjugorje and those stressed by Baba in His recent discourses. Some examples follow:

BABA: "Let me assure you that this dharmaswarupa, this Divine Body, has not come in vain. It will succeed in averting the crisis that has come upon humanity."—Baba (1980)

MARY: "An evil which threatened the world, according to the seventh secret, has already been eliminated through prayer and fasting."—Mirjana

Chapter Thirty-Six

BABA: "It is the mind which is responsible for the state of affairs in the world and for the condition of human beings. No physical, external effort you make to solve the problems of the day will solve them. The mind must be changed. There is no limit to the power of the mind." —Baba (1987)

MARY: "You have forgotten that with prayer and fasting you can ward off wars and suspend natural laws." —Mary

---

BABA: "I do not want your praise. I want your transformation." —Baba (1987)

MARY: "This time is a period of grace and conversion. After the visible sign, those who are still alive will have little time for conversion." —Mary

---

BABA: "If there is no spiritual transformation in your way of life over the years, you are guilty of having wasted all your energies, time, and opportunities." —Baba

MARY: "Convert yourselves as quickly as possible. Open your hearts to God." —Mirjana

---

BABA: "You have been coming to Prasanthi Nilayam for many years and have been listening to My discourses, but your desires continue to increase. The spirit of renunciation has not developed. Sooner or later you will have to give up your attachment to family members and material possessions. Only that one is a hero who gives up his possessions before they are taken from him."—Baba (1987)

MARY: "The only word I wish to say is '**conversion**'! To the whole world, I ask only for conversion. Give up everything that goes against conversion."—Mary

---

BABA: "Do not give room for differences and misunderstandings among yourselves. Work with Unity. Love Divinity. Serve the needy and helpless, and sanctify your lives."—Baba (1988)

MARY: "Peace, peace, peace. Be reconciled with one another." —Mary

---

BABA: Baba has repeatedly stressed the need for family sadhana—especially the regular singing of devotional songs. He is diligent in manifesting and blessing sacred objects for the individual and the home.

MARY: "The Madonna said that we need communal prayer and family prayer. She stressed the need for family prayer most of all. She also said that every family should have at least one sacred object in the house."—Mirjana

---

BABA: "Cultivate the habit of remembering the Lord with every breath; then only can you remember Him with the last breath."—Baba

Chapter Thirty-Six

MARY: "Everyone should be ready to die tomorrow. They should accept God now so that they can be at peace in their hearts. If they are committed to God, He will accept them."
—Mirjana

BABA: "There are three supreme maxims which should be ever remembered: Have love for God; fear sin; and observe morality in society.—Baba (1988)

MARY: "The greatest danger to mankind comes from Godlessness."—Mirjana

---

BABA: Baba has always emphasized the importance of character. He says that one of the results of His mission will be the permanent establishment of character: "I have come to inscribe a golden chapter in the story of humanity wherein falsehood will fail, truth will triumph, and virtue will reign. **Character** will confer power then, not knowledge, or inventive skill, or wealth. Wisdom will be enthroned in the council of nations."—Baba

MARY: "The devil manifests most through people of weak character, those who are divided within themselves."
—Mirjana

BABA: "Why fear when I am here?"—Baba

MARY: "Why should I be afraid when God is with me? God gives me whatever strength I need."—Ivanka

BABA: Peace (shanti), transformation, fasting one day a week from food and continually from bad company and bad thoughts, serving God by serving man, and prayer (sadhana), are Baba's instructions.

MARY: "The messages are peace, conversion, fasting, penance, prayer." —Ivanka

---

BABA: "Education must remove hatred between the pilgrims on their various roads to God. There is only one God, one goal, one law, one truth, one religion, and one reason." —Baba

MARY: "The Madonna said that religions are separated in the earth, but the peoples of all religions are accepted by her Son." —Ivanka

"One cannot be a true Christian if he does not respect other religions. You do not really believe in God if you make fun of other religions." —Mirjana

---

BABA: Thursday, Guru Day, is the day set aside by Baba for worship.

MARY: Thursday is the day that Mary appears each week to Marija to give her messages for the parishioners of Medjugorje. It is also the day that She appeared to Bernadette (Lourdes, France).

Chapter Thirty-Six

BABA: Monism is Baba's highest teaching. It was given to Moses as "I Am That I Am" and to the Vedic seers as "Tat Thwam Asi." Baba usually refers to it as advaita (nondualism). In a discourse given in November 1987, He stated: "I have resolved to teach advaita tatwa, or nondualism, as the spiritual path from this time forward. We have followed the paths of action and devotion and must enter the path of wisdom now. You must put forth every effort to make the necessary changes to achieve the goal of Oneness. These changes are not related to any lapses or faults on your part, but are related to the situation prevailing in the world today."—Baba

MARY: Mary's strong statement of monism to Bernadette—"I Am The Immaculate Conception"-was unacceptable to the church hierarchy at Lourdes and was used in an effort to discredit Bernadette's visions. Bernadette refused to change the words which Mary had spoken to her even though intimidated by church authorities.

Statements of spiritual identity and Oneness of The Creation have been misused and abused by the unenlightened throughout recorded history. The seers of Medjugorje say that once the secrets revealed to them by Our Lady have been realized, life on earth will change. What a wonderful change it would be if all men realized their oneness with God and with each other. I have been told that Sathya Sai Baba has recently installed a statue of Mary, mother of Jesus, at Prasanthi Nilayam, proving once again His total commitment to unity of all religions.

"There is no stepping down in your Godward march. It is a continuous journey through day and night, over hill and dale. Where the road ends, God is attained and the pilgrim finds that he has journeyed from himself to Himself....

"No matter where you go, always know that I will be there, inside you, guiding you every step of the way. In the years to come, you will experience me in different manifestations of my form. You are my very own, dearer than dear to Me. I will protect you as the eyelid protects the eye."

—Baba
Sanathana Saranthi, February 1987

37

"YOU WILL EXPERIENCE ME IN DIFFERENT MANIFESTATIONS OF MY FORM"

"Firmly believe that God is in every human being. If you do not recognize this truth, you are wasting your time in scholarly discussions.... Every man who wants to recognize the Divine and realize the truth should worship God in all human forms."

—Baba
November 23, 1988

It was early one Spring morning, and I glanced up to the pictures on the wall of my bedroom. There were seven pictures of Baba, a stitchery, two Van Gogh prints, and a picture of Mary holding the baby Jesus in her arms. As my attention had so recently been on the occurrences at Medjugorje, it seemed natural that my gaze lingered on the picture of Mary and Jesus. I had purchased the print in Italy when I was visiting there in 1967. On several occasions I had considered replacing it with a picture of Baba, but the size of the Baba pictures I had did not fit the frame and so the picture of Mary and Jesus remained.

Now I looked at it searchingly. I suspect that this was the first time I had really seen it since I had hung it there. Somewhat playfully, but with an undercurrent of sincere questioning, I addressed Mary. "You say that you are available to everyone who calls on you. Why, then, have you never made yourself known to me? I have on many occasions admired the amazing equanimity with which you accepted your role as Jesus' mother. You didn't waver even when Joseph would have refused to marry you, thinking your holy calling to be evidence of impure behavior instead of the highest honor that can be bestowed on a woman. Won't you make yourself evident now? I am watching and waiting for your appearance."

With no expectation at all of any response to this musing, I left the bedroom and went to the family room. It is my custom to sit in the same chair each morning and have some herb tea before beginning the day's chores. As I moved toward the chair, I looked to the east. The suns rays were streaming through our windows, and I saw a phenomenon which I had never seen before. Even though nothing had been changed or moved in months, a brilliant cross appeared to me with the suns rays streaming through it and straight toward me. I felt as if I were being enfolded in them, and that they were entering my heart chakra. It is my prayer that those rays strengthened within me the surrender to God's will and the equanimity which Mary expressed so beautifully.

I have, of course, pondered this little "miracle" many times. The cross was formed by the juxtaposition of two flower pots which sit atop an eteger. They have been there for years, and the light must have come through the opening between them every morning. The only part of the miracle which had been missing was my AWARENESS of it. Is that not true of every beautiful thing? Is it not true of Baba's presence in our heart and in our house? We have to ask to see it, and then open our eyes to become aware of its presence, which has been there all along.

Mary's son said, "Those who have eyes to see, let them see." Please, Mary/Jesus/Baba/Buddha, grant me the ability to love those who slander my best deeds and criticize me for the

Chapter Thirty-Seven

qualities I have struggled so long to develop. Let me feel only gratitude to them for the opportunity to develop and strengthen my character and to be a more worthy instrument for Baba's use.

"Let the petty wishes for which you now approach God be realized or not; let the plans for promotion and progress which you place before God be fulfilled or not; they are not so important after all. The primary aim should be to become masters of yourselves, to hold intimate and constant communion with the Divine that is in you as well as in the Universe of which you are a part. Welcome disappointments. They toughen you and test your fortitude."

—Baba
Words of Jesus and Sathya Sai Baba

38

"WHY FEAR ... SIN?"

"Study to show thyself approved unto God, a workman who needeth not to be ashamed, rightly dividing the word of Truth."
—II Timothy 2:15

In a discourse which Baba gave in 1988, He said: "There are three supreme maxims which should be ever remembered: Have love for God; fear sin; and observe morality in society." Loving God and observing morality are not easy to practice, but they are injunctions to which the average person can accede without argument. However, I had a little difficulty in reconciling the instruction to "fear sin" with my metaphysical mindset. Baba Himself has said many times: "Why fear when I am here?" Then why does He tell us to fear sin?

I had not totally resolved this within myself, when during a meeting of our Center's study circle, the three maxims were mentioned in connection with the teachings of Baba which were being studied. One gentleman in the group asked the other members for help in understanding why Baba would tell us to fear sin. He said that he had been taught that there was really no such thing as sin—that the word "sin" only meant to "miss the mark"—therefore, why should it be feared? Listening to the various comments, I realized that the group generally felt no more security in their understanding of the need to fear sin than I did. The gentleman did not get a satisfactory answer to his question, and he has never attended another meeting of the study circle.

I determined to study more diligently to understand this hard teaching—not so much for myself, because I accepted it in devotion and obedience to my Lord, but in order to be more helpful to those who might not be sufficiently grounded in their devotion to be able to accept until understanding came about naturally.

The dictionary is a valuable instrument when studying Baba's teachings. Those who have listened to His discourses at Prasanthi Nilayam know that He is very precise in His use of language. Even though He delivers the discourse in Telegu, He is quick to correct the translator if He is not satisfied with the English word which has been used in the translation. One definition given for "sin" in the **Webster's New World Dictionary of the American Language** is: "to commit an offense or fault of any kind—especially willfully." Immediately following, however, is another definition which reads: "acceptance of defective behavior, even though without action." Those two definitions clearly pinpoint the problem areas and highlight the need for discrimination in thought and action. Most of us will agree that we wish to avoid sin, but do we want to fear it?

Fear is the general term for the anxiety and agitation felt at the presence of danger. Its meanings range from apprehension to terror. To be terrified is to be intimidated by the source of danger. Baba's strong emphasis on the need for self-confidence and courage would preclude "terror" as being the appropriate definition of fear as He has used it in this maxim. However, when we look at the word "apprehend" in connection with sin, the meaning becomes quite clear. To apprehend sin is to be able to quickly see it and understand it—to recognize it for what it is.

Chapter Thirty-Eight

It is the conscience which causes apprehension or that slight feeling of uneasiness when we observe or participate in faulty behavior. Swami has told us that the conscience is God within and that we must listen carefully to its prompting. He certainly did not and does not want us to feel abject terror of anything, but He does want us to be discriminating, to feel an uneasiness about faulty behavior which will cause us to avoid it. He wants us to be aware of the counterproductivity of faulty goals and unfeeling behavior wherever they appear, without judging or condemning those who seem to us to be missing the whole point of their sojourn on Earth.

Let us take, for example, students who cheat on examinations. In a recent incident, a student caught cheating on college qualifying examinations told the press: "Everyone cheats; the only mistake I made was in getting caught." His attitude was based on the failure to set worthwhile goals for himself. From the shortsighted point of view that his goal was to pass the examination, he drew the faulty conclusion that the end justified the means. Had he been taught from early childhood that the only goal worth achieving was to bring his human actions into line with his divine Being, cheating could never have been considered to be a viable behavior. He would choose to act in the way which would enable him to be a person of fine character, thus setting an example for others who might be temporarily missing the mark, and also accelerating his progress toward his own goal.

We walk a tightrope when we are striving to achieve perfect balance and unity within ourselves. To bring our behavior into line with the laws of the Absolute, to abide by principles which are in tune with the Ideal Man, does not give us the right to judge, condemn, or attempt to reform others. Self-righteousness misses the mark also. We will never be able to live up to high ideals until we look within ourselves for them. We will never be able to correct faulty behaviors until we correct them within ourselves. Social consciousness begins with a selfsearch and ends with exemplifying those behaviors which we want to become predominant in the world. Then, whenever our duties fall into a category which entails identifying, legislating, or correcting faulty behaviors, we can perform those duties with self-confidence and love for our fellow man.

******

"The law was planted in the garden of the Brotherhood
to enlighten the heart of man
and to make straight before him
all the ways of true righteousness:
an humble spirit, an even temper,
a freely compassionate nature,
eternal goodness, understanding, and insight,
a mighty wisdom which believes in all God's works,
and a confident trust in His many blessings,
a spirit of knowledge in all things of the Great Order,
loyal feelings toward all the children of truth,
and a radiant purity which loathes everything impure. . ."

from the Manual of Discipline
of the Dead Sea Scrolls

39

THE MIRACLE OF MIRACLES

On the morning of December 1, 1988, I sat in ecstasy, watching as Bhagavan Sri Sathya Sai Baba made the rounds of the darshan area, accepting a letter or two here, manifesting vibhuti for someone there, giving joy to all who could witness his graceful walk and loving glance. It was my seventh trip to Prasanthi Nilayam, the first having been in 1981, and each visit has been as thrilling as the first. Even though Baba always follows a familiar routine, somehow each darshan is unique. One can never predict what He will do or who He will call in for an interview. Having only arrived the previous afternoon, I was caught completely off guard when I looked up to see my husband signaling me from the veranda. Before I could quite comprehend what was happening, the volunteers had taken hold of my wheelchair and pushed me up to the veranda. Baba greeted me, spoke to the friend with whom I had traveled, then came toward me with His arms stretched out as if He were going to take hold of my hands, but then, without touching me, He said, "Get up, get up!" I got up. It would never occur to me not to do anything Baba asked. The reaction of the group assembled for darshan surprised me: everyone clapped.

His remarks during the course of the interview seemed to me to center around the theme of Self-confidence. He spoke of the importance of having faith in God, faith in one's Self, and faith in the Self as God. I am sure that many of the devotees from Holland, Germany, India, and the United States, who were in that same interview, heard different things; but, for me, these were the central points. As the interview came to a close, Baba walked out and I followed. The wheelchair was waiting for me there on the veranda, and I realized that I had a choice. I could return to the chair, wait to be pushed back to Round Building One (a distance of about two city blocks, part of which is uphill and uneven with the additional hazard of loose stones), or I could accept the healing which had been offered. It was up to me. I chose to go forward, leaving the chair behind. My friend brought the empty chair as she left the veranda.

The questions I asked myself were: Do I have faith in Baba as God? Do I have faith in myself as God? Faith is the key issue. All Avatars, Masters, and healers have recognized the power of faith as the healer. Even allopathic physicians acknowledge the healing effect of the placebo and recognize the importance of the faith of the patient in the physician. Jesus told those that He healed: "Thy faith has made thee whole." Baba's mission, like Jesus', is not to do our work for us but to show us how to master the body and the senses.

The fall in which Baba fractured His hip was a vivid example to all of us of the importance of rising above pain. When asked, He said that His pain was great. He stressed the fact that His body was subject to natural law the same as ours. When we fall, the body reacts with pain. His does the same. But He was able to get up immediately to unlock the door of His room and only a few days later He stood for two and one-half hours in order to serve the devotees who had come to celebrate Onam at Prasanthi Nilayam. It was, He said, a matter of not allowing the mind to dwell on the pain. Whatever we give our attention to will assume importance and reality for us; therefore, to constantly repeat the name of God—to continually remember whatever

Chapter Thirty-Nine

form of God you love, and to accept your Self as God—these are the thoughts which will guide us into perfect equanimity and permanent peace.

I have suffered from painful knees since birth. The doctors called the condition "growing pains" when I was a child. They removed my tonsils and adenoids in an effort to alleviate the pain, but no treatment was ever effective. Many times in my teen years I had to withdraw from activity and retire to my bed, doubled up in agony. During college, motherhood, and a career in education, I was not bothered a great deal by the condition. However, twelve years ago, the pain and weakness increased to the point that I was barely able to walk. A team of specialists at Kaiser Permanente Hospital, California, U.S.A., took a series of X-rays and made extensive tests. The diagnosis was deterioration of the knee-joints which would progress with time. They recommended immediate surgery to replace the defective joints with artificial ones. However, they also told me that the success rate for such surgeries was low. (I understand it has since increased.) It was my decision to accept the crutches they offered me, rather than the surgery. As the condition worsened I went from crutches to a walker and finally to a wheelchair.

On my first visit to see Baba, I asked only for His love and for the opportunity to be His instrument. It was not until the third trip that I mentioned my physical problems to Him, and His response at that time was: "Forget it!" As I look back to the events of the past seven years, I see that there has been a steady and easily definable program of regeneration which has been going on in all of my attitudes and activities. I estimate that the same amount of progress might have taken lifetimes to achieve without the benefit of Swami's grace.

There were emotional problems, mental confusion, and ignorance to be overcome. These were brought to the surface one by one—sometimes through Baba's direct intervention and at other times through what appeared to be just coincidences. Some of these experiences have been mentioned in previous chapters. To quickly summarize, they involved learning to surrender the ego-will to the Divine Will (humility), balancing the male and female qualities, learning to love the Divine in others even when appearances might make them seem to be enemies, and many other developmental tasks easily recognizable to pilgrims on the spiritual path.

Last year, when Swami asked my husband what he wanted, he asked that Baba heal my knees. Baba placed His hands on my knees, indicated that He would do as Raye had requested, and said, "I will give her a lingam before you go." We thought that meant He would manifest a lingam for me, as He has done for others. However, in the second interview, He manifested a crystal japamala for me, but no lingam. This was a mystery to us until several months later we saw this quotation in *Sanathana Sarathi*:

"Swami is the very embodiment of compassion. He will pardon all errors. This principle which guides and guards you along the spiritual path is the lingam that is the center of consciousness, clustering around the inner and outer senses"

—*Chinna Katha,* page 155

I had realized, then, that the lingam which Baba had given me before I left was the pardon of my errors. They were not forgiven so that I could be free from punishment, but they were being corrected in order that I might not repeat them. The process has been dramatically difficult over the past year. Two major crises occurred which forced me to give up longstanding mistaken behaviors. Perhaps these behaviors had been obstacles to the healing of the knees.

Chapter Thirty-Nine

After Baba told me to "Get up!" I was questioned by physicians who were witnesses to the event, interviewed by editors from various publications, and photographed standing, walking, and sitting. The major question asked was: Was this a genuine miracle? I attempted to answer each question as factually as possible. In terms of any physical change, since there has not yet been (and probably will never be) any comparison of before and after X-rays, I can report only this: Prior to December 1, whenever I walked only a few steps, inflammation of the joints was so great that there was considerable heat and greatly increased pain for several days following. During the first two weeks of December, after walking more than I had walked for several years, there was no inflammation of the joints at all—no heat. Muscles which were being used after years of relative idleness reacted with soreness, but this was not out of the ordinary. Whether the condition will return or be permanently vanquished, remains to be seen. Swami has done His job. Now it is up to me to do mine.

I am, of course, extremely grateful for every aspect of this experience, but I know that Baba wants us to understand His adherence to the fulfillment of the law. He does not want anyone to be deceived into thinking that He has supernatural powers which are not available to everyone. He has continually stressed that He is God, and that each of us is God—that whatever He does is possible for us to do also. If rearranging molecules or exchanging one substance for another is considered miraculous, then He does perform miracles. Many hundreds of people can testify to witnessing such events. Regenerating a badly deteriorated knee joint is no more difficult than causing a ring to slip on the finger easily when seconds before no amount of force could push it on.

However, the miracle of all miracles is the unwavering, unchanging love which He pours out freely to everyone who will open his heart to receive it. What has happened in my experience is only a tiny speck of what has happened in the lives of hundreds of thousands of people. The miracle of miracles is a life regenerated. Baba's mission is to regenerate lives—and through such regeneration, to guide us into the realization of Advaita (unity with God) and the experience of peace on earth.

[This chapter was published in **Sanathana Sarathi,** January 1989]

40

"YOU ALWAYS WANT TO DO EVERYTHING JUST RIGHT"

For about two weeks after I had left the wheelchair behind, I walked from Round House One to darshan and back twice a day. My knees were quite free. The pain was either considerably less, or else I was successfully directing my attention to other things, or both. The muscles which hadn't been used to that extent for some time complained a bit, but that was not what put me back in the wheelchair. It was a respiratory condition.

I had been having difficulty with a lung or chest congestion situation for three or four years which had limited my ability to speak forcefully. The demands placed on me by walking required more oxygen and hence deeper breathing. In my opinion, this breathing caused some of the congestion to break up and enabled me to rid myself of it. However, I was unable to convince anyone else that the hacking, coughing, and spitting was a healing process. Everyone else was sure I was in the last stages of pneumonia and that I required medical help. My loving friends provided me with a homeopathic remedy, an herbal remedy, an ayurvedic remedy, and traditional over-the-counter remedies. I couldn't use them all, but the love which prompted the giving of them blessed me, warmed my heart, and certainly contributed to the healing which we all need so desperately: healing of our sense of separation from the All.

So it was back into the wheelchair while this bodily process was taking place, and that brought on another aspect of healing that was needed: pride! I wanted so much to continue walking, and I was obviously still attached to what others think. Even though I knew myself to be much freer of dependence on others to evaluate my worth or shortcomings, total independence was not yet a reality. Some only looked sad to see me back in the wheelchair, but others openly reacted, asking questions which bordered on being critical or unkind. Finally, one friend went to the hospital and asked that a doctor visit me in my room. She told me this only after she had done it, saying that the doctor would be there as soon as she had completed her rounds at the hospital. When she came, I immediately felt the love with which she practiced her profession. I explained to her that I preferred not to take antibiotics. She took my temperature and found it to be perfectly normal. Leaving the thermometer with me, she asked that I take my temperature four times a day and write down the readings for her. She came to see me daily, but never attempted to force me to do anything which conflicted with my own inner guidance. When it seemed that the worst of the accumulation of mucous had been eliminated, I elected to begin walking again in the mornings while my energy was high, but gratefully accepted the generosity of friends who volunteered to push me in the afternoons.

Then the next challenge presented itself. A minor abrasion on a toe became infected. I dabbed a little medicine on it, cleaned it with alcohol two or three times a day, but it continued to get worse. When one of the friends who sometimes pushed the wheelchair for me in the afternoons saw it, he was quite disturbed. That afternoon he took me to the apartment of a doctor from California, who is also a friend, and asked that he look at the toe. By this time, I must admit that it was not a pretty sight. He prescribed both antibiotic ointment and oral antibiotics, and said that it was not at all wise to be walking on a foot

Chapter Forty

in that condition. I acquiesced. Again, I felt love to be the active ingredient; it was there in generous amounts. And I became a full-time wheelchair patient again.

The toe was almost completely healed when the time of my visit came to an end, but the real healing was the one which took place inside. Swami so often says: "Both are right," when referring to a disagreement between two devotees. I saw quite clearly that the only illness from which I—or anyone else—suffer, is ignorance. And in this case, the ignorance (ego) showed itself as pride and judgment. I judged myself to be better when I walked than when I had to be pushed. Then I judged myself to be better when I abstained from antibiotics than when I accepted them. I realized that I had fallen into the right/wrong good/bad trap again. Oh, dear Baba, thank you for giving me the experiences I need to draw closer to realization of everpresent, all-inclusive rightness.

He began working with me on this lesson before I had been in the ashram twenty-four hours, both providing the experience which would bring about awareness and stimulating the self-inquiry which would result in knowledge. During the interview, He gave me an oral examination. Questions and answers are not only a good teaching technique for an entire class, but they become indelibly engraved on the mind of the one who is being asked. One of the questions He asked me was: "What is religion?" I replied from the standpoint of knowledge and sophistication, saying, "It is a systematized series of beliefs." His response was: "Oh, no. A religion is a path to God." He was pointing out to me—and to approximately thirty others in the room—that all religions are right! Not all are appropriate for me—not all are appropriate for anyone—and there are some people for whom none are appropriate at their present stage of development; but everything that is, is right, useful, and purposeful for someone at some time. It is not my business to judge them, to give them negative labels, to call them good or bad, right or wrong. Each of them is a legitimate growth experience for those who choose them.

Then He added still another experience to help reinforce the lesson. One morning, as I sat in the wheelchair waiting to be allowed to go through the gate, a lady whom I could not recall having ever seen before came up to me as if we had been friends for a long time and were now reunited. She leaned over and hugged me with great enthusiasm. She mentioned something about seeing auras and what a beautiful soul I was, while I was trying desperately to place her. She spoke English with an accent I couldn't identify. She was statuesque, dressed with exquisite taste in a silk sari embroidered with gemstones, and—as it was later revealed—I had never seen her before.

She was from Denmark. This was her first trip to see Swami, but she had been consciously following a path toward God since early childhood. She sometimes burst into song spontaneously and said that she frequently seemed to know things about people without the knowledge coming through what we consider to be the normal channels. She offered to come to our apartment and give each of us a massage, and we sidestepped the offer. She came anyway, and her massage was very relaxing. During the time she was there, she suddenly began singing what sounded like an aria from some unknown opera, and her voice had the power of a well-trained contralto. Raye and I expected to be waited upon by the accommodations office for disturbing the peace, but there were no such repercussions.

I was constantly trying to fit her into some familiar category, but she wouldn't fit conveniently into any slot my mind devised. For one thing, she smoked! Obviously no one who is seriously on a spiritual path smokes—right? And she drank coffee—frequently. Well, a cup of coffee now and then is not so bad, but I felt that she undoubtedly had exceeded the limit.

I not only judged her by externals, but I realized later that I had been judging myself as unworthy of receiving her loving

Chapter Forty

attention. She sent me roses on several occasions and each time I accepted them I felt slightly uncomfortable. Then two or three days before Christmas, she came to the apartment and brought a gift for me. It was a heartshaped box of typical Indian craftsmanship and inside was a beautiful brooch. She said, "I have brought you some garnets." The brooch was in the form of a spray of flowers and was made up of rhinestones and darker stones, which I presumed to be garnets as she had said. Then she continued very confidently: "If you will take this with you to darshan the morning after Christmas, Swami will come right to you and will bless it."

Well, that statement confirmed all my previous suspicions. Nobody predicts what Swami will do! I had no intention whatsoever of taking the box to darshan the day after Christmas. My early training surfaced, and I tried to figure out how to give the brooch back to her without hurting her feelings. "You just don't accept gifts from strangers," was deeply engraved on my neural pathways from frequent repetition by parents, relatives, teachers, and friends. So the box sat on the table in our apartment for two or three days. The day after Christmas, as I was preparing to leave for darshan, I saw it sitting there and debated whether or not to drop it into my shoulder bag. "Well, it can't hurt to carry it," I decided. So I arrived at the ladies' gate with the heartshaped box and the brooch. While I was waiting for the Seva Dals to signal that they were ready for us to go in, someone came up to me, handed me three roses, and said that the Danish lady had sent them.

At that moment we were called to go in, so with no time to give the whole dilemma any further consideration, I went in and took my seat as directed by the volunteers. When we were all seated, I became aware that the lady next to me was going through her purse frantically. She took everything out finally and shook her purse, looking quite distressed. I glanced over to see if I might be of any help, and she told me that this was her last darshan. She had to leave. She had not been called in for an interview. This was her first trip to see Swami, and she hadn't really had any interaction with Him at all. She had written Him a letter, but through some mix-up (or leela) she had left it in her room.

She seemed so disturbed and disappointed that I felt led to try to help. So quickly asking Baba to use me as His instrument, I suggested that she have someone give Him the letter for her at a later darshan. Then I held out the three roses to her. I said, "Take one of these." There was one red, one white, and one lovely shade of pale orange. She selected the orange one. I said, "When Baba comes, hold out the rose to Him. Whether He takes it or not, He may pause long enough for you to tell Him that you're leaving today." She seemed much happier, sitting there with the rose in her hand. We watched the corner of the veranda intently, waiting for the first sight of Baba's approach. Would He come to the chairs, or would He head straight for the ladies' gate without giving us even a glance? He had done the latter day after day until the "chair people" hardly dared to hope any more.

We caught a glimpse of orange. Could it be coming toward us? It was! We held our breath, and there He was. My new friend was holding out the rose to Him, saying "I'm leaving today, Swami." He replied, "I know, I know. You two were sitting here talking about the letter." He touched the rose and turned to me. I had the box with the brooch in it in my hand and He took it. He opened the box, lifted the top layer of cotton, looked intently at the brooch, then returned it to me, saying, "Keep it!"

We were in bliss as Swami continued His rounds, selected those for interview, and disappeared with them into the interview room. My friend was carefully placing her rose in an envelope, and she said to me: "This will be my most valuable possession." In a few seconds, Baba had given one devotee proof that He knew everything she thought and everything she said. She left, feeling that she had the answer to the question she had come with. Yes, He is just what He says He is. He can know even the most insignificant details about the lives of thousands upon thousands of people and confer upon each just what he needs to move him along his desired path to union with God.

As for me, He had driven home once again the lesson which seemed to be one of the most important ones of this trip. I was judging again, according to my old moralistic, behavioristic standards—not according to the divine reality of the Atma within every one. When He said, "Keep it!" in those two words He wiped out all of the right/wrong good/bad thoughts I had been attempting to use as a basis for my decisions. For reasons which I did not need to know or attempt to analyze, my Danish friend was doing whatever she needed to do to carry her along her chosen path. She had been Swami's instrument in providing the rose which brought such joy and validation for a devotee on her last darshan. And she had been the instrument Swami used to help me learn the thing I certainly needed to learn: unconditional love for myself and for others.

When I had the opportunity to tell her what had happened, she seemed pleased, but not at all surprised. After Swami had told me to keep the brooch, I took it out of its box to really look at it. As I did, I noticed immediately that the darker stones were not garnets. They were amethysts. I showed the brooch to her and pointed out that the stones were amethysts and not garnets as she had mentioned that they were. She replied, "They were garnets when I gave them to you."

I don't know whether they were garnets or amethysts. It doesn't strike me as being nearly as important as learning the good/bad lesson through such a pleasant and entertaining experience. However, other interesting tidbits were added to the feast when, upon return to our home and Center, I was sharing the experiences of our trip with other devotees. As I finished telling the story of the brooch, one member remarked, "It was an amethyst that was given to you on a previous trip by Marie Idol."

And I said, "That's right!" Marie and I had discussed the ring on this last trip, but the connection had not occurred to me. I had received amethysts as gifts twice in Prasanthi Nilayam. A coincidence? Then another gentleman spoke up: "I just happen to have brought these two pages with me today." And he held up two loose pages which he had copied and brought with him. The title on the heading was: "The Transformational Properties of Gems and Minerals." Another coincidence? He left the pages for me and after the meeting was over, I began reading about garnets and amethysts.

"**Garnet** — strengthens, purifies, vitalizes, and regenerates bodily systems, especially the bloodstream. Has strong affinity with root chakra, helping to harmonize the potent forces of the kundalini. Stimulates pituitary gland. Aligns subtle bodies. Love, compassion. Enhances imagination. Chakras: root, heart.

"**Amethyst** — A variety of quartz. Strengthens endocrine and immune systems. Enhances right brain activity and pineal and pituitary glands. Powerful blood cleanser and energizer. Helps mental disorders. Purification and regeneration on all levels of consciousness. Transmutes one's lower nature into the more highly refined aspects of their higher potentials. Physical representative of the Violet Ray of alchemy and transformation. Cuts through illusion. Enhances psychic abilities. Excellent for meditation. Calming, strong, protective qualities. Healing, divine love, inspiration, intuition. Chakras: third eye, crown."

Had I been offered the opportunity to choose between the two, I think I might have chosen the amethysts. Perhaps someday Swami will tell me something that will shed more light on whether He had anything to do with them being amethysts or not.

Chapter Forty

As I pondered these experiences, I recalled a comment that Baba had made to me last year. When I asked Him to please tell me if I had done anything wrong or said anything in my book which was not correct, He replied: "I know, I know. You always want to do everything just right." I thought at the time that He had paid me a compliment! I thought that in order to be right, I had to do right—which brought about the logical conclusion that for others to be right, they had to do right. Now He was teaching me that right and wrong is only a part of the delusion—the ignorance from which the ego suffers. It is only when the positive and negative come together into a blissful unity of Being that we can even begin to see Light at the end of the dark tunnel. But our path is easy and our way is clear when Baba, who is the Light, is here to transform our lower nature into the more highly refined aspects of the Self, to provide the gems of experience from which we can best move onward and upward, and to guide us safely home to merge into the Light with Him.

"Love yourself and love others. This is true worship."
—Baba
November 23, 1988

I LOVE MYSELF THE WAY I AM

I love myself the way I am
    There's nothing I need to change.
I'll always be the perfect me
    There's nothing to rearrange.
I'm beautiful, I'm capable
    of becoming the way I began,
And I love myself just the way I am.

I love you the way you are
    There's nothing you need to do.
When I feel the love inside myself
    It's easy to love you.
Behind your fears, your rage and tears,
    I see your shining star,
And I love you just the way you are.

I love the world the way it is
    'cause I can clearly see
That all the things I judge are done
    By people just like me.
So tell the world of peace on earth
    That only love can bring
And help it grow by loving everything.

I love myself the way I am
    And still I want to grow
For change outside can only come
    When deep inside I know
I'm beautiful, I'm capable
    Of becoming the way I began,
And I love myself just the way I am.

—J. Josephs

41

"BLESSED ARE THEY THAT MOURN..."

It was my intention that, sometime during our stay at the ashram in 1988, I would ask Baba to clarify His teaching in regard to sympathy. He says, "Feel another's pain or sorrow as though it were your own." I don't seem to have too much difficulty doing that, but I have always questioned the value of it. It seemed to me that to sympathize with anyone was to simply take on another's pain and hurt along with the sorrowful one, thus two people suffered and nobody gained. I knew I must be missing the point in some way because I've learned that Baba's teachings are not to be questioned. His personal direction may vary from person to person and from situation to situation, but His basic teachings are Truth of the highest order.

When we were called in for interview, all of my questions were swallowed up in the joy of being in Swami's presence. I couldn't even remember what I had wanted to ask. But He always knows and answers, whether we remember or not. If we stay tuned in by keeping our Awareness turned on, we will hear the answer quite clearly.

Each morning and afternoon at darshan, in the ladies' chair section, we naturally saw the same people. Our chairs would be arranged differently but since we were so few in number, we frequently sat by or near the same person. One of the ladies was of Indian descent, but she had been born in London and had always lived in England. She had come to see Swami to seek His help for her baby who had been brain damaged by the use of forceps in delivery. Baba had spoken to her very lovingly on several occasions and had manifested vibhuti for her and her child two or three times. I have a precious picture in my photograph album of Swami putting vibhuti on the baby's forehead. However, He did not call her in for an interview. When the time came for her to leave, she had a letter she hoped to give Him, but He did not come to the chair section that day. I was sitting next to her, and I could feel her pain very much as if it were my own. I struggled to hold back my tears, and she did the same. We said our good-byes. She gave me the letter she had hoped to give to Swami, asking that I try to give it to Him before I left. Her pain was with me intensely that day and was renewed each day as I held her letter in my hand, hoping to hand it to Him. But He did not come near.

There was another lady that I had seen frequently in the chair section. The first day she arrived at the ashram, I had noticed her. She had on a white eyelet embroidered sari, so I knew that her husband was deceased. (Only widows wear white in India.) She was not Indian, but I knew that she would have been advised of the custom wherever she purchased the sari. When I attempted to tell her how attractive her sari was, she did not understand right away. I realized, then, that she spoke very little English. She was from Luxembourg and spoke mostly German. She was able to say, in response to my comment, that it was her birthday. We smiled at each other, for smiles require no interpreter, and I thought no more about her.

I had selected four of the nicest medallions from those my husband had painstakingly sought in the shops, and hoped that Baba would bless them. I wanted to give one to the lady from London for her baby. That day He came to the chairs. What a glorious day it was! I held out the medallions to Him and He gave

Chapter Forty-One

them a touch with His hand, imbuing them with His vibrations and His love. After He had gone over to the men's side and we could no longer see Him, I gave the little plastic envelope with the four blessed treasures to the baby's Mother and she picked out the one she wanted for her son.

When she handed the envelope back, I remembered the lady from Luxembourg and that it was her birthday. As she was sitting about a half-dozen seats away from me, but in the same row, I passed the envelope to Roxanne Morgan, a friend from California who was about halfway between us, and asked that she pass it down with the message that the German-speaking lady could choose whichever she wanted for her birthday. When Swami had gone inside with those He had selected for interview, Roxanne handed the envelope back to me with the two remaining medals.

Days passed. The baby's mother pinned his medallion on his little blue corduroy overalls each day, and I always felt happy to see it. The lady from Luxembourg also wore hers every day. She had bought a very pretty chain to go with it, or perhaps it was one she had brought with her, but, at any rate, it was just right. I felt a warm glow, knowing that they were happy to have Baba's picture always near their hearts.

Then a few days after the baby and his mother had left, my German-speaking friend was leaving, too. It was her last darshan. She had not been called for interview, and she had a letter she wanted to give Swami, but He did not even glance in our direction. Again I felt an overwhelming sense of sorrow for her pain. I had never told her that I had been the one who had sent the medallion to her, thinking that it was dharmic behavior not to look for any credit for good deeds or thanks for gifts. Then I suddenly realized that she did not know that Baba had blessed the medallion. I quickly had to decide which behavior was, in fact, the most dharmic under the circumstances. If I told her, I might lose credit for a selfless service, but if I did not tell her, I would rob her of the comfort of knowing that she had an object in her possession which had been blessed by Swami. I decided to tell her. When I told her what had happened, she seemed to understand every word. She said she was very surprised to learn that it had been a gift from me because she had thought it had come from the other American lady, but her joy that it had been blessed by Swami was all that mattered. She handed me the letter she had written to her beloved Lord and asked me to try to give it to Him for her. As she saw my moist eyes, she pointed to hers. She said in perfect English, "I have tears in my eyes, too." We embraced each other, sharing both our pain and our love.

A week later, I was still carrying both of the letters which had been entrusted to me. Swami had not been to the ladies' chair section for over two weeks and now it was my last day at the ashram. I prayed very hard that He come to us—that He at least give a little glance in our direction—but neither prayer was answered. I had wondered what I would do if such a thing happened. My sorrow when it had happened to the others was so deep and so painful, I had thought it might be unbearable if it happened to me. I could see that others were feeling for me. So much love surrounded me, I felt wrapped in the warmth of it. To my great surprise, instead of being plunged into depression and despair, I felt a great peace. Joy seemed to come from deep inside me, expanding and expanding into an unbounded bliss. I was able to say my good-byes to all of the beautiful souls who had been serving Swami so faithfully day after day, never thinking of themselves or their needs, but paying very close attention to see that all of our needs were met. I passed the two letters on to Roxanne, hoping that she might be able to give them to Him.

My husband was waiting for me near the gate. As soon as he could, he spoke to me to tell me that Swami had come to him. When he had told our Baba that we were leaving, He had replied,

Chapter Forty-One

"Be happy!" He had not looked in my direction. He had not called me for a second interview, which I had prayed for, and He had not taken the letters I had so hoped to give Him, but He knew all about them. He had answered the question which I would have asked Him in the interview, and I know that He answered the letters also.

The bliss which I was feeling was greater than happiness. It was a calm, peaceful, unshakable joy. It continued through the hectic last minute details of storing the furniture in the kitchen, getting the suitcases to the cab, and dealing with all of the demanding porters. It surrounded us on the long, rough, dusty ride to Bangalore. It was with me as we arrived at our hotel, settled into our room. The desk clerks, room boys, doorman, and waiters were all so happy to see us. They were especially delighted to see me walking. When I had arrived only a month before, I had been unable to walk to the elevator. Now I was going all over the hotel, leaving the wheelchair in the room. The bliss I felt seemed to be contagious. Our overnight in Bangalore was a joy, and our trip on to Madras a pleasure. The feeling of all-pervading bliss gradually dissipated, but I feel it again whenever I remember.

After I arrived home, Swami gave me the words to go with the experience. My thought turned to the Beatitudes. The one: "Blessed are they that mourn, for they shall be comforted," had always been a mystery to me. I had pondered its meaning numerous times without ever feeling any sense of resolution. But now I knew exactly what it meant, and I knew the answer to the question I had wanted to ask Baba. Those who mourn for others, feeling their pain as though it were their own, are blessed. And the blessing is that when they themselves have to go through hard experiences, they are comforted, not only by the love which flows abundantly through others, but also by the Bliss which is God. It is the Ananda, the essence of their own Being which is experienced. My soul is blissful; my intellect is satisfied;

and I'm closer to my Lord than I could ever have been in darshan or an interview. I am truly comforted.

But the story was not yet finished. It may never be. Growth and expansion may be the law of Being. I have on my desk a birthday card from my stepfather which says "To a Wonderful Daughter." And it's true. I am full of wonder at the beautiful ways our Swami works to bring about Love in the world.

As for being much of a daughter to my stepfather, however, I'm afraid I've been pretty much of a failure. He married my mother after I had married for the second time and was living in California with my husband and the two children I had brought to the second marriage from the first. It must have been about 1956 or 57. Mother was visiting us in California. Her home was in Florida. And this man she had met when he was vacationing in Florida called her at our house and asked her to come to Chicago and marry him. I didn't know him and didn't really care to get acquainted. I would have preferred to keep my mommy all to myself. I had never gotten over the deprivation of love that I experienced when we were separated for eight very important years in my childhood. Subsequently, my mother and I worked through our relationship and achieved a very peaceful love between us that was seldom contaminated by attachment.

But by then my stepfather and I had each settled into the rut of a non-caring relationship. He was openly hostile and critical of me at times (especially about my "kooky New Age beliefs"), and I was indifferent to him. However, when my mother became ill, he cared for her so lovingly that I began to see him in a different light. He became even more critical of me, however, feeling that I was not as attentive to my mother as I should have been. I spoke to mother on the telephone frequently, and she knew that I loved her very deeply. We both understood that our relationship had matured—grown beyond any need for each other's physical presence. If my own health had been more vigorous, I would have gone to help with the chores. But since they lived on the

Chapter Forty-One

second floor of a condominium complex, I felt that my presence would not have been of any help at all—rather it probably would only have made things more difficult for Frank. Even though he is small, wiry, and in excellent health, he is eighty-four years old and does not need any unnecessary stress.

When my mother shed her body, he called as he said he felt it was his duty to do since I was "the daughter." But he made it fairly clear that I hadn't been much of one! I dealt with grief for a time, but Swami's teachings about death made it much easier than I could have imagined. When Frank called again to tell me that he had decided to keep my mother's ashes in the apartment with him "because I have no one else to talk to," I felt my heart break. It broke open to let this man in that I had kept out for so many years. Swami says, "Sometimes I have to break a heart in order to get in." And both He and Jesus teach: "Inasmuch as ye have done it unto the least of these, my brethren, ye have done it unto Me." And so I determined that, whether Frank wanted to hear from me or not, I would write to him as often as I could. I would try to be the kind of daughter for him that he wanted—one who was dutiful and attentive. His own daughter's death some fifteen or twenty years ago had caused him great suffering.

And so I began to write short letters to him, in each one telling him that I loved him and expressing an interest in his activities and his welfare. Occasionally I got an answer, very impersonal but less critical. On February fourth (my sixty-third birthday) I received a card from him which read: "Daughter, some things change, but you just go on being wonderful." It was the best birthday present I could ever have received. It proves that "Love is reflected in Love." If we want to be loved, we must love. I am so grateful to our precious Baba. He heals all of our relationships as well as all of our diseases. And I can testify from the standpoint of experience that when we feel another's pain as our own, He comforts us by giving us the greatest of all experiences: the Bliss of Being, the deep joy of Awareness.

And the mundane wants get taken care of also—not as we outline with our own little desires for everything to go just as we have planned—but in His perfect timing and delicately balanced design, He gives us every good thing. The two letters which I had left with Roxanne were still undelivered when it was time for her to leave the ashram and return to the States. She passed them to Sundarum, another devotee who was staying longer, and asked that every effort be made to give them to Swami. Both she and I felt a wonderful sense of comfort and completion when she received a letter saying: "About a week after you left, Swami took the letters. He looked at them with great interest. He didn't say anything, but your friends will be glad to know that they did get into His Divine Hands. The date was Sunday, January 8, at morning darshan."

42

"WHAT IS YOUR NAME?"

Swami asked me the question: "What is your name?" in 1987, and I told Him. Again in 1988 He asked, "What is your name?" I replied, "Joy, Swami." And He continued, "Second name?" I responded, "Thomas." At the time, the question seemed to me to be almost a rejection. "Doesn't He even know my name?" I thought. He knows everything; why does He have to ask me my name?" Happily I did not have to be stuck in such ego-musings for long. It was not a logical reaction. I know that Swami does not ask questions of us for His information, but for our transformation. Thus his question: "Second name?" was the beginning of the Thomas story for me.

It had been a continuing saga with Raye for several years. Someone had mentioned to him that Thomas, Jesus' disciple called Didymus, had established a church in Madras, India, and that it could be visited. He had attempted in 1985, 1986, 1987, and again in 1988 to schedule enough time in Madras to visit the St. Thomas Church, but something had arisen each time to make it impossible or, at least, very inconvenient. On the last day of our 1988-89 trip, Swami came to Raye in darshan and Raye said, "Leaving today, Swami." Baba replied, "Leaving? Be happy!"

On arrival in Bangalore, we found that our flight to Madras had been rescheduled to leave early the following morning instead of in the afternoon. This meant that we would have an unexpected layover of several hours in Madras. From that point on, everything that happened seemed programmed toward a visit to the St. Thomas Church. With the extra time in Madras, we made a hotel reservation. The hotel shuttle bus was waiting for us on our arrival and we were comfortably settled in our hotel room twelve hours before the departure of our flight to Singapore. Raye asked the clerk at the desk if he knew where to locate the church, and he replied, "Of course. You can see it from here. Come, I'll show you." A few minutes later, we were in a taxi, winding our way up a narrow dirt road to a church on a hilltop.

The church itself was a modest gray building; but, on a promontory overlooking the valley, stood a beautiful statue of Jesus on the cross with a man and woman at the foot of the cross—presumably Mary, the mother of Jesus, and the Apostle Thomas. We were somewhat at a loss, however, to know how to go about getting answers to our questions as there seemed to be no one around. A plaque near the statue marked the spot that Pope John Paul II had stood when, in 1986, he had addressed the St. Thomas Christians seated on the slopes below.

We went inside the church to see if we could learn more about Thomas and found another plaque with this inscription: "It was here that St. Thomas the Apostle was pierced with a lance and killed. There is now evidence that the stone cross on the altar was made by St. Thomas himself.... The picture of Our Lady seen on the main altar was brought to India by St. Thomas when he came here."

While Raye was taking a picture of the plaque so that we could have the information on it without having to copy it off, I sat on one of the pews in back of the church where a nativity scene had been placed in a niche. Two nuns were standing in

Chapter Forty-Two

front of the small creche in an attitude of devotion. When they turned and started to walk away, I suddenly felt guided to speak to them. "Do you speak English?" I asked. One of them indicated that she did. I asked her if she could tell me more about the church and about Thomas. She said that Thomas had come to India in the year 52 A.D. He landed at Cranganore and built seven churches there before coming to this area. He had lived at Mylapore, preached at Little Mount, and was martyred on this site, which was called St. Thomas Mount, in 72 A.D.

I was surprised to learn of the other two churches nearby which were so closely connected with Thomas, but since our taxi driver spoke no English and seemed not to know anything about any of them, it was highly unlikely that we could find them. It then occurred to me to ask the Sisters if they would be able to help us direct the taxi driver to find the other two sites, possibly even to go with us there so that we might get some information to help us know what we were seeing while we were there. They said that, as a matter of fact, they could and would be very pleased to do so.

Suddenly we became a party of four friends, touring the historical spots relating to Thomas. The Sister who spoke English was a teacher of the deaf in Kerala State, and her companion was a working Sister, both Indian. We went first to a church which had been constructed over an underground cave. The entry to the cave was in the foyer, down a flight of stairs, and through a very narrow opening. Sister explained that Thomas had been meditating and praying in this cave when he was set upon by a band of persecutors. He managed to slip away and get to Little Mount, but they followed, caught up with him, and murdered him with a spear.

We proceeded from there to the place of his burial. After duly noting the points of interest, we asked the Sisters if we could take them to wherever they were staying. They said that their boarding house was just across the street from where we were, so it was not necessary to take them anywhere. They said that they had not been inconvenienced in any way by taking us on the tour because they would have had to take the bus back. By riding with us in the taxi, they had been able to serve as our guides and yet arrive at their temporary residence at just about the same time that they would have, had they taken the bus.

At one point during our tour, wanting to write something down, I had started fishing into the collection of miscellaneous accumulation in my huge handbag in an attempt to find a pen. The teaching Sister had opened her very small cloth purse and taken out a little plastic ball point pen and lent it to me. Knowing how highly prized ball point pens are in India, I was careful to return it and Sister replaced it in her little zippered bag. As we were saying our good-byes, she again brought out the pen, handed it to me, and said that she would like me to have it as a gift with her good wishes for a very happy journey back to the United States. My first impulse was to say, "Oh, no, I can't take your pen!" I knew that in the bottom of my handbag, which now seemed to me to be too big and to contain too much, there were probably a half-dozen pens. But I could not refuse the love with which the pen was offered. It was a true gift and would, therefore, bless both the giver and the receiver.

How good our God is! He fulfilled Raye's desire to see the St. Thomas Church more fully than he ever expected. As He had told us in 1981, "I am prepared to give you whatever you want." Then He told him to "Be happy!" and provided the one experience which would give him the greatest happiness. Baba further stimulated my desire to understand my true nature, as indicated by my second name, Thomas. And He showed me His love, expressing it through the instruments of the two dear nuns. He provided additional income for the taxi driver, an opportunity for the Sisters to serve others, which was clearly understood by them to be serving their beloved Lord, and a very pleasant day for all concerned. Our stay at the hotel was relaxing and our

Chapter Forty-Two

departure from Madras the easiest we had ever experienced.

I knew that my own part of the Thomas incident was not yet complete. At this time, I still only identified him with the appellation "Doubting Thomas," and I was not at all clear how this applied to me. If I was one of little faith, I did not yet know in what area this manifested itself or how I could correct it. I turned all of this over in my mind a number of times on the way back to Los Angeles and asked Baba in my prayers to please help me learn whatever I needed to learn.

We arrived at the Los Angeles airport late on a Friday evening. The following Sunday morning I turned the television station to a program that a friend had mentioned as being new since I had left and one that I might enjoy. To my delight, it was announced that the topic for the program that day was *The Gospel According to Thomas.* This was more serendipitous than I could have imagined. The announcer even gave the address of a bookstore from which the book could be ordered, and I phoned in my order the same day.

I began to read the book immediately upon its arrival. It not only had the 114 verses attributed to Thomas, but it also contained several complementary texts. It was from these scholarly treatises that the completed message emerged. Elton Hall wrote in an essay entitled "The Gnostic Transmission": "'Doubting Thomas' is often thought of as the weakest of the disciples because he questioned whether the being who appeared to the disciples after the resurrection was Jesus.... The Gnostic gospels do not portray a vacillating Thomas. Rather, he is initiated into the Mysteries by Jesus as a spiritual companion. Presumably his 'doubt' is the insistence on seeing firsthand the marks of the Initiate, symbolically given as the wounds suffered in the crucifixion." I realized, then, that Thomas, understanding the tremendous difference between knowledge and Awareness, did not want this momentous event to become mere knowledge for him. He did not want to pass up the opportunity to increase his Awareness.

If you would like to experience the difference between these two, just take two beautiful pictures and place them before you. Be sure that one of the pictures is of a place you have seen in person and that the other is not. You will note that you have a much more intimate feeling for places which you have visited than you have for those you have not seen before—no matter how beautiful the latter may be.

When my beloved Baba (in the flesh) asked me where I had come from, I kept trying to tell Him I had come from California. He refused to accept that simplistic response, continuing to ask the question until I opened my heart to hear the answer. Then it came from within: "You have emerged from Me and you will merge with Me again." He might easily have told me the answer to His question, but He wanted me to experience having the answer come from Omnipresent Wisdom, in order that I might feel a more intimate identification with it. Now He was asking for my name—my identity. Again, He was unwilling to accept my superficial reply. He doesn't want to know what name is shown on my passport. He wants me to know my true identity—my true nature. As in the first instance, when ruminating on the question brought about a Holy message and a deep inner knowing, I had to continue searching for the answer until it came—not through books or anyone else's words, but through my own firsthand experience. I saw so clearly that Thomas was not a doubter; he was only unwilling to accept secondhand information about anything so intimately connected with his beloved Jesus or about anything with such enormous implications for him in his search for his own identity.

And so I began to ask: "What is my name? What is my nature? Who am I really?" Oh, I could have given a discourse in reply to those questions, but this time I knew that I did not want a mind-answer. I would continue asking until I received a heart-reply from deep within my Self. Finally it came. It was not an unfamiliar reply. But I was beginning to be able to tell the

Chapter Forty-Two

difference between the voice of the intellect and that of the heart. From deep within my Soul came a faint echo, a sound from very far away, and it uttered three words: "**Sat-Chit-Ananda** (Being-Awareness-Bliss)."

I was left with no doubt. My name, my nature, is Being-Awareness-Bliss. These were no longer just words; I had felt them, experienced them firsthand. Being had been experienced when He had graced my meditation with the utter stillness of which one is aware only in the absence of thought. Awareness was experienced when His persistence in questioning resulted in my increased attention, alertness to the little incidents of His drama which I call my life. And Bliss was experienced when I no longer attempted to separate Being and Awareness or to allow them to seem separate to me. Being was seen to be the essence of Becoming; Becoming, as the expression of Being; and the Bliss of their Oneness, as who I am.

Frequently I have felt a need for validation after such a revelation, but no such desire was present following this one. The experience was complete, but validation came anyway. It was evidence of His love, the abundance of the Grace with which He showers us. As I continued reading **The Gospel According to Thomas**, I came to the first validation in stanza 13. After Jesus had questioned His disciples in regard to who He was, Thomas had replied: "Truly, Master, my mouth cannot bring itself to utter comparisons." Jesus commended Thomas with the words: "I am no longer your Master. You have drunk from the bubbling fountain which I brought, and you are drunk [God-intoxicated]." Thomas had drunk from the living water—the Truth of Being—which Jesus came to reveal to all who would see and hear. Now he would no longer need to partake of Jesus' inspiration. He would be drinking from the fountain of Omnipresent Wisdom. The verse continues: "He took Thomas aside and said three words to him." My soul knew those three words; they were Being-Awareness-Bliss.

I continued reading. All of the words were illumined. When I came to stanza 50, I found further validation. It reads:

> "If you are asked your origins, answer: 'We have come out of the Light where the light came of itself. It rested, appearing in their Image.' If you are asked your identity, answer: 'We are His sons, the Elect of the Living Father.' If asked for a sign of your Father, answer: 'Movement and Repose.'

This was Advaitic teaching, the Oneness which Baba is emphasizing more and more in His discourses today. He tells us that He identifies Himself with the ocean (Movement and Repose), but that we identify ourselves only with the waves (Movement). How can the movement of the ocean be separated from the ocean itself? We emerged (Movement) from the Light where it rested (Repose). We are His sons (Movement), set apart by the divine favor of the Living Father (Repose). When we become aware of our true being, we will rest in action (change) and continually progress in unchanging Bliss, all-inclusive, all-expressive Divine Love.

Feeling completely enfolded in that Love, that Bliss, I read on. It was on page 70 that the entire experience was brought into perfect focus in a few words. Elton Hall, further elucidating the teachings of the Gnostics, states:

> ...the descent of the Logos is the revelation of the Name. The emancipating reversal of consciousness is effected by the discovery of one's real name. The Christos, who is the Name of the Unnameable, descends as a Light consubstantial with the imprisoned Light that constitutes the essence of every human being. Man discovers the greater Light by releasing the Light within himself. This epiphany [intuitive grasp of reality] is epistemic, [gnosis or

esoteric knowledge of spiritual Truth], for evil, corruption, delusion, and confusion are the result of ignorance (agnosis), a deficiency of unbound Light. Freedom consists in self-knowledge, a discovery of one's name (that is, real immortal nature) through hearing the teaching of the Name, who is the Christos. Self-knowledge leads to—and in fact is identical with—knowledge of the Father, because all human beings are sons of God. This spiritual knowledge is Truth, and its ontic correlate in consciousness is indescribable joy, the unconditional Bliss which is the afflatus [gift] of the Unnameable, the Ananda of Hindu and Buddhist traditions.

Baba has told us all of these things in His discourses, and therefore we have heard the teaching of the Name again and again. This has prepared us for the experience of self-knowledge through discovery. He stimulates our inner search by asking questions and providing experiences which will lead us inexorably home to Him and enable us to dwell forever in the Abode of Eternal Peace.

Sarvadharma Emblem
Unity Of All Religions

43

DANTE CALLED YOU BEATRICE

"[Mohammed remained] days and nights together in prayer and meditation... At length, it is said, what had hitherto been shadowed out in dreams was made apparent and distinct...."
—Washington Irving
The Life of Mohammed

Oh, my beloved, what shall I call you? My Swami, my Baba, you have been so dear to my heart through eons of time and in All which is timeless. How can it be told to those who will not hear? How can the music of the spheres be made appreciable to the tone-deaf? Can the blind see the delicate colors of the rainbow, or the wingless feel the thrill of flight?

Shall I tell them: "When you have prepared a place for Him, He will come. Make of your heart a Prasanthi Nilayam, and He will abide with you for ever"? It has all been said over and over again, but unbelievers remain unbelievers still. Gautama called you Nirvana. Mohammed called you Gabriel. Saint Paul called you Christ. Jesus called you the Kingdom of Heaven or the Kingdom of God. If I call you My Heart, My Swami, My Baba, there are some who profess to know You who will stand aghast. But those who truly know You will rejoice.

You have come again and again, but not yet to stay, as You promised. With each visit, Love has expanded, fear has decreased, Joy has blossomed, and sadness has almost entirely disappeared. Understanding has been recognized to be secondary to Peace, and Contentment is among all things most desirable. I can now accept You, surrender to You, and trust You, because You have patiently given me many validations of Your trustworthiness. How can I deny You, sell You for a price, or recant words which You Yourself have given? No longer can I be an ego-pleaser. To please all of the egos on the earth for years cannot compare to one moment in Your embrace.

Oh, my dearest One, I did not see the end from the beginning. You were the One who drew me ever closer, urging me to record the struggles and the pain, each ending in some slight victory or some little gain. Will this small volume encourage some other pilgrim on his way? Have I been a faithful instrument, writing only for You? If You are pleased, though all the world revile my words, I am fulfilled. This mortal self, lighting its little hour or two, will sink into oblivion; but our friendship, our love, is forever new, eternally blissful, and ever pure. It can never pass into nothingness. Its loveliness increases.

Only because I have completely surrendered to You can I say "You are mine." You are mine because I am Yours. When You placed Your ring on my finger, I accepted it as a sleepwalker might—not seeing or understanding. I changed my name to Yours, but, for the most part, Joy was only a name. Now I know Joy to be my nature, my Self, my identity. The Joy, the Peace, the Love I know in You is in All, and We are now and forever One.

BIBLIOGRAPHY

[1] Baylis, Janice, *Sleep On It! The Practical Side of Dreaming.* 1977. DeVorss & Co., Marina del Rey, California.

[2] Case, Paul Foster, *The Tarot.* 1947. Macoy Publishing Co., Richmond, Virginia.

[3] Cirlot, J.E., *A Dictionary of Symbols,* 1971. Philosophical Library, New York, N.Y.

[4] Sechrist, Elsie, *Dreams, Your Magic Mirror.* 1968. Cowles Education Corp., New York, N.Y.

[5] Weible, Wayne A., "*Miracle at Medjugorje,*" 1985. Weible Columns, P.O. Box 2647, Myrtle Beach, S.C. 29578.

BOOKS BY AND ABOUT SRI SATHYA SAI BABA

Available from:

Sathya Sai Book Center of America
305 West First Street
Tustin, CA 92680

Sri Sathya Sai Baba Books and Publications
Prasanthi Nilayam
Anantapur District
Andhra Pradesh 515134
India

Images of Sai Baba, original drawings by Alexi Allens, Masterpiece Publishing Co., 8830 Evergreen Way, Everett, WA 98204

PERIODICALS

Sanathana Sarathi
Prasanthi Nilayam P. O.
Anantapur District
Andhra Pradesh 515134
India

Sathya Sai Newsletter
1800 East Garvey Avenue
West Covina, CA 91791
U.S.A.

Notes